Passage to Alaska

DEDICATION

For my mother, Jackie Lydon, for a lifetime of support.

Passage to Alaska

Tim Lydon

hancock
house

ISBN 0-88839-523-X
Copyright © 2003 Tim Lydon

Cataloging in Publication Data

Lydon, Tim, 1967–
    Passage to Alaska / Tim Lydon.

    Includes bibliographical references and index.
    ISBN 0-88839-523-X

    1. Lydon, Tim, 1967– —Journeys—Inside Passage. 2. Inside
Passage—Description and travel. 3. Kayaking—Natural history—
Inside Passage. I. Title.
FC3845.I5L92 2003   917.11'1   C2003-910566-0
F1089.I5L92 2003

Editor: Nancy Miller
Production: Andrew Jaster
Cover design: Theodora Kobald
Cover photos: Tim Lydon
All photographs by Tim Lydon unless otherwise credited.

*We acknowledge the financial support of the Government of Canada through the
Book Publishing Industry Development Program (BPIDP) for our publishing activities.*

Published simultaneously in Canada and the United States by

HANCOCK HOUSE PUBLISHERS LTD.
19313 Zero Avenue, Surrey, B.C. V3S 9R9
(604) 538-1114 Fax (604) 538-2262

HANCOCK HOUSE PUBLISHERS
1431 Harrison Avenue, Blaine, WA 98230-5005
(604) 538-1114 Fax (604) 538-2262
Web Site: www.hancockhouse.com *email:* sales@hancockhouse.com

Contents

Acknowledgments 6
Preface 7

Part I — British Columbia — Getting Started

Preparing for Two Months in a Sea Kayak 11
To the Lighthouse—First Miles, First Storms, First Friends 26
Fear and Loathing in the Sound—Twelve-Foot Seas in a
    Seventeen-Foot Boat 48
Reaching Safety—Discovering the Nature of
    the Inside Passage 69
Cold Rain and Snow—Weather in the Inside Passage 92
Legacies—Human History in the Inside Passage 131
A Walk in the Woods—Getting to Know the Rain Forest 152
The Big Tease—Hard Lessons About Winds and Tides 173

Part II — Alaska

Back to the Grind 197
High and Dry on the Stikine—Big Rivers in the
    Inside Passage 220
The Land that Ice Built—Dodging Icebergs in LeConte Bay . .242
Humpbacks, Eagles and Bears—Wildlife on Admiralty Island .259
Back to the Future—A Visit to Sumdum 282
Taku—Parting Lessons 305
Culture Shock—Learning to Walk Again 327

Bibliography 332
Index 333

Acknowledgments

Thanks for the interest, support and patience from my family. Thank you, Malinda. Kacey, Rob and Meg, you made the Falcon an unlikely but productive base and provided much-needed doses of insanity. Sally Greenwood, I think I would still be fumbling around for direction if it had not been for your clear and direct guidance. Bill Bastian, thanks for paddling and remaining a friend through harsh storms. Thanks Patti Smith for food deliveries and years of friendship. Mark Johnson, thanks for the Dean Martin album and other therapeutic mailings and for continued interest and support in the years that followed. Thanks Mickey and Sue for a computer and years of steady encouragement and interest. Thanks to my Forest Service friends on the Tongass (John, Laker, Ken and many others) who helped me understand southeast Alaska. And thanks to those soaked kayak rangers, Kevin Hood in particular, who over the years inspired and shared adventures of questionable sensibility and severe discomfort-each an incredible journey into the heart of the Inside Passage. To the Rose family, the Egg Island lightkeepers and Belle Eaton and family: your hospitality was an inspiration and will always be remembered warmly. Sharing your passion for your home was a special gift. To the residents of Port Hardy, Klemtu, Hartley Bay, Prince Rupert, Ketchikan, Wrangell, Petersburg and Juneau who helped on this expedition and subsequent journeys: thanks for your hospitality and insightful stories. And thanks David Hancock for a nice phone call in February and Nancy Miller for helpful editing.

Preface

In April, 1996, my friend Bill Bastian and I set out on a sea kayak trip through the Inside Passage from northern Vancouver Island to Juneau, Alaska. In the following two months we paddled roughly 1,000 miles, camping nearly every night on the thin margin between the high tide line and the forest. Following the mainland most of the way, we paddled along vast stands of temperate rain forest below snowy mountains that grew more spectacular as we traveled northward. Signs of bears, moose, wolves, otters, mink and deer were usually present at our camps. On the water, whales, seals and sea lions were common, sometimes approaching within a few feet of our kayaks.

Of course, weather in the Inside Passage is a challenging combination of rain and cool temperatures. We experienced poor weather on most days, which often concealed the scenery and led to at least two cases of mild hypothermia. Although winds were usually calm, we experienced several days of rough water, the worst a long crossing through twelve-foot breaking waves and wind-driven rain. Had we begun our travels in May or June, we probably would have experienced better weather, but April was the only time that worked for us. Even so, I have experienced plenty of fifty-degree rainy July days in the Inside Passage.

My fascination with the Inside Passage began in 1991 when I spent a summer working for the U.S. Forest Service in southeast Alaska. I have spent a large part of the twelve years since then exploring and working in the region. Each stay has only inspired further exploration. Even on the most miserable, rain-soaked adventures-when warmth and comfort seemed impossibly distant-the region's glacially carved landscape and intimate mixture of land and sea have always been magical and luring to me. Its rain forest, glaciers, snowy mountains and narrow channels have always provided new insight into a dynamic natural history. And its bad weather, cold water and steep terrain have always offered new adventures and challenges. One could easily spend a lifetime exploring the place and never cover it all.

While this book focuses largely on the 1996 trip, it relies heavily on subsequent adventures and is the result of a long-standing fascination with the Inside Passage. In it I have attempted to provide an introduction to the region's human and natural history, with stories that illustrate the harshness of its weather and terrain and the challenge of traveling the area. I regard this book as much as a story of the coast itself as a story of kayaking it.

But it is a huge place, and this book only scratches its surface. It tells a few stories, like those of Admiralty, LeConte, the spirit bears, George Vancouver. Sitka, the outer coast, Glacier Bay, the Unuk and Pitt Island offer other anecdotes, along with countless bays, islands, rivers and valleys throughout the region. And that's the beauty of the Inside Passage: it is too vast and wild to be covered in one book, leaving much to be discovered by residents and visitors. There are countless stories out there to discover, beaches to camp, bays to explore, valleys to hike, mountains to climb. Each location is rich with history of Natives, explorers, miners, loggers, dreamers, entrepreneurs and adventurers.

This book is not meant to be a guidebook. It represents only one route through an enormous region. Myriad other routes exist, many are more interesting and challenging than ours. You can put your finger anywhere on a map of the Inside Passage and discover glaciers, bays, forest, inlets and wildlife that are centuries removed from the Lower 48.

The Inside Passage. is among the wildest coasts left in the temperate zone, and through its defenses of steepness and bad weather it has retained a pristine condition that is a treasure in the early twenty-first century. Its Native culture is still intact and vibrant, and its spectacular nature offers many lessons on the interconnectedness of the earth's processes. I hope this book provides an introduction to this fascinating place and that readers will use a map and their imaginations as a guide.

PART I

BRITISH COLUMBIA—
GETTING STARTED

CHAPTER ONE

Preparing for Two Months in a Sea Kayak

B ill took a long sip from a bottle of beer and stared through the passenger window. He hadn't said a word in half an hour. Jenn and Karen were in back, under the camper shell, sprawled amid dry bags, backpacks, food boxes, paddles and sleeping bags. I could hear them laughing through the open window between the cab and its shell. Cassidy, Jenn's yellow dog, poked her head into the cab, her big tongue hanging from the side of her mouth, and looked eagerly at the winding two-laner ahead. I had a beer between my legs and both hands on the steering wheel. I moved the wheel back and forth, surprised at how little it affected the truck's course.

The truck was a 1979, two-wheel-drive Toyota. It was a long-bed model and looked like a dwarf cousin of the larger four-wheel-drives that had been passing us for a week. The dented and scratched body was a faded off-white with a tan camper top. It seemed to have a rattle, shimmy, shake or clunk for each of its 188,000 miles. In motion, the combination was cacophonous.

The truck's ignition had seized years earlier, and I kept a screwdriver on the dashboard to start it. Bailing wire lashed the hood shut on the highway; a pair of vise grips operated the driver-side window. The rubber boot around the gearshift had disintegrated, providing a blurred view of the pavement below, and I used a broken ski pole to prop open the camper shell's back window. The front-end could no longer be aligned; keeping the truck pointed straight required some effort. Every few months, I replaced the resulting worn tires with used ones bought at a junkyard for twenty dollars apiece. A custom-cut piece of plywood held one of the headlights in place, although I never adjusted the aim correctly-not even close: At night it

11

focused a bright beam at a fifty-degree angle to the tops of trees beside the road.

I built a homemade roof rack from eyebolts, galvanized pipe and plumbing insulation, and a few days before our arrival on Vancouver Island, Bill and I secured two brand new sea kayaks to it with a combination of rope and cam straps. The kayaks obviously exceeded the truck's worth by many times, and by the looks of our vehicle it was easy to see our sea kayak trip lacked corporate sponsorship.

It was April 11, 1996. The four of us, Cassidy, the two kayaks and all the gear and food in back were making that tired four-cylinder engine perform miracles. As I considered the truck, it seemed silly to be reviewing the logistics of our expedition. Inventorying the toolbox and reviewing the procedures of transmission or head gasket replacement seemed more fitting. But with each dozen or so miles I realized we were fast approaching the northern tip of Vancouver Island. Port Hardy was less than 60 miles away, which meant we would soon run out of road. It amazed me that the truck was actually going to make it—I realized that if we reached the end of the road, Bill and I would have to go through with the big sea kayak trip we had talked about for nearly an entire year. Suddenly my stomach tightened. No wonder Bill was so quiet: This was insane!

As we drew closer to the road's end I began thinking in detail about the risks associated with our proposed expedition. I thought about twenty-foot waves, hypothermia and the murky depths of a deadly cold sea. Soon I was listening carefully to the engine. Maybe it *would* break down. Maybe it *could*. Maybe I should push this old beater up to eighty and try to blow it up. The more I thought of it, the more I preferred being stranded on the side of the road than bobbing helplessly on the surface of the sea. Undaunted by my thoughts, the vehicle continued northward.

It had been a hectic week and, nervousness aside, I was eager to get out of the truck. Our travels had begun on Sunday, when Bill Bastian arrived at Denver International Airport from New York City. I picked him and his kayak up at the airport, and we drove west for two hours to my home in the Colorado Rockies. "What vehicle are we taking to Vancouver Island?" he eventually asked, absent-mindedly peeling off part of the dashboard.

We spent Monday putting my belongings in storage and packing the truck and at night said goodbye to mutual friends at a barbecue. I found it hard to believe that in twenty-four hours we would be out of the Colorado River's drainage, driving somewhere beside the Snake or the Columbia and coming into America's rain forest. The thick, wet majesty of Douglas firs, Sitka spruces and western red cedars would replace the thin lodge poles that surrounded my home. I could not imagine how it felt to Bill, who was replacing fiords of steel and seas of concrete with something entirely alien.

On Tuesday we left for Oregon. Although heading immediately west would get us there quicker, we had to first drive east, back to Denver. There, at the U.S. Geological Survey office we bought $100 worth of topographic maps, which would cover our route through the Alaskan portion of the Inside Passage.

We drove through the night, taking turns napping amid the gear in the back of the truck. After a 1:00 A.M. gas stop, police pulled us over in a small town near the Idaho-Oregon border. A young officer informed me that one of my headlights was out, and after another officer arrived with lights flashing, they searched my truck as Bill and I stood on the side of the road. The officers were not impressed when I revived the headlight by banging my fist on the truck's hood. Its beam pointed upward into the night, illuminating dust and insects above our heads.

By midday Wednesday we were in Mosier, a town of 250 along the Columbia River Gorge. The town is only a few miles east of the crest of the Cascade Range and occupies a unique position between two very different ecosystems: Oregon's high desert to the east and the rain forest to the west.

My friends Jenn Mawn and Karen Rudert shared a beautiful house in the woods outside Mosier, where rent was cheap and they enjoyed a life of part-time employment. Jenn and I had guided commercial raft trips in Colorado a few years earlier. She had since chosen Mosier as a quiet place away from the growing crowds and spreading glitz of Colorado's high country. That afternoon the four of us sat in warm sunshine on their porch overlooking the Columbia River. Although we told stories, laughed and drank beer, Bill and I were aware that something very big was looming, and our thoughts were never far from the long list of things we needed to accomplish in the next few days.

1.1: THE BASICS

The following is a list of basic equipment and supplies for an extended sea kayak expedition in the Inside Passage:

- Two- or three-season tent with water resistant rain fly and durable ground cover (Two-season tents are light, but three-seasons provide more rain and wind protection.)
- Sleeping bag (Although down bags are lighter and pack smaller, synthetic bags dry faster.)
- Thermarest inflatable sleeping pad
- At least one tarp with twenty feet of florescent cordage from corners and sides (Several brands of freestanding tarps with aluminum poles are available; they are convenient for beach camping, but occupy considerable storage space.)
- Two compact stoves and MSR fuel containers (White gas burns efficiently and doesn't produce the waste of propane or butane.)
- Durable cook-kit with three pans, including a large one for pasta and lids that double as frying pans
- Plastic cutting board that can be rolled for packing
- Mixed set of small Tupperware containers for spices, cooking oil, milk/juice, leftovers
- Two 100-foot sections of nylon rope and several marine carabiners for hanging food (Bear canisters are effective, but require exces-

Bill and I departed for Seattle on Thursday morning and late that afternoon arrived at the Capitol Hill doorstep of two college friends, Stephanie and Brian Rapp. They offered their house and yard as a staging area for our trip; we spent the afternoon and all of Friday buying supplies and food. We needed another tarp, more rope, two more dry bags and ammunition for the rifle. We spent $200 on a marine radio and another $300 on nautical charts we had ordered six weeks earlier. We bought enough groceries to last the first fourteen days of the trip, plus three extra days, just in case. Then we bought food for the two-day drive up Vancouver Island. As we checked off each chore, we thought of two other things we should take care of while still in Seattle: buy a bilge pump for Bill and a new headlamp for me. Once we left the city, we would be in more remote areas where stores had less variety and higher prices.

When we finally finished shopping, we piled all of our gear and food in the yard and spent almost an hour throwing away excess packaging, then packed the boats to make sure everything we had purchased fit inside their storage compartments. Neither of us had used the boats for extended trips, so we spent a couple hours figuring out how to fit the gear in each kayak. As with a long road trip, each item had a place where it fit best.

Next, we cut the maps down to size so they would fit into our 18 x 13-inch, waterproof map case. We had twenty-five topographical maps, from which we only needed to cut away about two inches of margin, but our twenty nautical charts, which averaged three feet by four feet, required more extensive editing. We carefully determined which parts of the charts we needed then cut away the rest. It was frustrating to throw away large portions of maps that cost $300, and while amassing the unused portions in a ball, Bill suggested we return them for store credit.

After hours of busy activity, we ate a late dinner with Stephanie and Brian on Friday night. Although visiting friends and enjoying a great meal, our nervousness was impossible to hide. We were fidgety and could not stay focused on one conversation. The size of our trip seemed absurd, the amount of money we spent seemed foolish, and the impending dangers clouded our thoughts. As we passed plates of food between us and laughed at stories from when we had last been together, I found myself thinking mostly about a stretch of coast several hundred miles north of Capitol Hill.

Jenn, Karen and Cassidy arrived in Seattle shortly after noon on Saturday. After we ate lunch and reorganized the gear in my truck, we departed for Vancouver Island. It would take the remainder of Saturday and most of Sunday to reach the

sive space. Bear-resistant food bags have yet to prove totally effective.)
- Six or more nylon stuff sacks for hanging/storing food
- Very durable rain gear and layers of fleece
- Durable dry bags with sizes ranging from five to twenty liters (The variety enables efficient packing; larger than twenty liters uses too much space.)
- Quart-size plastic water bottles and two 2.5 gallon collapsible water sacks (One five-gallon sack uses too much space.)
- Water filter, cleaning kit, spare cartridge (Silty water, common in the Inside Passage, quickly clogs water filters.)
- LED headlamps, flashlight, extra batteries kept in Ziploc bags inside dry bags
- Knife (Leatherman-type knives include screwdrivers, saw, can opener and more.)
- Watch (Essential for reading tide books.)
- Several tide books in Ziploc bags distributed throughout dry bags
- Waterproof map case
- Fifty feet of extra rope, several spools of extra cordage (florescent), extra lighters in Ziploc bags distributed throughout dry bags, trash bags, loads of quart- and gallon-sized Ziploc bags, extra marine carabiners, sunglasses/sunscreen
- Nylon cockpit covers to keep rain from filling boats at night
- Collapsible camp stool, a luxury item worth the space it occupies

northern tip of the island, where Jenn and Karen would drop us off, then go camping for a few days before returning my truck to Seattle. Stephanie and Brian had no driveway, but they would move the truck often enough during the next three months to ensure it did not get towed. Listening to this plan, Jenn recommended we name our endeavor "Shoestring Adventures."

It was around two in the afternoon on Sunday when Bill took that long sip of beer, Jenn and Karen laughed in the back of the truck, Cassidy looked eagerly at the road and I moved the loose steering wheel back and forth without effect. My nervousness had escalated to genuine panic attacks, and I could not stop reviewing the schedule, gear, menu and a few terrifying scenarios. Foremost on my mind was the open water of Queen Charlotte Sound, which would influence seas during the first forty or fifty miles of our trip.

The Inside Passage is a complicated series of inland waterways between Olympia, Washington, and Skagway, Alaska. For almost 1,500 miles, the waterways wind between several thousand closely spaced and mountainous islands that shield mainland shores from the stormy waters of the northern Pacific. While high winds and big waves slam against the archipelago's outer coast, the water beside the mainland, sometimes less than twenty miles away, is often flat-calm under light breezes. The consistently calm waters have provided safe passage for early inhabitants in dugout canoes, eighteenth-century explorers and fur traders and present-day cruise ships.

Although mostly protected, two large openings within the Inside Passage enable rough seas to reach mainland shores. The largest opening is Queen Charlotte Sound, which is more than 6,000 square miles-larger than Connecticut and Rhode Island combined- and fills the opening between Vancouver Island to the south and Haida Gwaii (Queen Charlotte Islands) to the north. Along its eastern boundary, dozens of islands protect all but about forty miles of mainland coastal B.C. northeast of Vancouver Island. Several shallow banks offshore provide some protection, but the waters bordering this area of mainland are some of the most dangerous in the Inside Passage.

Unfortunately, the first days of our trip required paddling from Vancouver Island to the mainland across Queen Charlotte Strait, then traveling north along roughly forty miles of exposed coast in

South Passage. Only shallow banks and offshore rocks separate the passages from Queen Charlotte Sound, where seas can build to fifty feet. Neither Bill nor I had ever paddled in anything so open. If we encountered bad weather I estimated it could take close to a week to get through the area, although I knew it could easily take longer.

I was fixated on Queen Charlotte Sound as we approached Port Hardy. What if a storm developed and seas became rough? From autumn through spring each year, an almost constant progression of low-pressure systems barrels into Queen Charlotte Sound from the Gulf of Alaska. It was likely we would encounter rough conditions. I also wondered how well Bill and I would handle a bad situation. If one of us capsized several miles from shore, would the rescues we had practiced in calm pools work in waves, wind and rain? With average April water temperatures in Queen Charlotte Strait just 45°F, hypothermia would be an immediate and life-threatening con-

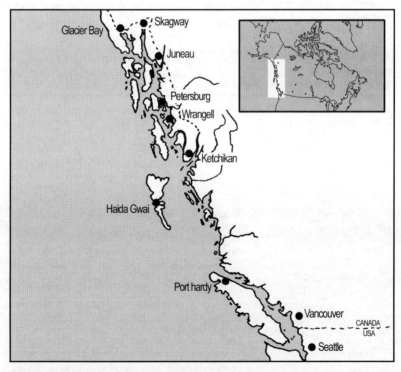

Map 1.1: Inside Passage, with Puget Sound in the south and Haines and Skagway in the north.

17

1.2: SAFETY GEAR

The following is a list of safety equipment for kayakers, regardless of trip duration:

- Coast Guard approved Type III personal floatation device (Many PFDs are made specifically for kayakers.)
- Durable spray skirt with neoprene cockpit cover
- Spare paddle, at least one per pair of kayakers
- Inflatable paddle float, stored on deck
- Bilge pump, stored on deck (Pump is essential in a capsize and convenient on rainy days.)
- Whistle
- Marine radio and understanding of its function and protocol (See sidebar 12.1.)
- Comprehensive first aid kit
- Personal survival kit (See sidebar 5.2.)
- Kayak repair kit
- Two compasses and accurate maps of large enough scale for navigation
- Towline

cern if someone capsized. Rescues sometimes take several attempts, but in cold water each failed attempt increases the likelihood of drowning. Even with a successful rescue, severe hypothermia could easily develop during the crossing to land.

With both hands on the steering wheel, I pulled myself forward and craned my neck toward the sky. The seamless clouds that had blocked the sun since our arrival on Vancouver Island promised imminent rain, but the tops of the trees showed no sign of wind. I eased myself back, dissatisfied. Encouraging weather observations made from the cab of my truck would not amount to very much; I knew conditions could either clear completely or go to hell in minutes. I just hoped for one or two days of calm weather to get us across the opening between Vancouver Island and the mainland. From there, we could paddle close to shore in South Passage or simply wait ashore for violent weather to pass.

Northern Vancouver Island is sparsely populated, mountainous and heavily forested. It is the traditional land of the Kwakuitl, whose ancestors arrived in the area at least 8,000 years ago. Early people fished salmon, hunted animals with stone arrowheads, gathered berries, clams and seaweed, and made giant dugout canoes from the red cedars of the temperate rain forest. Like other northwest coast Natives, they developed an advanced and politically complex culture, and their unique artwork is still prevalent throughout the region.

The fur trade brought the first wave of whites to northern Vancouver Island in the late eighteenth century. In 1792 George Vancouver sailed past the island's northern tip while searching for the Northwest Passage. Sea otters were abundant, and their pelts fetched high prices in Asia and Europe for several decades. In 1849 the Hudson's Bay Company established Fort Rupert, a fur-trading post near present-day Port Hardy, for years it was the only European settlement on the northern third of Vancouver Island. Its residents trapped beaver and hunted otters, and the settlement became a supply post for trappers and miners traveling the Inside Passage.

Port Hardy began as a store and a post office in the early twentieth century. In 1912, the Hardy Bay Land Company offered cheap land in the area, advertising it as a growing port town, but new arrivals were often disappointed by the cool, wet climate and impenetrable forest. Although many abandoned their land, Port Hardy had a school, church and sawmill by 1920. The town continued to grow slowly in the following decades, but in the 1970s a copper mine opened nearby and the population boomed. By the mid-seventies, it reached its current level of approximately 5,000 people.

Today Port Hardy is the largest settlement on the northern third of Vancouver Island, with most neighboring towns supporting populations of less than a thousand. The towns have similar histories and have long relied on logging, mining and fishing. However, as automation, resource depletion and stricter environmental laws have hurt extractive industries, tourism has grown sharply, with kayaking, fishing and whale watching being a few of the big draws. Port Hardy also acts as the southern hub for ferry traffic to British Columbia's north coast. The steady flow of ferry passengers ensures the continued significance of tourism to the economy.

From Olympia to Gustavus, the scattered settlements of the Inside Passage share a similar story. The first humans arrived at least 10,000 years ago and by 2,000 years ago had developed a unique and sophisticated culture. By the eighteenth century, hundreds of thousands of aboriginal people from more than twenty distinct groups occupied the region widely. In the early and mid-1700s, Russian fur traders became the first whites to visit the area, and within fifty years fur traders from Europe and America were traveling the Inside Passage extensively. After nearly exterminating the sea otter, many whites left the area by the mid-1800s, but soon the search for gold brought far greater numbers. They settled dozens of towns, began steamship routes through the protected waterways and opened missionaries, canneries and sawmills. They also introduced diseases and alcohol to many Natives, who perished in great numbers by the early twentieth century. While major cities developed near Puget Sound, timber, fishing and mining supported smaller communities in the northern Inside Passage. But toward the end of the twentieth century, tourism challenged extractive industries as the primary source of revenue in an increasing number of towns.

■ ■ ■

Light raindrops struck my windshield as we arrived in town, representing only a fraction of Port Hardy's seventy-four inches of annual precipitation. Like most of the Inside Passage, the nearby ocean keeps winters too mild to produce much snow at sea level-almost all of Port Hardy's precipitation arrives as rain. The temperate climate and heavy precipitation are a perfect recipe for the lush rain forest that carpets the Inside Passage.

For Bill, Port Hardy was a new and strange land. He had lived briefly in Colorado and traveled a few times to the West Coast, but had spent most of his life in New York. He was born and raised on Long Island and went to college in the Hudson Valley, then spent the six years preceding our trip in Manhattan, where he waited tables, acted in theater productions and practiced hypnosis and massage therapy. With his wiry build, shaggy blond hair and sharp blue eyes, he traveled between his occupations at break-neck speeds on his roller blades, thriving on the concrete, noise and motion of the city.

Bill visited me in Seattle eleven months before our arrival in Port Hardy, and after sea kayaking in Puget Sound one afternoon we sat down to a map of the Inside Passage. I outlined my dream of paddling the coast and talked of bears, whales, glaciers and vast swathes of rain forest. Of course, I also talked about the likelihood of miserable weather and the torturous tedium of twenty-mile days. I didn't think the trip would interest him, but after laying out a brief itinerary, his eyes focused on mine and he said, "Let's do it." Two months later he phoned to tell me about his new sea kayak, and from that moment we planned seriously for the trip and looked forward to our arrival in Port Hardy.

Part of what brought Bill to Port Hardy was the novelty of the trip. He is curious and has always enjoyed the challenge and adventure of immersing himself in new realms. Paddling a thousand or so miles of remote coastline was a departure from his urban life too radical to resist. The endurance required of the trip also appealed to him. As a marathon runner, he welcomed the physical and mental challenges of paddling long distances, enduring terrible weather and camping nightly. Of course, the opportunity to visit Alaska was also enticing. He knew the scenery would provide constant amazement, even after the novelty and challenge waned.

My reasons for paddling the Inside Passage were different. Unlike Bill, I had been there before, spending three summers in the early nineties working for the U.S. Forest Service in southeast Alaska. I was a naturalist at a visitor center, then a laborer on a trail crew and, finally, a wilderness ranger traveling largely by sea kayak. Much of the work required hiking or flying to remote backcountry locations for up to eleven days. Upon arriving in Port Hardy, I had been away from Alaska for nearly three years, but my fascination with the Inside Passage had not diminished.

Above all, the Inside Passage is a vast mingling of land and water. The glacier-carved landscape, with thousands of closely spaced islands and countless narrow inlets, ensures visitors are never far from mountains or the ocean. Between Puget Sound and Skagway, Alaska, a little over 800 miles of latitude, the islands and inlets form over 25,000 miles of coastline. North of Vancouver Island, the severity of the mountains and the abundance of water isolate most towns from roads.

The boundary between land and water is often obscured, especially by the weather. Pacific moisture washes over the area, draping mountainous islands and mainland peaks with low-lying clouds for days and sometimes weeks-creating patchwork scenery of water, forest, rock and ice. Abundant rainfall creates thousands of swift streams that erode forest soils into the ocean, and deep mountain snows bury peaks and form glaciers that creep seaward through barren valleys. Between rain, snow, ice and the ocean, water intercepts the land in countless ways.

The Inside Passage is also about abundance, with its mixture of land and water providing diverse habitat for thousands of species. Its rich waters provide abundant fish for killer whales, humpbacks, gray whales, seals and sea lions while many species endangered on other parts of the continent thrive ashore, including wolves and brown bears. Otter, mink, moose, deer and black bear also inhabit the area in great numbers, as well as North America's largest population of bald eagles. Rivers and marine waterways provide vast wetlands for millions of migratory birds each spring and fall, and just as many songbirds inhabit the expansive rain forest. Each summer salmon choke the region's numerous streams.

The Inside Passage also contains the largest remaining tract of old-growth temperate rain forest in the world, part of a larger rain forest that stretches from Cape Mendocino, California, to Cook Inlet in Alaska. Receiving between fifty and 200 inches of annual precipitation, the forest and its understory cover islands and mainland slopes to within a few feet of tidewater. It is home to some of the biggest trees on the planet and its dynamic ecosystem provides clear lessons in interconnectedness. The most obvious example is the annual arrival of salmon, which crowd streams to spawn and die and provide crucial nutrition to eagles, bears, ravens, gulls and a host of other species. Through defecation and abandonment of carcasses, scavengers and predators spread salmon flesh into the forest, where nitrogen from their flesh travels into tree roots and makes trees growing beside salmon streams some of the largest in the area. In turn, big trees keep sediment out of salmon spawning beds and fallen trees deposit nutrition into streams to feed young salmon.

For me, the kayak trip was an opportunity to reconnect with the dynamic nature of the Inside Passage. During earlier field trips with the Forest Service I had witnessed extraordinary events on a daily basis, including calving glaciers, breaching whales and competition between wolves, eagles and bears; after a few years in more populated surroundings I craved the region's real wilderness. I wanted to feel the solitude that big mountains, cold water and bad weather provide and see one more time the Inside Passage's textbook glacial features. As it turned out, two years after our trip I remained unsatisfied and returned to my job as a Forest Service ranger in southeast Alaska. For five more years, I spent six months there annually, traveling the area widely by kayak, ferry, foot and plane.

■ ■ ■

Port Hardy was quiet and dim the afternoon of our arrival. We went to the hardware store for duct tape and tide books, spent an hour in a coffee shop and then made phone calls to friends and family. They were odd calls, too much like goodbyes, and each one tempted us to stop the trip and return to our normal lives.

The final call was to our friend Patti Smith in New Jersey, who would handle our food deliveries. In the preceding weeks, she and Bill had visited bulk food and grocery stores in New York and created a menu for our trip based on caloric intake, quick preparation and minimal packaging. We aimed for 5,000 calories daily to fuel the constant exercise of paddling and to keep warm in the cool, wet weather and relied heavily on pasta and rice, which we could quickly prepare after long days. Since fresh meat and vegetables would be rare, we included a wide array of spices and sauces we could keep in small, waterproof containers and dried produce such as Portobello mushrooms, sun-dried tomatoes and a variety of beans.

The day before flying to Colorado, Bill gave Patti $650 and zip codes to four communities in the Inside Passage. We planned an average of fourteen days between each delivery and told Patti we would call her when we received each package to schedule the next delivery. On the phone from Port Hardy, we told her we were leaving in the morning and would need the first food shipment in twelve days.

"You boys be careful," she said, "and I'll talk to you in Hartley Bay."

Late in the afternoon, as the light in Port Hardy faded, we drove to a campground tucked in forest above a calm bay. I parked by the campsite closest to the water where we set our tents on grass under tall trees. It was nearly dusk under the canopy, where raindrops gathered on branches and fell in big drops that smacked the pavement without rhythm. We were the only party at the campground, and the host said we could stay for free. Without other campers, the place was eerily quiet.

After setting camp we walked across wet pavement to the bottom of a nearby boat ramp and looked into Hardy Bay. Light rain rippled on flat water at our feet and a breeze pushed damp air against our faces. Both the water and sky were steel gray. In the distance blue islands and peninsulas collided with each other, looking far more confusing than they appeared on our charts.

"This is good," said Bill, looking at one of our nautical charts, "I think this campground has the quickest route out of Hardy Bay." It seemed funny to be excited about shaving a few miles from the beginning of a two-month trip, but we were eager to get across to the mainland.

We chose Port Hardy because it is the end of the road. It is not only the end of the North Island Highway, but it is also the end of a network of roads bordering North America's western coast beginning in Guatemala. But north of Port Hardy, glaciers, fiords and steep mountains have prevented the construction of roads to all but a handful of small communities: Kitimat, Bella Coola and Prince Rupert along the British Columbia coast and Hyder, Haines and Skagway in southeast Alaska. North of Port Hardy, approximately 100,000 people inhabit only a few dozen generally small communities, and almost half that number live in two cities, Prince Rupert and Juneau, leaving thousands of miles of undeveloped coastline.

We would have seen more of the Inside Passage if we started from somewhere in Puget Sound or Johnstone Strait, but paddling that area would have meant passing continuous roads and towns and widespread clear-cut forests. With more than 700,000 people occupying Vancouver Island, more than two million more along its adjacent mainland, and several additional millions living along Puget Sound south to Olympia, the region's nature is cloaked by massive development. In contrast, the isolation north of Vancouver Island would enable us to view parts of the Inside Passage as they were a thousand years before my truck squealed into Port Hardy. It would also introduce a meaningful remoteness to our trip-without roads, mistakes and illnesses carried greater stakes.

We piled back into the truck and drove toward town for food. Halfway there, the sky collapsed into big raindrops that covered the windshield in a layer of running water. A steady breeze quickly pushed the rain to an angle and swayed the tops of trees. The boats were right-side up atop the truck and began filling with water.

"Well, at least it's raining," I said in mock relief.

"Phew!" Bill agreed, wiping mock anxiety from his forehead, "It's about time! For a minute there I thought the sun was going to come out!"

Although I laughed, I was beginning to think our situation had the potential to become decidedly unfunny very soon.

Bill and I convinced Jenn and Karen to help us by advertising our drive up Vancouver Island as an all-expense-paid vacation. Partly to fulfill the promise, but also to give ourselves a good send-off, we drove to the best restaurant we could find and ran to its doors as fat raindrops nailed the parking lot. By the time we sat down the parking lot, forest and view of Hardy Bay had all disappeared into darkness, with lights from houses shimmering on the wet windows. We spent the following three hours laughing and eating, our conversation weaving together our lives in Alaska, Mosier, Colorado and New York and gusty winds lashing rain against the window near our table. I didn't think much about the big waves the storm was likely creating in Queen Charlotte Sound. That could wait for the morning.

We left the restaurant shortly after ten, gorged with food and our faces aching from laughter, and drove through steady rain to the campground. Karen, Jenn and Cassidy climbed inside one tent, Bill disappeared into another and I crawled into the back of my truck. I lay awake late that night, knowing that it was my last night with luxuries such as my truck, its stereo and a group of friends. The rain fell in thick sheets and the wind rushed ominously through the trees.

CHAPTER TWO

To the Lighthouse—First Miles, First Storms, First Friends

Jenn, Karen and Bill were already up when I crawled from the back of my truck at seven the next morning. We walked to the boat ramp and once out of the forest were surprised to find mostly clear skies over Hardy Bay. Spreading our life jackets and rain gear on wet pavement, we sat in patches of sunlight and shared bananas, bagels and a jug of orange juice. In strengthening sunshine, gulls cried from a nearby beach, and a few boats motored from Hardy Bay. For a place where storms can last for days, I considered the clear weather exceptionally good luck.

After breakfast, we broke camp and carried the kayaks to the water, then spent two hours pulling gear from the truck, packaging it into dry bags and organizing the dry bags inside our boats. Finally, at nine-thirty, I stuffed the last dry bag into my forward compartment and laid my paddle across the deck. Bill, already done packing, was up by the truck talking with Jenn and Karen. With the loaded kayaks at my feet and the sea lapping gently at their bows, I looked into Hardy Bay and tried to imagine the small boats conveying us safely all the way to Alaska. It seemed impossible.

I rejoined my friends, and we had a good laugh as I checked the oil and explained a few of the truck's idiosyncrasies to Jenn and Karen.

"Remember," I said, shoving the dipstick back into the engine, "after you check the oil, always tie the hood shut. It's a drag when it opens on the highway. And don't move the heat from defrost because it will totally stop working."

I let the truck's hood slam shut, which punctuated our laughter. Looking down, I absently kicked together a pile of hemlock needles on the wet pavement.

"That's it, then," said Bill, and started walking toward the boats.

At the bottom of the boat ramp, we exchanged hugs and a few last jokes, then Bill and I climbed into our boats. When Jenn and Karen gave us a ceremonial push our heavy sterns scraped off the pavement and bobbed on the calm water. We made a few tentative strokes, our paddle blades sloshing softly in flat water, then turned simultaneously to Jenn and Karen, who were staring at us from the edge of the water.

"Okay, we're going to paddle to Alaska now," Bill joked. "We'll see you in a bit." Then we waved and turned our backs. Jenn would comment later that it was both odd and kind of sad to see us paddling into the unknown.

A few minutes later, I looked back to see the truck roll out of the campground and felt a visceral longing to be sitting between Jenn and Karen. I knew that by late afternoon they would be in Victoria or camping on Vancouver Island's coast, and in another day or two they'd be back in wonderful Seattle, drinking lattes or shopping for CDs. Each image seemed far better than paddling into the loneliness of Hardy Bay.

As Jenn and Karen left the campground, I thought about the position Bill and I were in. Port Hardy is remote, with the winding North Island Highway the only access by car and no ferry service southward. If one of us freaked out and decided to turn back, we would be stranded in lonesome Port Hardy while our only friends on Vancouver Island puttered steadily southward. Our only way back to my truck would have been by hitchhiking, a difficult task with two big boats, sixty pounds of food and a ton of camping gear. Our only realistic option was paddling north toward Queen Charlotte Sound.

For the sake of morale I kept my thoughts to myself, but I didn't need to. I glanced over in time to see Bill exhale a long breath, the kind a protester might give before standing in front of a tank. I thought it was not the way a great vacation should start.

■ ■ ■

Sitting in a sea kayak is quite comfortable for the first hour, moderately comfortable for the next and increasingly uncomfortable after that. Over the course of a few hours, the limited cockpit leads to cramped legs and sore butts. Eventually, feet fall asleep, bladders fill and moods sour—usually in that order. Because discomfort can be distracting, resulting in inefficiency and a compromised sense of safety, we agreed to paddle in intervals averaging a couple of hours.

Stopping every two hours ensured regular opportunities to eat and evaluate the weather. Like climbers suffering from "summit fever," kayakers can set unrealistic goals or stay out too long without food or rest. Just as on mountains, the weather at sea changes quickly, and kayakers can inadvertently paddle too long in deteriorating conditions. Stopping every two hours provided the opportunity to change course and destination, review the maps and observe the weather.

During our first two hours we paddled out of Hardy Bay, then made a two-mile crossing north to a chain of small islands covered in forest. The shock of being left alone along the giant coast faded as we paddled on water that was blue and calm, with waves less than a foot high. A bright sun shone from light blue skies, and giant balls of cottony clouds clung to the green and blue mountains of Vancouver Island and the mainland. It was useless to imagine being with Jenn and Karen any more and time to get on with the business of paddling to Alaska.

After a little more than two hours, we pulled our boats onto a beach only thirty feet long and covered in grapefruit-sized rocks. With steep bedrock bordering each side unevenly about five feet above the water, it was the best landing we found after searching the steep islands for twenty minutes. Standing beside our boats we consulted our chart and found we had traveled eight nautical miles and reached the edge of Queen Charlotte Strait. The speed was slightly more than our anticipated average of three knots, which bolstered our confidence.

We snacked on granola bars, drank water and looked about the wide expanse of our new world. The sea was calm and dark blue, with shifting sparkles of sunlight, and Vancouver Island was a mountainous mass of green forest filling the south and west. Although we could see several boats near Hardy Bay, Port Hardy was around a corner and out of sight. Four miles to the northeast, a group of forested islands were green against the blue sea, too distant to distinguish individual trees. The mainland lay beyond them, nine miles to the northeast, with thick, white clouds capping its blue hills.

After snacking, Bill set the map case between us. During the next few days Calvert Island, about forty miles to our north-north-west, would be our ultimate goal. Thirteen miles long and eight miles wide, it was the first location to our north where a large island protected the mainland from Queen Charlotte Sound. From Calvert Island northward, we would enjoy protection from an island chain almost 250 miles long before reaching Dixon Entrance. But first we had to paddle across Queen Charlotte Strait to the mainland, then at least thirty miles in South Passage along exposed coastline. It was the part of the trip that had made me nervous for months.

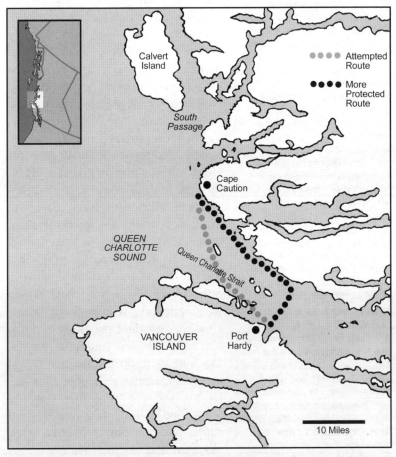

Map 2.1: Queen Charlotte Strait and South Passage. The light dotted line shows our attempted course to Cape Caution; the dark dotted line shows a course that would have been more protected by Vancouver Island.

2.1: KAYAKERS AND HYPOTHERMIA

Hypothermia, a potentially fatal cooling of the body's core temperature, is a constant threat in the cool, wet climate of the Inside Passage. It can occur quickly or over the course of several hours, and knowledge of its causes and effects is a paddler's first line of defense.

The most obvious cause of hypothermia in the Inside Passage is submersion in cold water. With water temperatures in the low fifties Fahrenheit in summer, and much colder water near glaciers, hypothermia begins within minutes of submersion as cold water quickly robs heat from a victim's body. Because heat loss quickens with movement of cold water, swimming increases hypothermia. Unless very close to shore, the best way to stay alive in cold water is remaining as still as possible and bringing the knees close to the chest to conserve heat near the vital organs. Even if a victim is pulled quickly from the water, cold and wet clothes will still lead to hypothermia.

Even without submersion in cold water, the cool temperatures and frequent rain of the Inside Passage create a perfect recipe for hypothermia. Wet clothes combined with cool temperatures and even light breezes can steal heat from the body just as effectively as submersion. Cotton clothing, which absorbs moisture, increases the threat. Because this kind of hypothermia may not occur as quickly as with

From our tiny beach, we had several options across Queen Charlotte Strait. By the easiest and safest route the mainland was a little less than eight miles away at a northeast heading of twenty-five degrees, a distance we could easily cover that afternoon. With two small groups of islands on the way, the longest stretch between land was only three miles. Seas during the short crossings would likely remain calm, even if winds increased, because the route was tucked safely between Vancouver Island and the mainland. However, it was not the most direct course northward and would ultimately add mileage to Calvert Island.

A more direct course required paddling northwest at 300 degrees for eight miles along our island chain, then cutting due north across roughly fourteen miles of Queen Charlotte Strait to a prominent mainland point called Cape Caution. It would be a slightly more direct course that brought us to the mainland thirteen miles closer to Calvert Island, which we believed would save time. However, it would also bring us much closer to Queen Charlotte Sound, exposing us to open water that would become dangerous in poor weather. During the fourteen mile crossing only Pine Island, four miles from shore, and the Storm Islands, three miles further, would provide opportunities to land.

We could also take any number of

routes between the two outlined above. The safest, less direct routes involved varying degrees of island-hopping, relatively short crossings and an overall shorter distance to the mainland. Those closer to the sound required longer crossings, more exposure, but perhaps a shorter distance to Calvert Island. In the end, clear skies and calm seas gave us the confidence to choose the shorter and riskier route. This choice ultimately cost several days and endangered our lives. Staying within the lee of Vancouver Island for as long as possible would have been much smarter.

■ ■ ■

We paddled northwest along the islands under clear skies, with temperatures around sixty and light breezes blowing through gaps between small islands. The water was calm and cold, somewhere near forty-five degrees, and several times I dipped my hand into it, allowing the cold to bite at my skin. I tried to imagine how immersion would feel, knowing hypothermia and cold-water drowning were threats we would face every day for the next two months.

If one of us capsized, we would rely on an Eskimo roll to right our boat without leaving the cockpit, but with loaded boats and rough seas a roll can fail, forcing a victim to exit the cockpit and rely on a partner's assistance. However, in forty-five-submersion, paddlers may not notice its effects until it is well advanced and potentially dangerous.

In mild hypothermia, the brain pumps blood from extremities to the body's core to protect vital organs from damaging cold. Shivering, the body's attempt to warm itself, is one of the first symptoms. As more blood flows to the core, nonessential functions such as speech and dexterity suffer, making slurred words and clumsiness other early symptoms. Simple tasks such as setting a tent or tying knots may become difficult at this stage. Grogginess and poor judgment are signs the condition is worsening, leading to severe hypothermia, which is potentially fatal.

Severe hypothermia occurs when the body temperature drops to the low nineties, a level difficult to rebound from without professional help. As the victim loses energy, shivering stops and grogginess, confusion and apathy increase. A victim may express more interest in sleeping than changing clothes or lighting a fire. As the remaining energy is devoted to protecting vital organs, depressed vital signs-slowed pulse, faint heart beat, shallow breathing-and unconsciousness will occur. Without immediate and professional medical attention, ventricular fibrillation and death are likely at this point.

For paddlers it is important to have proper clothing and judgment and realize that conditions do not need to be extreme for severe hypothermia to develop.

degree water, less than half the warmth of the human body, the average person begins losing dexterity within only a few minutes. With a good life jacket but no dry suit, most people become mildly hypothermic in less than thirty minutes and severely hypothermic inside of an hour, causing muscle cramps, exhaustion and unconsciousness. Most people die of severe hypothermia within three hours. Swimming or otherwise moving in cold water quickens heat loss and decreases survival time.

But the calm conditions and warm temperatures made the risks of hypothermia seem remote, and we paddled at a leisurely pace, enjoying the sights and sounds of the coast. We passed a dozen bald eagles, usually perched high in tall trees at the forest's edge, and saw oystercatchers, cormorants, gulls and terns. They fed in the intertidal zone, flew low over beaches or floated quietly on the water. Early in the afternoon, two harbor porpoises swam within 100 yards, breaking the surface with smooth, gray backs. Soon after, a harbor seal stared curiously at us from twenty-five yards as we dragged our boats ashore for lunch.

It took just hours to appreciate the hundreds of species that thrive in the rich waters of the Inside Passage. A large tidal exchange occurs twice daily, keeping the cold, deep water in motion and continuously stirring nutrients from the coastline and ocean floor. Erosion deposits organic matter into the water from the nearby rain forest, creating some of the most nutrient-rich waters in the world. Plankton, krill, shellfish, herring, cod and salmon are just some of many marine species that contribute to a food chain that includes sea lions, seals, porpoises, humpbacks and orcas. The benefits also reach land, where mink, otter, wolves and bears fish near shore or feed in the intertidal, later spreading ocean nutrients to the forest in a subtle blending of land and water.

We paddled for another hour after lunch, then stopped on a narrow beach inside an intimate cove 100 yards deep. Like our first two beaches, steep bedrock surrounded a small area of cobbles, and thick vegetation overhung the water in tangled shocks. Landing there would have been difficult without the small beach, with rock too steep to haul our heavy boats onto and thick vegetation covering every comfortable place to eat. Camping would have required a chainsaw and dynamite.

Small, rocky beaches, often at the mouths of streams or the

heads of bays, are the norm in the Inside Passage, where most of the coastline is steep bedrock and piles of broken boulders. It is increasingly the case in the north, and in the following weeks we paddled along miles of coastline without finding adequate beaches for landing or camping. It was a big reason we spent $400 on maps; we needed to know in advance of long stretches of steep shores, especially during rough weather.

Four miles from our cove Pine Island jutted stubbornly from Queen Charlotte Strait, looking like a small tropical island in the middle of blue water. Distance blurred its forest a uniform green, only the canopy revealed the ragged tops of a few individual trees. Its steep shore was a gray line between green forest and blue sea. Cape Caution was a pale blue nub ten miles past the island, with cottony clouds atop the mainland's mountains beyond it. At three in the afternoon, after paddling sixteen nautical miles, we easily could have relaxed for the rest of the day, but instead we agreed to paddle to Pine Island. It seemed a better use of the remaining daylight and good conditions, and if the weather changed overnight we would be glad for the head-start across the strait.

We checked our charts before leaving. They showed steep shores around all but a small inlet on the north side of the island, where it looked possible to land. If not, a very small cluster of islands lay less than a mile to the northeast. Although their shores also looked steep, we thought there was a good chance of finding a landing somewhere among them. Before strapping the map case to my deck, I noted the massive opening west of Pine Island, a broad invitation to the Pacific's rough weather.

Thirty minutes after leaving the wind increased from the southeast, creating closely spaced waves of one and two feet that hit against our beams. The waves shifted us from course, even with our rudders down, and we made frequent sweep strokes to remain pointed at Pine Island. In the middle of the crossing the waves increased to three feet, and we repeatedly leaned into them to steady our boats. They broke against our beams; the wind, steady at more than ten knots, blew water against our sides and faces each time we lifted our right-hand paddle blades. We quickly grew chilly as the sun, which had felt warm on the beach, dipped low in the sky.

We were tired, wet and paddling in waves to four feet when we reached Pine Island, where fifty-foot black cliffs rose sharply from the water. The waves crashed against broken rocks below the cliffs, pounding loudly and sending spray ten feet high. A foamy surf zone surrounded the steep shores, where confused waves collided. Keeping fifty feet from the rough water, I steered toward the north end of the island, hoping to find the small inlet on our map. But then I heard Bill yelling over the waves from about a hundred feet behind me. I turned quickly and saw him pointing upward at the island and yelling something. Back-paddling toward him, I saw two men standing above the cliffs, shouting for us to paddle to the south side of the island.

As we turned around the waves pushed me uncomfortably close to the surf zone, and my ears filled with the thunder of breaking waves. I paddled quickly toward Bill, but a series of loud splashes from behind startled me—and I thought I heard angry barking. I looked quickly to shore, to particularly turbulent water, and saw seven sea lions bobbing in the waves. Four more slid sloppily from uneven rocks, barking loudly and falling into the water with loud splashes. They looked at me with apparent irritation; as my adrenaline subsided and my muscles relaxed, I wanted badly to be ashore.

The south shore of the island was rough and steep. Black rock sloped upward ten feet before reaching tall grasses that covered a lumpy headland, which climbed fifty feet to the edge of a shaggy forest. The two men stood at the edge of the rocks and waved to us, with the wind leaning the tall grass over at their ankles. One at a time we paddled to a barely protected nook, and as the waves banged our boats against the rocks the men leaned down to help us ashore. Then they helped hoist our heavy boats from the water. After a few minutes of busy activity, with the wind blowing steadily, they introduced themselves as Dan McMurry and Dennis Rose.

When Bill and I decided to paddle to Pine Island, we did not notice the purple teardrop on our nautical chart pointing to the island. We soon realized the symbol indicated a lighthouse, which Dan and Dennis informed us was one of few manned lighthouses left in North America. Most others were already automated.

"Are you hungry?" asked Dan, smiling.

"We will be soon," answered Bill.

"Well, you're just in time. Dinner's almost ready."

"We'll help you with your stuff," offered Dennis.

34

I was baffled. Dinner? What the hell could that mean out here on Pine Island? And what "stuff" should I bring? Things were moving too fast.

"Are you sure you have enough? We have plenty of food with us."

Dennis waved his hand, brushing aside my comment. "C'mon, we've got plenty," he said. "You can stay with us, too, so bring some dry clothes."

We followed them along a thin, brown trail beneath tall trees. Thick vegetation, downed branches and a carpet of green moss covered either side, and far overhead the treetops swayed in the wind. It was after six, and the light beneath the canopy was dusky. After ten minutes we took a break to reorganize gear, and Dan pointed to a hole in the soft earth between two big roots.

"Auklets," he said.

"Bird kill?" asked Dennis, looking up at the dead tree.

They explained that auklets burrow between tree roots to build their nests. Some say they can cause enough root damage to kill trees.

"Auklets are funny," said Dan. He was in his mid-fifties and six feet tall with a strong build and gray hair cut military style. "They fly well enough, but they have yet to learn how to land. We hear them hit the windows of the house all the time. Here in the woods they just dive-bomb the ground. Sometimes they hit trees and lie there stunned for a little while. That's why we have such healthy eagles on Pine Island."

We came to a grassy opening with two neat gardens. We passed a shovel stuck in the dirt and a wheelbarrow lying on its side by a garden hose as we walked across grass and onto a cement walkway leading to three houses. Beyond them, the Pine Island light rotated in a tower above a high cliff. Each building was red and white, the colors of the Canadian Coast Guard, and faced Queen Charlotte Sound. Whitecaps dotted the water below, and to the south a layer of clouds stole the tops of mountains on Vancouver Island.

Inside the middle house, Dan and Dennis led us into a warm kitchen where the air was moist and delicious, and steam covered a window above the sink. A woman sat at the table with three children; another woman rinsed a pot in the sink. Dan and Dennis laughed at a joke as a radio crackled a weather report in the background, then the woman at the sink dried her hands and walked toward us.

"I'm Cynthia," she said with a smile and shook my hand firmly. She was around thirty, strong and attractive, with slightly curled light brown hair to her shoulders. She wore an apron and held a serving spoon in her other hand.

Then Fil stood up from the table and introduced herself quietly. She was in her fifties and shorter than Cynthia, with short, black hair and a tan complexion. Next, Cynthia introduced her children, Heather, Sylvia and Patricia, who were seven, five and four. Each had blond hair, and they sat at one end of the table looking up with caution and curiosity.

"I hope you like ham," said Cynthia, loading fresh cuts of meat onto a plate with heaps of potatoes, cooked string beans and a warm, buttered roll. She served everyone as her husband Dennis pulled extra chairs to the table.

The warm kitchen, friendly people, and big meal were the last things I imagined when we left Port Hardy nine hours earlier, and I wished Jenn and Karen could see how our first night was going. Conversation was lively around the crowded table as we introduced our lives to each other. Fil was a native of Portugal. She and Dan had met in Prince Rupert and married seven years earlier. They had been on Pine Island for a few years and talked about retiring in Portugal.

Dennis was affable and tall with scrambled brown hair and baby-fat cheeks. He and Cynthia had been on Pine Island for six years. Cynthia's grandfather had been a lightkeeper out of Halifax and her father had been in the navy and had also spent a short time as a lightkeeper on Canada's east coast.

The sun disappeared into high clouds as we ate. And by eight o'clock, with Queen Charlotte Sound consumed in darkness, light rain began falling. Cynthia cleared the dishes, the children left the table to do schoolwork and Fil served coffee as the conversation moved to our trip. Among other things, our hosts wanted to know how we were getting our food, how long we thought it would take to get to Juneau, and whether we were prepared for hypothermia. Dennis brought maps to the table, and we discussed possible routes through the area. I felt relief when our plans met their approval.

At nine o'clock, still sitting at the table, Cynthia served ice cream and pie. The world outside was oily black and fast raindrops smacked the big living room window. They ran down the glass in defeated streams that sparkled silver in the kitchen light's reflection. Gusts of wind howled outside the door and shook the window.

At ten o'clock Dennis leaned back in his chair and stretched. Fil had been quiet for a while, and her eyes were tired. Dan stood and switched on the marine radio by the window, which crackled to life with a constant flow of weather and sea-state information. After a few minutes it broadcast reports for northern Vancouver Island and Queen Charlotte Sound. We listened quietly as it called for heavy rain, gale winds and seas to fifteen feet the following day and three consecutive low-pressure systems in the days ahead.

"Well, I don't know if you'll be making your crossing tomorrow," Dan sighed, "it sounds like the storm will last through the day. You might be able to get across in the break between lows the day after. We have spare rooms and you're welcome to stay here until the weather improves. In fact," he chuckled, "we have a whole spare house for you."

The spare house was thirty yards downhill and was used when maintenance crews came to work on the light. Dennis led us inside a kitchen cluttered with fishing gear, an old sink and some tools. Young pepper plants filled trays on the window sills, old issues of *National Geographic* lined a bookshelf beside an unplugged refrigerator and a bare light bulb hung from the ceiling, illuminating plain walls. Walking down a hallway, Dennis showed us to rooms with clean linens and windows facing the sound. After chatting briefly he walked out into wind and rain, and Bill and I fell asleep quickly in our rooms.

■ ■ ■

Although Russian fur traders reached southern southeast Alaska by 1741, white traffic in the southern Inside Passage was not common until after James Cook's explorations of 1778. Cook died in Hawaii in 1779, but his crew returned to England with news of the region's abundant sea otters, creating the first rush of whites to the area. However, traffic in the inland waters, made hazardous by strong tides and uncharted rocks, remained light until the gold discoveries of the mid-1800s.

With increasing shipwrecks, British Columbia built its first lighthouse near southern Vancouver Island in 1860. Eleven others followed by 1895, most of them within the 300 miles of tricky channels between Vancouver Island and the mainland. But the Klondike gold rushes of the late 1890s, which brought tens of thousands of gold-seekers through the Inside Passage, prompted new lights from Vancouver to Prince Rupert. Twenty-three went into operation between 1898 and 1909, including Pine Island in 1907. They came at a time when radar was uncommon. In fog, storms and darkness, the lights provided the only indication of dangerous rocks, shallows or the safe route through tight passes with swift tidal currents.

Early lightkeepers, both men and women, worked endless hours under grueling and dangerous conditions. They chopped kindling and shoveled coal to feed steam engines and repaired faulty gas lights at all hours, regardless of the weather. Each time a boat approached, they ran out to rocky points, often in blowing rain, snow and surf, to hand-crank deafening foghorns. When diesel and gas replaced steam, they hauled heavy fuel barrels over rocky headlands and steep hills to hand-pump fuel into loud engines. Sleep came only in catnaps, as they broadcast weather every three hours, and many risked their lives in rowboats to rescue shipwreck victims in heavy seas. They constantly battled the weather and sea to keep their lights standing, repairing boardwalks, towers and quarters after each stormy winter and frequently cleaning lenses, overhauling engines and painting everything.

Winters brought endless gales of rain and wet snow with surf exploding 100 feet into the air. In 1947, high seas demolished the Egg Island Light in Queen Charlotte Sound twenty miles north of Pine Island. Before their rescue, the keeper and his family spent five days huddled in wet woods without food or fresh clothes, slowly dying of hypothermia. In 1967, a giant wave destroyed the Pine Island Light and its helicopter pad and heavily damaged its living quarters. The lightkeepers spent a miserable night in the woods around a small fire, and the light was later rebuilt on higher ground.

Access to the lights was difficult, and many keepers received provisions and mail only once every six months. Some lights were on large islands or the mainland, where gardens, deer or small game augmented provisions, but others were on barren islands with no such opportunities. In emergencies, lightkeepers rowed small boats through rough seas or hiked for days through thick rain forest to reach help.

Early lightkeepers received little pay for their risks and hard work. Many earned only a dollar a day after paying assistants from their own pockets, which left almost nothing for medical bills or schooling for their children. In addition to the cost of food, they paid for delivery of provisions to their remote posts, supplies that were sometimes lost in the rough landings. They received no holidays or overtime. If they needed to leave their station, even for health reasons, they had to find and pay a replacement.

Even as traffic increased in the Inside Passage, raises were meager and uncommon. Pensions were small and without guarantee. After decades of service many lightkeepers retired in poverty, while others succumbed to madness, depression or alcoholism. A few committed suicide or simply disappeared, and some drowned in rough seas while rowing after mail, food or mere contact with the outside world. British Columbia lightkeepers were not granted annual leave until the 1940s, and an eight-hour day with paid overtime did not come until 1971. By far, they were the lowest paid government employees.

But many loved the beauty and hard work of the coast. In long letters written from their remote homes, they told their families or lovers hundreds of miles away about sunsets, gales, solitude and freedom from supervision. They raised children safe from society's hazards and passed long nights reading books or bundles of outdated newspapers delivered with their food. They fostered strong friendships with other lightkeepers and the crews of ships.

By 1960, when the last British Columbia lighthouse was built, there were close to fifty staffed lights from Vancouver to Prince Rupert. However, about three-quarters of the lights on Canada's eastern coast were already fully automated, and in the 1970s British Columbia began automating its lights, too. When Bill and I arrived on Pine Island thirty-five staffed lights remained, vestiges of a disappearing lifestyle. Eight more were automated by 2002, including Pine Island. Passing it aboard ferries several times in the late nineties, I wondered what had become of its keepers.

■ ■ ■

Life for Dan and Dennis, the only Coast Guard employees on Pine Island, was much better than that of their predecessors. Their remuneration included housing, food and full benefits for themselves and their families, and although they still issued weather reports every three hours, maintaining and operating the light did not always amount to forty hours per week. In their spare time, they maintained a chicken coop and two big gardens and kept busy with letters, books and hobbies. The children attended correspondence school, and the marine radio provided contact with other lightkeepers.

Although only nine miles northeast of Vancouver Island, Pine Island was extremely remote. Its residents received mail and food via helicopter once each month, and while boats were common in Queen Charlotte Sound, visitors were very rare. The steep shores made use of a boat difficult, and rough winter seas prevented construction of a dock. Leaving Pine Island required expensive helicopter time, and although the Coast Guard provided free flights to Port Hardy for vacation and other necessities, Cynthia and Dennis had not left in eight months and Dan and Fil had been there for eleven months.

In 1860, when all North American conifers were commonly called pines, a survey crew named Pine Island for its thick forest rising abruptly from Queen Charlotte Strait. The forest consists of mature cedar, spruce and hemlock surrounded by lush understory and grows to the edges of the island's steep shores. The island is only one square mile in size, and its highest point is just under 100 feet above sea level. It takes less than fifteen minutes to cross it in any direction.

Pine Island is virtually defenseless from northwesterly winds and seas from Queen Charlotte Sound and southeasterlies from the gap between Vancouver Island and the mainland. Winter storms pack hurricane-force gusts and waves to forty feet. Cynthia provided vivid accounts of helicopters blown toward the house while attempting landings in December and January. She pointed to the window facing the helicopter pad and explained how she would sometimes duck, sure that the winds would deliver a helicopter into their living room. Sometimes food and mail were delayed for days.

For four days high winds and big seas marooned us on the island, and we easily slipped into what Dan called "Pine Island time," a dimension where life moved slower than for the rest of the world and where conversations were long and entertaining. Each day our hosts invited us to one of the houses for lunch or a midafternoon "cuppa," a caffeine fix involving an hour or more of conversation. And each night as the storms faded into darkness they invited us to share delicious dinners. Afterward, we engaged in winding conversations covering everything from politics and international affairs to the cost of marriage. Jokes were frequent and lulls were rare, and each night we staggered back to the spare house exhausted from food and conversation, but thoroughly entertained.

Bill and I had endless questions about their lives and the coast, which they rewarded with wild stories: rescues, drownings, shipwrecks, big winds. They told us of a man shipwrecked for a few months on a remote island bordering the sound and a kayaker found upside down in his boat, snarled in a crabpot line. Apparently, he had been helping himself to a free meal when he capsized.

"Do you see many kayakers?"

"We've had a few come visit," Cynthia told us. "We still keep in touch with...oh Dennis, what's their names?"

Pine Island had an oral history. The couples knew each other's stories well and nodded or coached each time someone shared a good anecdote. When names or locations could not be remembered, the others filled in the blanks.

"Honey, did ya hear that Lester Winthrop got in another helicopter crash?"

Routine conversation sometimes revolved around extraordinary events, like the fact that Lester had the misfortune of more than one helicopter crash.

"What will you do when they automate the light," I asked one evening.

"Lightkeepers do one of three things when they retire," responded Dan. "They either build a boat, write a book or build a boat *and* write a book."

With wind lashing rain against the windows, we traded stories until well after dinner. In addition to stories, we gained the invaluable benefit of local knowledge. We pored over maps, and they showed us where bears were common, fishing was good and the tide ran fast. They showed where we might find nineteenth-century totem poles and pointed out other manned lights where we might be welcome. Dan and Dennis were particularly knowledgeable about

Beaufort Number	MPH	Km/h	Kts	Observations on Land and Sea
0 (calm)	0	0	0-1	Smoke rises vertically; sea like a mirror
1 (light air)	1.2-3	2-5	1-3	Smokes moves slightly, showing direction of wind; ripples with scales
2 (light breeze)	3.7 - 7.5	6-12	4-6	Wind felt on face and leaves rustle; small wavelets are glassy, not breaking
3 (gentle breeze)	8 - 12.5	13-20	7-10	Small branches sway, light flags extend; large wavelets with scattered whitecaps
4 (moderate breeze)	13 - 18.6	21-30	11-16	Dust, sand rise, larger branches sway; small waves, frequent whitecaps
5 (fresh breeze)	19.3 - 25	31-40	17-21	Small trees sway; moderate waves, getting bigger, whitecaps, some spray
6(strong breeze)	25.5 - 31	41-50	22-27	Large branches in motion, whistling in wires; large waves, abundant whitecaps, spray
7 (moderate gale)	32 - 38	51-61	28-33	Large trees in motion, resistance while walking; sea heaps in large waves with foam and spray blown in streaks
8 (fresh gale)	39 - 46	62-74	34-40	Twigs and small branches break from trees; moderately high waves of greater length with crests breaking, foam, and spray blown in streaks
9 (strong gale)	47 - 55	75-89	41-47	Branches break from trees, slight structural damage; high waves, rolling sea, dense foam, spray can limit visibility
10 (whole gale)	56 - 64	90-103	48-55	Trees are uprooted, considerable structural damage; high waves with overhanging crests, sea looks white from foam and blowing spray, visibility reduced.
11 (storm)	65 - 74	104-119	56-63	Widespread damage; sea rolling and white
12 (hurricane)	75+	120+	64 +	Structural damage on land and storm waves at sea

Figure 2.1: Beaufort Wind Scale

the weather and sea. Looking through their windows at stormy weather, they taught us about wave height, swell direction and storm patterns. And they warned us about areas like Cape Caution, where shallows and offshore rocks created dangerous seas.

Standing by the living room window on the third afternoon, I asked Dennis about the wind speed in Queen Charlotte Strait, where whitecaps dotted the gray water. He estimated the seas at ten feet and the wind between twenty-five and thirty knots, and then retrieved a Beaufort scale from a nearby desk. The scale correlates observable sea conditions with wind speed; "popcorn" surf, whitecaps and blowing spray each occur at certain wind speeds. Sometimes the visit felt like an introductory course to paddling the Inside Passage.

Each day we felt increasing guilt about staying so long and accepting their food, and we offered to help with chores whenever we could and repeatedly tried to use our own food.

■ ■ ■

The wind blew persistently at thirty-five knots with gusts to fifty on the fourth morning, covering Queen Charlotte Sound with white-caps. They absorbed light from below heavy clouds and shone brightly against the dark gray sea. Frequent gusts stripped spray from the tops of waves, whipping it over the water like blowing snow. I wondered how we would ever get off Pine Island.

Late in the morning Bill and I hiked to the south shore and crouched by our boats. The wind rustled grasses and whipped our hair; waves foamed inside crevices in the rocky shore, rising six feet then dropping with a loud sucking sound. The biggest waves ham-mered the rocks and shot spray upward into blowing rain. Simply getting the boats into the surf zone was beyond my comfort level. I thought paddling in such conditions would be terrifying. I wondered how Natives had navigated through the rough waters in dugout canoes and began feeling unqualified to paddle the coast.

In the distance heavy clouds appeared ready to crush the low, blue mountains of the mainland. We discussed our food delivery that was due soon in Hartley Bay, nearly 200 miles away by kayak. In four days we had covered only eighteen miles, and we worried the food would either perish before we reached it or be returned by the postmaster if we were too late. If we arrived in the remote vil-lage and the food had been returned to New Jersey, we would be in serious trouble. It was unlikely a small village could provide enough provisions for the next leg of our trip. I felt our plan unraveling.

Bill returned to the house to read, and I went to explore Pine Island's small forest. Standing beneath a tall spruce, I watched an auklet-fattened eagle drop silently from a high limb, its wings extending gracefully to catch its heavy weight. It flew overhead with powerful wing beats as I reached a high point on the northeast edge of the island. Below, big waves hurried northward toward

2.2: ESKIMO AND ALEUT ORIGINS OF THE KAYAK

Although common in the Inside Passage today, kayaks were not traditionally used in the region. Instead, they were developed between western Prince William Sound and the Aleutian Islands and in northern latitudes between eastern Siberia and Greenland. They varied greatly across this vast region due to differences in geography, environment and food sources.

Original kayaks were fast, highly maneuverable skin boats with low profiles and shallow drafts and were used for fishing, whaling and hunting shorebirds and sea mammals. With narrow, double-bladed paddles made of wood and bone, hunters traveled great distances in short periods, protected from rain and surf by spray skirts made of skins and intestine. Some skirts were attached to jackets and hoods with sinew drawstrings that tightened around the cockpit combing, hood, wrists and waist. The boat's low profile cut through wind and enabled hunters to silently approach prey, and its light weight helped them portage across ice and land.

Like today's boats, original

Cape Caution. They stood tall, crested, then toppled as they rushed past the island. A sea lion smoothly broke the surface of the moving water, blowing mist from its nose and swimming effortlessly toward Cape Caution. There were gulls, too, coasting northward in the wind, and a couple brave captains pushed small boats in the same direction. I shook my head: everything capable of movement seemed headed easily for Cape Caution, a battered nub of coast impossible for us to reach.

Cape Caution. What a name, I thought. It had been on my mind for days, and I even recalled seeing it weeks earlier on the map in Colorado, a rounded protuberance sticking westward into the sea, stubbornly defying the big water of Queen Charlotte Sound. I had looked at it with curiosity and fear, picturing an age-old contest between land and sea, with great explosions of surf sending water and earth dozens of feet into the air.

My spirits sank as I walked back to the house, knowing I had nothing to do there but listen to the weather and stare out at heavy seas. I felt discouraged about losing four days of travel and guilty about all the food we had accepted. Under gray-washed skies, the surrounding seas looked too cold and bleak for a paddle trip, and I succumbed to a sense of failure I had tried to resist for days. I was sure Bill felt the same.

Back at the house we listened to

the forecast on our small radio. It predicted the departure of one low early the next morning and the arrival of another that afternoon, with seas to fifteen feet by nightfall. After trying to guess whether the seas would diminish significantly between the lows, we agreed to make an attempt to leave the island early in the morning. We spread the maps on the kitchen table and plotted a course directly for Cape Caution, ten miles away at a heading of 350 degrees. We could rest on one of the small Storm Islands three miles into the crossing. If the seas grew too big we could either set camp there or head twenty degrees north-northeast to a piece of mainland five miles away and five miles south of the cape. By either course, we hoped to reach mainland by afternoon.

We were up at six and finished breakfast by seven-thirty. We thanked our hosts profusely, exchanged addresses and promised to keep in touch. An hour later we reached the south end of the island and looked nervously down at four-foot swells rising and falling against black rocks. We knew the water would be bigger further from the island.

The rocky shore was too steep and the surf zone too active to enter the water in a conventional manner, leaving a seal launch our only option. We positioned Bill's boat on a sheer bench five feet above where the highest waves struck the island. His seat

kayaks were between fifteen and twenty feet long, eighteen to thirty-two inches wide at the cockpit, and eight to sixteen inches deep. They had sloping decks that drained rain and surf and deck rigging made of sinew thongs stretched between adjustable knobs of wood, bone or ivory. Hunters kept lances, harpoons and floats made of seal bladder on deck, along with trays that held harpoon line. The boats had removable seats, sometimes long enough to accommodate outstretched legs, that prevented sand and shells from tearing the skin covering. Most kayaks had one cockpit, but some had two back-to-back.

Early kayaks were sturdy, with continuous frame pieces often made of willow fastened to gunwales by wood and bone pegs and sinew lashings. Dried skins from seals, walrus, sea lions and other animals were sewn with braided sinew, then soaked in hot water and stretched over the frame. They were only attached at the cockpit. Where skins were joined, double seams, blubber and melted tallow provided waterproofing. Heavy coats of fish or animal oil provided additional but temporary protection. Where sea ice was common, plates of bone lined the hull at the bow and stern.

Both men and women contributed to kayak construction, with men typically constructing frames and women sewing skins, but only men hunted in them.

balanced at the edge of the rock, and his bow overhung the water by seven feet. Sitting on his stern I stabilized the boat as he climbed into the cockpit and secured his spray skirt.

Waves usually arrive in recurring patterns, with isolated big waves followed by a few smaller ones. Watching the waves for a few minutes we tried to predict when the largest would arrive. Launching into the biggest wave would minimize the drop to the water and take advantage of the smaller waves that would follow.

"Are you ready, Bill?"

"Are you sure you've done this before?" It was an understandable question from a man about to be pushed off a cliff into rough seas.

"Trust me," I said, hoping it would work.

As a high wave broke, then flooded against the rocks below Bill's boat, I gave his stern a hard shove. What followed seemed to occur in slow motion. His bow, laden with gear and food, sunk into the ocean, and his stern rose into the air above the ledge. Then the boat slid forward, plunging into the water at a forty-five degree angle. His entire bow submerged, foam and white water encircling it greedily, and the front of his cockpit started sinking. It looked like his boat would simply dive to the bottom of the sea. My mouth opened wide, and I think I raised my hands in the air. I should have pushed harder.

But suddenly his stern cleared the rock and fell toward the water. His bow rose quickly, surfacing like a submarine with water sliding off its deck. Off balance in the waves, Bill braced hard with his paddle gaining support by leaning on its shaft while pressing its blade horizontally against the water. A moment later he looked back with a big smile, surprised and ecstatic. But from land I could only focus on the wave building in front of him. If he doesn't stop looking at me and start paddling, I thought, he'll be slammed against the rocks.

"Paddle!" I yelled.

His smile vanished, and he turned his head quickly. Just in time, he gave a few strong strokes and his bow pierced the oncoming wave. It launched into the air and slammed down with a splash. Moments later the wave swelled against the rocks and turned to white water. Safely beyond the surf, he turned to me again with a broad smile.

"Let's go!" he shouted, his paddle high in the air.

With no one to help me into the water, I managed only half-hearted enthusiasm. Nervously, I balanced my boat on the ledge and climbed inside, my fingers trembling as I lay my paddle across my cockpit and looked down at the waves. As a big mound of water built toward shore, I swallowed hard and put my hands on the wet rocks beside me. Then I shoved with all my strength and grabbed my paddle as my boat tilted over the edge and slid forward. But my stern hung on the ledge, and when the wave receded my bow wedged against a rock, leaving me precariously balanced at a thirty-degree angle. A few seconds later, the next wave engulfed my bow and shoved my boat partially onto its side. I jammed my paddle blade against the shore to stay upright and, with my heart racing, I expected the next wave to dump me into the surf.

But as the next wave lifted my bow I dug my paddle into the water and made desperate strokes. Much to my surprise my boat moved forward, its stern clearing the ledge and slapping the water. I paddled hard and my bow pierced the next wave, rising into the air and returning to water with a loud smack. A few seconds later I rafted alongside Bill, safely away from shore. I was shaking, but we both wore broad smiles and enjoyed the subsiding adrenaline. Four-foot rollers bobbed our boats up and down.

"Not so bad, huh?" I asked, slightly out of breath.

"I can deal with this," Bill laughed.

I was unaware I was about to face the most prolonged period of fear of my life.

CHAPTER THREE

Fear and Loathing in the Sound—Twelve-Foot Seas in a Seventeen-Foot Boat

Windier, huh?" Bill's face looked serious.

"Yeah, with these waves—" I stopped as a wave lifted my boat surprisingly high from behind. My stomach dropped as I slid down the crest's back. Only a quarter mile from Pine Island the wind had increased significantly. The waves rose to six and eight feet, tossing our boats around. Cold rain stung our faces.

"We better cut toward the south side of the Storm Islands," I called over the rushing wind and waves, "and head straight for the mainland. We'll worry about Cape Caution later." We were twenty feet apart, bracing on both sides against big waves.

"Okay," I said, "see the mainland hill south of Cape Caution, the one behind the Storm Islands?"

"Yeah, it slopes to the south, right?" He sounded nervous.

"Yeah…let's head for the part of the Storm Islands directly below that."

Our new course required paddling northeast for eight miles to a point six miles south of Cape Caution, the quickest route to the mainland. After three miles we could rest or camp on the Storm Islands before the remaining five miles of open water. Unfortunately, the southeasterly waves would hit us at the quarter-stern, about a forty-five degree angle from behind, the whole way, each wave threatening to broach our boats and make us highly susceptible to capsize. Preventing a broach would require frequent braces and corrective strokes. We were both nervous, having never been in waves that big, and knew seas near the Storm Islands, the most exposed part of the crossing, would likely be even bigger.

The weather was another concern. The morning forecast still called for the departure of one low in the morning and the arrival of another in the afternoon, but left us wondering when or if a lull between lows would occur. As we maneuvered our bows at the Storm Islands through heaving water, I worried that we were already in the lull and that the big waves and blowing rain represented the best conditions of the day. I tried to reassure myself that we were still experiencing the end of the departing low, which meant conditions could soon improve. But what if the new storm arrived early or, worse, what if it had already begun? Conditions would deteriorate as we approached the most exposed section of the crossing.

Struggling to stay pointed northeastward, we quietly wondered if we were qualified for the crossing. The unspoken truth was that if one of us capsized and was unable to pull a roll, an assisted rescue would be extremely difficult—the waves would hamper each attempt and the cold water would quickly incapacitate the victim. Continued attempts would put the rescuer at risk of a capsize, which was almost a hopeless situation. Even just a quarter mile from Pine Island, swimming ashore was impossible in the cold water, and with the lighthouse on the opposite side of the island, no one would see us if we were in trouble. Suddenly, I wondered if we were being foolish. After all, we left the island to avoid the embarrassment of staying longer and the frustration of a fifth day without progress. Pride and impatience didn't seem good reasons to risk our lives.

"You sure about this?" I yelled to Bill.

"I could *definitely* turn back!"

While truthful, it was not the response I wanted; I had hoped for reassurance. Looking back at Pine Island I envisioned us returning to the house, and when I realized we would be just in time for lunch my face flushed.

"You have the marine radio close, right?" I shouted.

"Yup." He nodded toward a dry bag secured to his deck.

"I'm willing to give it a try. The radio's a good safety net."

He nodded.

"If something happens," he said, "we'll pull parallel for a rescue, right?"

"Yeah, with rescuer upwind."

The Storm Islands were a thin line facing northwest, as if blown into formation by southeasterly winds. The largest were less than half the size of Pine Island, with low forest hunkered against the wind and looking bent to the northwest atop their highest points. Many of the islands were much smaller, and some were just barren rocks. From three miles away we could see white surf surrounding their rocky shores. Beyond them the mainland was blue and formless. It looked too far to be reached in a single day.

The wind intensified as we paddled beyond the protection of Pine Island, and soon we were in waves to twelve feet, with their crests breaking and piles of white water rushing loudly a few feet down their faces, creating a continuous roar. With our legs and butts slightly below the surface, the waves appeared huge; fearing they would surf us into each other, we put more than fifty feet between us. When we sank into the troughs, we couldn't see each other or any land, just twelve-foot walls of steep green water about twenty feet apart rushing stubbornly northwestward. They formed terrifying prisons of cold water, with wind occasionally stripping spray from their tops.

After a few seconds in each trough big waves lifted us from the quarter-stern. We rose quickly to their tops, where crests crumbled into white water on either side. Rain and spray stung our faces, and gusty winds yanked at our paddles. With the taste of salt on our lips, we squinted into blowing water and glimpsed islands, mainland and each other before sliding down each wave's back. Bill looked small and vulnerable as he rose and fell on the heaving waves. The sea was like a mad bull trying to throw him from its back.

When waves broke under me I leaned into them and braced hard with my paddle. Sometimes they surfed my kayak forward on their crests, my bow suspended over the trough ahead. When they finally slid beneath me my bow pointed skyward, and I sank down the wave's back. Other times the size or direction of waves surprised me, bullying my boat one way then the other, or dropping me suddenly into a deep trough. It was occasionally nauseating, and a few times I braced quickly, sure I was about to capsize. Maintaining our course required frequent corrective strokes, and broaching was a constant threat. Breathing hard, with my heart beating fast, I spoke aloud—to myself, my paddle, the sea—in an effort to claim control of the situation.

Temperatures remained around fifty with moderate showers.

Blowing rain and spray soaked my fleece hat and matted my hair against my forehead. After ninety minutes in twelve-foot seas we drew within a quarter mile of the Storm Islands, where surf roared above the wind and waves. Waves rolled over and exploded against rocks, trapping pockets of air that thudded like bombs and pitching water thirty feet into the air. A tumult of white and green water surrounded each island and sounded like a freight train.

We paddled north along craggy shores looking for a lee-side landing and giving wide berth to the violent surf. Rough headlands covered in blowing grass led up to stunted forests, where trees swayed in the wind. They leaned to the northwest with few branches growing on their south sides, like the islands had never seen a calm day.

Near one of the northern-most islands we reached the mouth of a narrow inlet partially protected by a rocky point. Five-foot rollers disappeared between cliffs thirty feet high, but we could not see where they landed. I waited for a series of small waves, then paddled cautiously into the opening to see if it led to a beach. I paddled thirty feet and rounding a bend saw the inlet narrow abruptly into a bouldery notch where waves stood to eight feet and crashed against a thick log crammed into the rocks 100 feet away. I suddenly realized I was too close to the end of the inlet, with the waves drawing me further inside, and began back-paddling frantically. The inlet was too narrow for turning around, and I looked over my shoulder at big waves approaching fast from behind. My stern rose over one wave as I moved backward, but a second engulfed my stern and slammed against my back, breaking under my cockpit and moving me forward again. As the inlet ahead filled with white water I back-paddled with all my strength, afraid the next wave would surf me against the rocks. I rose over two more waves, then exited the inlet and turned around.

"How's it look?" Bill asked as I paddled alongside him.

"No way," is all I managed to say. My hands were shaking and my heart was beating so hard I could feel it pounding against my life jacket through layers of fleece and rain gear.

We continued to the north end of the islands, where the waves diminished to four feet but collided against each other from different angles. They formed steep pyramids that lifted and dropped our boats quickly—I didn't know if I would capsize or vomit first. But with hard strokes and frequent braces we broke into the lee of the islands and rose and fell on mellow rollers only three feet high. Approaching the rocky shore we found another narrow inlet, this one between three tightly spaced islands. We surfed a small wave through the inlet and arrived in a lagoon fed by two other inlets, where two-foot waves milled around confused. A solid raft of about fifty logs diffused the waves, and after forcing our way through them we landed on soft sand between piles of jagged boulders.

With a small patch of blue sky opening overhead amid thick clouds, we clambered over broken rocks into a stunted forest of spruce and mountain hemlock. We climbed fifty feet above the water and sat on a ledge facing Queen Charlotte Sound. The sea was dark gray and dotted with whitecaps; the surf broke loudly below us. With wind rushing through the trees overhead, we ate granola bars and hot soup from thermoses, but before long started shivering in our wet clothes.

We climbed back down to our boats, then forced our way through the floating logs with our paddles. At the mouth of the inlet we agreed on a mainland bay five miles to the northeast, then returned to the big, breaking swells and high wind. Clouds swallowed the patch of blue sky, and soon the wind drove raindrops against our faces.

But the wind slowly diminished after ninety minutes, and the waves decreased to eight feet, then six. We were still a few miles from shore but had reached the lee of the mainland to our south. Regardless of how hard the wind blew in the strait, the conditions would continue to mellow as we approached land. Soon the waves stopped breaking and shrank to five feet, and I began believing we would survive the crossing. Slowly, a long sand beach ahead gained detail, with waves breaking on black boulders in the intertidal and tough grasses swaying above the high tide line. We could see branches shaking in the wind on trees that had been a blue blur four hours earlier.

But two hours after leaving the Storm Islands my relief turned to overwhelming fatigue. My leg muscles cramped, my knees felt sore and I developed a headache, the result of drinking too little water. The light fiberglass paddle began to feel like a two-by-four, and the water took on the consistency of molasses. And that's when the headwind blasted us. It seemed to come directly from the beach ahead, a constant force that pushed hard against our progress, and although we paddled with all our remaining strength I sometimes felt no progress at all. Each time we rested, the wind stopped us immediately and shoved us backward.

After battling the wind for thirty minutes, we finally reached the edge of the surf zone, where waves stood to five feet before breaking against a long, sandy beach about fifty yards away. Great sheets of spray blew from their tops and trailed seaward in silver manes. With spray lashing our faces, we held our position at the edge of the surf zone by paddling forward with moderate strength. We watched the waves, trying to determine when the largest would arrive. A large wave would deliver us high onto the beach, while smaller ones would strand us in the surf zone to be hit by waves as we exited our boats.

We chose our wave after a few minutes. As it approached quickly from behind, rising to five feet, we paddled hard to stay in front of it. Looking back, I saw the wind peel a layer of water from its top and shoot it seaward.

"Here it comes!" I yelled as it broke.

A pile of roiling foam sped toward us, and we leaned hard to the right, angling our beams at it for stability. The pile jolted our boats and sped us toward the beach as we leaned and braced our paddles against it. In seconds it delivered us through the surf zone and ran our boats high onto the sandy beach. As it receded, we jumped from our boats and dragged them a short distance up the beach, then collapsed onto the sand and laughed. We lay there for half an hour, exhausted, wet and incredibly relieved, then it began pouring rain.

We scrambled to our feet and began unpacking the boats. We took the tent, sleeping bags, sleeping rolls and dry bags full of spare clothes to a flat spot in the forest, then carried the stoves, cook set and bags of food to the base of a cliff 200 feet away. With fat raindrops assaulting us, Bill set up the tent and I tied a tarp near the cliff to make our kitchen, then we hurried into the tent to change clothes and climb deep inside our sleeping bags. For a couple hours we napped and reminisced about the crossing while rain drummed steadily at the tent.

An hour before dark we walked to the kitchen and quietly ate a pasta dinner while looking out at Queen Charlotte Strait. Gray clouds moved busily above gray water, and waves toppled noisily onto our beach. An unbroken forest surrounded our bay, and strong wind gusted through the trees overhead. Light rain crackled on the tarp.

After dinner, we hung our food in a tree, washed the dishes at the edge of the bay, and tied our boats to drift logs at the head of the beach. As darkness fell, we stood at the water's edge and brushed our teeth in light rain, then retired to the tent. I tried to read but was too tired. Instead, I lay on my back and listened to the waves collapse on the beach. It sounded like a bowling alley on a Saturday night, with everyone hitting strikes.

■ ■ ■

By the early eighteenth century, Russian fur traders had overexploited fox and sable populations in Siberia and Kamchatka, threatening to end a lucrative fur trade with China. Hoping to find another fur resource, Vitus Bering made secret, Russian-sponsored expeditions north and east of Kamchatka during the first half of the century and crossed the North Pacific to Alaska in 1741 with Aleksei Chirikov. They soon reached southern southeast Alaska and became the first whites to contact Natives of the Inside Passage. Chirikov disappeared in southeast Alaska, but in 1743 Bering returned to Russia with sea otter pelts. *Promyshlenniks*, freelance Russian fur traders, soon swarmed to the area, crossing the North Pacific in inefficient, risky boats and establishing posts along the Gulf of Alaska. As they overhunted along the Aleutians and south-central Alaska, they pushed east, eventually settling forts at Sitka in 1799 and Wrangell in 1823. Although they received no protection from their government, whose capital was 7,000 miles away, their presence validated Russian claims to Alaska.

Due to Russian secrecy, promyshlenniks monopolized Alaskan furs for almost forty years, but in the 1770s Spain became concerned about Russian advances southward, fearing conflict with Spanish California. Beginning in 1774, Spain sent two expeditions to investigate Russian activity on the northwest coast and find the Northwest Passage, a navigable waterway rumored to link the Pacific and Atlantic Oceans through North America. The Spanish became the first Europeans to sail the southern British Columbia coast and claimed the region for Spain. But in 1778 British captain

James Cook sailed along the northwest coast from Oregon to far northwestern Alaska, also searching for the Northwest Passage. Among his officers was a twenty-one-year-old George Vancouver, and in generally poor weather the expedition mistook the outer coast of the Inside Passage for the continental shore.

The Spanish and British expeditions of the 1770s brought word to Europe and America of the fur resources of the Inside Passage, beginning a rush to the area. In 1788, British traders established a small post at Nootka Sound on western Vancouver Island, but the following year Spanish traders seized British ships, personnel and property there, which almost led the two countries to war. However, in 1790 they signed the Nootka Convention, which required Spain to return British property at Nootka and established shared hunting rights along the northwest coast. The treaty did not determine possession south of Alaska, and by the early 1790s British, Spanish, Russian and American traders were all traveling the Inside Passage.

As the sea otter trade grew, so did the importance of finding the Northwest Passage, which could give one country control over an essential trade route between Europe and Asia. Based on observations made by Cook in 1778, modern maps showed the passage flowing from Great Slave Lake to Cook Inlet. Another popular theory had it crossing the midcontinent and emptying into Puget Sound.

The Spanish led the race to find the Northwest Passage in the early 1790s, sending expeditions into Puget Sound and as far north as Yakutat Bay in the Gulf of Alaska, and by 1792 their repeated dead-end investigations had convinced many that there was no Northwest Passage. In 1793, Hudson's Bay Company trader Alexander Mackenzie provided further proof by traveling the Mackenzie River from Great Slave Lake to the Arctic Ocean and the Peace River to Burke Channel on the central British Columbia coast, becoming the first white to cross the North American continent north of Mexico. However, in 1791 England had already sent the Discovery and Chatham with roughly 140 men under Captain George Vancouver to find the Northwest Passage.

Vancouver's assignment from the British admiralty was threefold: to sail to Nootka Sound to accept the return of British possessions from the Spanish according to the Nootka Convention; to map in detail the continental shore of North America between thirty and sixty degrees north latitude, which would bolster British claims to the region; and to determine the existence of a Northwest Passage. After a yearlong voyage from England around the Cape of Good Hope, Australia and Hawaii, Vancouver arrived in the Strait of Juan de Fuca in June, 1792. Particularly through contact with the Spanish, he learned that a Northwest Passage was already considered unlikely, news that dampened his crew's morale as they began to see their mission as superfluous. However, rumors persisted, and Vancouver was determined to survey the northwest coast in detail.

Although he hoped to finish his surveys in the summer of 1793, the labyrinthine channels of the Inside Passage required a third season. Almost from the start, he disliked the region for its poor weather, disordered forests and endless amount of dead-end channels. Usually, the channels lacked sufficient wind and were too narrow for the Chatham and Discovery, forcing him to send crews in small boats for weeks at a time to meticulously survey narrow bays and inlets as the larger ships remained anchored in protected coves. After each season Vancouver retreated to the Hawaiian Islands, where his mentor James Cook had been killed thirteen years earlier in a fight with aboriginal people. The expedition returned to England in 1795, having lost only six members.

Vancouver spent the next three years working on his journals, which were published in 1798, shortly after his death, as *Voyage of Discovery to the North Pacific Ocean and Round the World, 1792–1794*. His uncompromising attention to detail produced charts of unprecedented excellence, which were used for more than a century, and he named more than 400 geographic features, usually after crewmembers, family, friends, mentors and prominent figures in England. Most of his names remain today, including Mount Rainier, Mount Baker, Whidbey Island and Puget Sound.

When we finally left the tent around nine the next morning we greeted a day similar to the previous four—gray and cool with intermittent rain and steady wind. It took more than two hours to eat, break camp and pack the boats. It was nearly midday when we sat down to our maps. Cape Caution, after occupying our thoughts for more than a week, was only six miles to the northwest, and we were eager to put it behind us and focus on Calvert Island and our entrance into calm water.

With four-foot waves breaking on our beach, we waited for a

series of small waves, then punched through the surf zone. Paddling northwest through the bay, we rose and fell on four-foot rollers, but after a mile we entered Queen Charlotte Strait, where a strong southerly wind created waves to eight feet. They rose steeply behind us with breaking tops that looked ready to crush our small boats. After a moment atop their crests, with rain and spray blowing past us, they dropped us suddenly into their troughs. Nervous, we sat too rigid, paddled clumsily and braced frequently, looking often to shore for bays that would offer some protection. We discussed going ashore for the day, but the waves

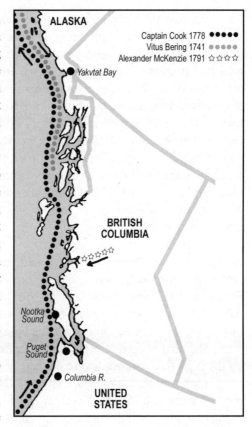

Map 3.1: Pacific Northwest showing English, Russian and Hudson's Bay Company routes from 1741 through 1794. Spanish and American traders and explorers also traveled the coast during that era.

pushed us northward so fast we missed the rare opportunities for good landings.

But after thirty minutes we became more accustomed to the steady rising and falling and after an hour began confidently surfing the waves forward. We found that paddling hard as the waves lifted us enabled their breaking crests to take control of our boats, speeding us northward with our bows overhanging the trough ahead. After fifty or more feet, the crests rolled ahead, releasing us into the next trough. We paddled slowly in the trough, then accelerated our strokes as we rose on the next wave. After much practice and a few panicked braces, we were actually laughing as we sped along the coast.

After less than two hours we approached Cape Caution, a low, flat headland covered in tough grasses, low shrubs and a few gnarled trees. One hundred yards inland, a low forest stood safely retreated from persistently violent surf, and to the west open ocean met gray skies. With our chart showing shallow water near shore, which would increase wave height, we gave the cape berth of more than half a mile, which also kept us out of confused seas likely reflected from shore. Raindrops tapped against our hoods as the waves carried us anticlimactically past the cape, which after so much thought I had come to expect as something violent or imposing, maybe crowned with a thick thunderhead or surrounded by cliffs a thousand feet high. Instead, it was just a storm-beaten headland gliding quickly into our past.

George Vancouver named Cape Caution for the "dangerous navigation in its vicinity" as he sailed past in July, 1792. He had spent the previous two months exploring Puget Sound and Johnstone Strait and determining the insularity of Vancouver Island, which until then was considered part of the mainland. Within hours of passing the cape he almost lost his boat *Discovery* to an offshore rock. The boat hung on the rock in rough seas, but was luckily freed by the high tide without severe damage.

Cape Caution marked our exit from Queen Charlotte Strait and our entrance into South Passage, where we continued north in eight-foot seas with the open ocean appearing infinite to our west. Shortly after rounding the cape, we caught our first view of the placid scenery of the Inside Passage. Calvert Island was about twenty miles to the north, with a solid layer of clouds 2,500 feet above the water engulfing its highest points and its steep hillsides plunging directly into the sea. To its east, across a narrow body of flat-looking water, steep hills on the mainland mirrored Calvert Island, with tops covered in clouds and hillsides sinking precipitously to the sea. Further north, steep hills lined both sides of the narrow water, each dropping sharply and overlapping the next. Fading gradually into the distance, they appeared endless. An unbroken forest colored the hills in the foreground dark green, and those in the background faded blue through gray, with the farthest appearing gossamer, sometimes disappearing altogether in thickening clouds. Misty air softened the details and made everything seem distant.

The Inside Passage appeared a place truly *inside*. It looked calm and enchanted. It even looked warm. The hills layering into the distance were luring and intimate, and the clouds formed a steely ceiling that further enclosed and softened the landscape. Rising and falling on breaking seas and bullied forward by a rain-stung wind, we knew for certain that we were *outside*. The calm of the Inside Passage, though now visible, seemed excruciatingly distant.

A hilly mainland littered with low clouds retreated east after Cape Caution, and soon we were more than a mile from shore. For the next two hours, we repeatedly chose points ahead to land for lunch, but reaching each point we found it easier to continue with the waves than to cross them to the mainland. We far exceeded our self-imposed paddling limit of two hours, and snacked on candy bars and trail mix, bobbing on the sea like flotsam. However, the snacks provided only temporary relief from our growing hunger; the exertion and cool rain quickly sapped our energy. Five miles north of Cape Caution and two miles from the mainland, I felt weak and distracted, but just a mile ahead a tiny island would provide a place to land without cutting across the waves.

Just then a deep sucking sound erupted from the water ahead, and my eyes bulged when I saw a section of the ocean turn suddenly turbulent 100 feet off my bow. At its center, white water spilled from a mound of sharp black rocks—an offshore rock like the one that almost sank Vancouver's *Discovery* more than 200 years earlier. Our low profile and the noise of wind and waves had prevented us from seeing the rock before we were nearly on top of it. Had we paid more attention to our chart, we would have seen it represented as a black asterisk. The chart even indicated the tide level when the rock is exposed.

Big waves toppled over the rock with loud, threatening splashes, then spilled from it in foamy water. Adding a sense of conspiracy, a swell surfed us directly toward the turmoil. Spending our last calories on expletives and corrective strokes, we narrowly avoided the danger, our boats skimming the boundary of the disrupted water as we paddled hard to the northwest.

Nearing the small island we saw a red and white lighthouse atop its highest point, roughly 300 feet above the sea. Our friends on Pine Island had encouraged us to stop there and even radioed the lightkeepers to tell them we were in the area, but we still felt guilty about

3.1: GETTING OUT OF TROUBLE

The following are a few rescue techniques every kayaker should know before hitting the water, no matter their trip duration.

Wet exits: Practicing wet exits, the process of evacuating a capsized boat, is a simple but important exercise. Familiarity with removing the spray skirt while upside-down and under water, which requires pulling the grab-loop toward the cockpit, will provide confidence while paddling and help a paddler calmly deal with the skirt in an emergency. It is essential in the confusion of a wet exit that a victim never let go of the paddle.

Eskimo roll: The beauty of a well-practiced roll is that the paddler can self-rescue without leaving the kayak, a potentially life-saving technique in the cold waters of the Inside Passage. A roll requires a capsize victim to position the paddle above the water and perpendicular to the kayak, then use the paddle as leverage while snapping the knee and hip on one side to right the boat. A roll usually takes a few sessions in a pool to learn, but requires frequent practice in cold and rough water to be reliable.

Self-rescue with a paddle float: Every kayaker should

spending so much time on Pine Island and intended to stop only briefly, then camp on the mainland. If the southerly wind continued, we could arrive close to the calm confines of Calvert Island by early evening.

The scene around the island was similar to that near the Storm Islands the previous day, with big waves exploding loudly against steep rocks and a wide surf zone of green and white water. We nearly circled the island, which was less than half a mile around, before finding a small, lee-side cove where we could safely land. As we climbed ashore on steep rocks, Glen Thomas and his wife Brenda approached from a long flight of wooden stairs leading up a steep hill. They helped us carry our boats to the bottom of a cliff, where we tied them to a huge log.

"We heard from Pine Island you guys were in the area. We actually thought we might see you yesterday. How was the paddling today?"

Glen was balding and rotund and spoke enthusiastically with a friendly smile, and Brenda was thin with long brown hair and let Glen do most of the talking. After a few minutes, they led us up 160 steps to a clearing of grass with two red and white houses and the light overlooking the surrounding water. The wind whipped angrily, driving increasing rain against our faces, and far below the sea was gray and dotted with whitecaps.

We followed them into the first

house, where we met Stan and Judy. Stan was stocky with a weathered face and a gruff voice. He walked to us with a slight limp and shook our hands firmly. Judy was pretty with blonde bangs and a warm smile and served coffee as the six of us sat around their kitchen table. After chatting for more than an hour, Judy invited us to stay for dinner, and with strong winds whipping tree branches and driving rain sideways outside the window, we were happy to stay off the water.

"It sounds like you two will be spending enough time inside your tent soon enough," Stan said.

Judy lent us towels, and we went upstairs and took long showers. It was the warmest I felt in two days, and I took my time rinsing salt from my hands and face and sand from my ears. Afterward, Judy served heaps of chili, and we talked for a few hours about our different lives and life on the coast. They had "been on the lights" since 1969 and in South Passage for eighteen years and possessed a wealth of information about the coast. But like our friends on Pine Island, Stan admitted he was leery of sea kayakers.

"Some people give your sport a bad name by coming here unprepared for the rough weather," he said, "We've had some that seem to think of the Coast Guard as a government service. They expect free food and a place to sleep on a rainy night."

carry a bilge pump and inflatable paddle float lashed to the deck. In the event of a failed roll, the paddler wet exits, rights the capsized kayak by grabbing the opposite side of the cockpit and sinking into the water, then inflates the paddle float and attaches it to one of the paddle blades. After pumping enough water from the cockpit that the boat will float with the victim inside, the victim places the paddle perpendicular to the boat with one blade on the deck and the side with the paddle float in the water. Using the paddle for leverage, the victim climbs belly-down onto the rear deck and corkscrews backwards into the cockpit while maintaining a low profile. Like other rescues, it takes hours of practice to become proficient, which is essential for paddling in cold water.

Assisted rescue: In an assisted rescue, the capsized kayak is placed perpendicular to the rescue kayak, then the rescuer pulls one end onto the cockpit while the victim, still in the water, pushes down on the other end, enabling water to empty from the cockpit. Next, the boat is righted, then they are placed parallel and the rescuer leans over the victim's front deck while the victim climbs onto the back deck, then corkscrews backwards into the cockpit while maintaining a low profile.

All rescues should be practiced repeatedly and in challenging conditions.

When we shared our experience paddling across Queen Charlotte Strait, Stan shook his head and said, "This can be a real not-nice coast sometimes."

We were up early the next morning. Stan warmed cereal for us as we discussed the impending lighthouse automations. Judy appeared and poured herself a cup of coffee, and after breakfast they walked us to the door and wished us luck. In the background, CNN showed live coverage of a memorial service in Oklahoma City for the first anniversary of the bombing. Catching the glimpse of news made me feel the remoteness of the coast.

Outside was gray and breezy, but without rain. We enthusiastically descended the steps knowing Calvert Island and water more typical of the Inside Passage were not far away. The doubt, fear and stress we felt since Port Hardy might finally turn to hope as we made real progress toward Hartley Bay and our food delivery. But as would happen many times in the weeks ahead, unforeseen challenges tempered our optimism. When we reached the bottom of the stairs, we found low tide had exposed an uneven and rocky intertidal fifty yards long and covered in seaweed, tide pools, algae and loose rocks. Sea anemones, cucumbers, barnacles and mussels added to the obstacle course, and it took more than thirty minutes to move all our gear to a shelf by the water. But just as we began packing the boats the advancing tide flooded the narrow shelf, forcing us to move everything back onto a ledge six feet above the water. Glen arrived after a while and watched with interest as we packed the boats. Finally, ninety minutes after leaving the house, we seal launched into the water.

"Now I'm going to have to buy a kayak," Glen said with a chuckle once we were in the water.

We waved goodbye and paddled northeast under gray clouds moving quickly across the sky. Overnight the wind had diminished to breezes, and the waves in South Passage were only four feet high. They moved northward toward Calvert Island, which stood tall and covered in forest only ten miles away. Six miles to its east, mainland hills rose abruptly from the water, overlapping each other into the distance. Between the hills on Calvert and the mainland, Fitz Hugh Sound formed a flat opening six miles wide and thirty miles long—a friendly invitation to the Inside Passage. By afternoon we would be within its confines, with land on every side and no more chances for twelve-foot seas.

After an hour we reached a square-mile island lying flat as a table at the southern edge of Smith Sound, which intruded the mainland for fifteen miles to our east. With our next goal a five-mile crossing to its northern edge, we landed for a break on a narrow beach facing the mainland and sat in wet sand sharing a bag of trail mix. A big bald eagle watched us from atop a nearby snag, and to the east a patch of blue sky opened, an island surrounded by gray clouds, letting a shard of sunlight land on the sea. It drew a shimmering silver line upon a small section of gray water, then disappeared after less than five minutes. We returned to our boats after thirty minutes, with the incoming tide nearly consuming our beach.

Confidently surfing the waves northward, we made the crossing in less than two hours, then continued north along the mainland for two miles. Under a ceiling of gray cloud at 3,000 feet, the layered hills of the Inside Passage gained detail, and soon we saw individual trees in the green blur of temperate rain forest on Calvert Island. The waves shrank to three feet and urged us listlessly toward Fitz Hugh Sound, where they dissipated in flat water. We paddled close to the mainland to find a lunch spot, moving easily between scattered offshore rocks that were no longer seething with surf like the previous day. Long pieces of kelp wavered northward in the direction of the flooding tide, and a family of harlequins hurried close to shore. Oystercatchers stood erect on the rocks, watching us with bright red eyes.

We veered east and paddled between two immense boulders standing thirty feet apart and forming open doors to a glassy lagoon about 100 feet wide. The various greens of cedar, fern, devils club and hemlock overhung its sides like jungle, and it ended 100 yards ahead at a small sand beach littered with gray driftwood and bordered by tall forest. The place was startlingly quiet compared to the riotous surf in Queen Charlotte Strait, with the only sound being my paddle blades sloshing in its flat water.

We sat on the beach eating soup, energy bars and peanut butter and jelly sandwiches, with the water lapping thirty feet away in waves two inches high. After eating, we picked through driftwood and broken shells at the water's edge, then took a short walk into the woods. Soft moss covered the forest floor; ancient cedars, hemlocks and spruces stretched into the sky. Enjoying calm conditions for the first time since Port Hardy, exploring the beach and forest felt like a much-deserved vacation.

Back on the beach, we studied our maps and planned our next route. Queen Charlotte Sound still opened west of our lagoon, but six miles to the northwest it disappeared behind the southern tip of Calvert Island. North of our lagoon, Fitz Hugh Sound narrowed and stretched indefinitely between Calvert Island and the mainland. On the mainland side, across the mouth of an inlet five miles wide, a series of rocky headlands and islands stood fully exposed to the south. If winds built from the south as they had in previous days, they could pipe rough seas directly into Fitz Hugh Sound. Anything with a southern exposure, like the southern tip of Calvert Island and the rocky islands and headlands to our northeast, would receive their brunt. If we paddled for either of those locations, big surf could easily pin us ashore for a day or more.

After considering a few protected bays on the mainland, we finally chose a northwesterly course of 340 degrees across Fitz Hugh Sound to a deep inlet on Calvert Island called Safety Cove. The diagonal crossing of the sound was twelve miles, which could take four hours, but during the last few miles we would be within a mile of Calvert Island if we needed to take a break. The cove had a good stream and only opened narrowly to the east, with steep hills surrounding its other three sides, providing excellent protection from wind. And since it was on Calvert Island's east side, it was totally out of the influence of Queen Charlotte Sound. If winds increased again overnight, it was unlikely they would delay us.

We arrived parallel to the southern tip of Calvert Island within the first hour. The southerly breeze had almost disappeared, and the waves were less than two feet high. To our southwest, we could still see open water, but land filled our view in every other direction. During the next hour two humpback whales surfaced a half-mile ahead, their sleek backs rising four times within a few minutes and exhaling plumes of gray mist before disappearing smoothly below the water. They reappeared several times within a mile to our north and east during the following half hour, then vanished.

We paddled within two miles of Calvert Island after another hour and could distinguish individual trees on its steep hills and occasional bald eagles perched in trees near the water, their heads appearing like golf balls suspended in the dark forest. To our east, steep hills on the mainland were between six and ten miles away on an uneven coast. The wind died, reducing the waves to one-foot rollers, and the clouds broke open, revealing large patches of blue sky. I remembered residents of southeast Alaska calling such openings "sucker holes" because they deluded people into believing the weather would soon improve.

Our progress slowed during the third hour and we began looking for possible places to camp, but found the shore too steep for landing and the hills too steep for a tent. The shape of Calvert Island's shoreline slowly unfolded as we paddled, with small indentations, rocky points and sharp hills dropping 1,000 feet in half a mile. Eventually we spotted the opening to Safety Cove five miles ahead. I was excited at first, knowing we could land soon, but after half an hour the cove didn't seem any closer. After an hour the forest near its opening still lacked detail, and I became frustrated.

Sea kayaking can be boring, and boredom combined with long crossings can be agonizing. The worst thing a paddler can do is fixate on a distant location, which inevitably makes the boat seem smaller and the crossing seem larger. Muscles become tense, claustrophobia can develop and breaking free of the obsession becomes difficult. I was well aware of the condition, but suddenly found myself trapped. No matter how hard I tried to think of other things, simply to let my mind wander, my eyes gravitated back to the entrance of the cove, and I was always surprised at how little we had advanced.

I tried to distract myself by talking to Bill, but he was not interested, obviously happy with the quiet. I tried to think of projects, hobbies, girls, the past, the future. I tried pointing out to myself what a wonderful day it was and how lucky we were to be on the wild British Columbia coast with nothing to do each day but paddle our little boats. But it was hopeless. My boat shrank, my paddle grew heavy and the water turned to peanut butter. The trees near Safety Cove gained detail so slowly that I sometimes felt we were making no headway at all.

Eventually, I got the absolutely silly idea to count paddle strokes as a meditative exercise that would force me to forget about the seemingly unattainable cove. I thought I would come out of the exercise either calm or ashore, but twenty-five minutes later, when

I muttered "one thousand," I was neither. In fact, the cove seemed just as far away as when I started. I glanced at Bill, who stared ahead, grinning peacefully.

The length of the crossing played a part in my frustration, illustrating the importance of regular breaks, but we had also slowed significantly, from both fatigue and tidal currents. While bordering the open expanse of Queen Charlotte Sound, the tides played only a minimal role in our speed, especially considering the winds, but beginning in Fitz Hugh Sound and lasting the rest of the trip, the tides became a much more significant force, sometimes propelling us forward and other times slowing us almost to a stop. Like most channels in the Inside Passage, Fitz Hugh's long, narrow shape funneled the big tides of northwest coast. The flooding tide we had experienced all morning had turned during our crossing, and the ebb worked against us as it emptied into Queen Charlotte Sound.

We finally reached the mouth of Safety Cove after another hour, making the crossing slightly more than four hours. Before entering the cove, I noted with great relief that land surrounded us on all sides. Vancouver Island, now fifty miles away, filled the distance to the south, the mainland filled our east and southeast and the closely spaced and densely forested hills of Calvert Island occupied everything else.

After eight days we were finally inside, and for the next 200 miles we would paddle surrounded by land. We would still make some significant crossings, but the chances of large seas were greatly reduced. As we headed into the cove, I contemplated the challenges we had overcome to arrive at that spot. It had been hard since the day we left Colorado: the near-sleepless, twenty-hour drive to Oregon, the long drive up Vancouver Island, the four days stuck on Pine Island with sinking morale and the two days of sometimes terrifying and always rough seas.

Naively, I had hoped to reach Calvert Island by the end of the fourth day, but it was already the ninth day and we were still only fifty miles from Port Hardy. Our food delivery was due 150 miles away in just three days, and the earliest I thought we could reach it was eight days. As we landed our boats in the cove, we agreed to paddle hard during the coming week to reach our food supply without further delay. After that, we agreed, we could relax our pace in order to enjoy the coast more deeply.

■ ■ ■

Two-hundred-and-four years earlier, in August, 1792, George Vancouver had anchored the *Discovery* and *Chatham* in the same cove. In high wind and rain, he and members of his crew, with a week's provisions, left the cove in five small boats to survey the many inlets along the mainland. When he returned a few days later, he found another British ship had joined his ships. It brought news that mail and provisions for the expedition had arrived in Nootka Sound. He waited another couple of days for poor weather to pass, then headed south for Nootka concluding the season's surveys. Vancouver named the cove Safety Cove. The surveys of 1793 would begin just north of there.

In October he returned south to investigate the Columbia River, which he had missed that spring. Unable to cross the bar at the mouth of the river with the *Discovery*, he sent the *Chatham* upriver approximately 100 miles to present-day Portland, the farthest any whites had traveled up the Columbia. Eleven years later, Meriwether Lewis and William Clark brought traced copies of Vancouver's charts on their expedition across the American west. Their belief that a small continental divide separated the Atlantic and Pacific Oceans was in part based on observations made aboard the *Chatham*.

■ ■ ■

Safety Cove was ideal. Its north side had a small, sandy beach great for landing and a mossy ledge above the intertidal with a flat spot about the size of our tent. Two hundred feet away, flat bedrock rose from the intertidal like a big table, providing a great place to cook and eat dinner. Nearby, a giant cedar extended a lone branch over the bedrock, perfect for hanging our food. And big pieces of driftwood shoved up against the forest edge provided a safe spot to tie the boats.

We divided the chores and within ninety minutes had set camp and prepared dinner. The tide was low and we harvested some limpets, a single-valve mollusk, which we added to our pasta sauce. Afterward, enough light remained for us to take a short walk along the shore. Of course, the shore was so steep, uneven and heavily forested that our walk was more a process of clambering over bedrock and forcing our way through vegetation. But it was an enjoyable treasure hunt that netted views to the mainland, a thousand shades of rain forest green and an eagle feather stuck perpendicular into the soft forest floor.

Bill fell asleep quickly that night, but I lay awake until midnight, reading and listening to the incoming tide calmly engulf our beach. By midnight, the water was less than ten feet from our tent. It sounded lazy as it repeatedly folded upon the beach in tiny waves, which was soothing compared to the roaring surf and rushing wind of recent days. It created a wonderful soundtrack as I released myself into the night.

CHAPTER FOUR

Reaching Safety—
Discovering the Nature of the
Inside Passage

B ill grunted, then mumbled, confused somewhere between a dream and consciousness. I opened my eyes to find his face just two feet from mine, the fleece pullovers we used as pillows nearly touching, and I smelled the previous night's garlic on his breath. I rolled onto my back, then sat up. When my sleeping bag fell from my chest, goose bumps quickly covered my skin. I reached through damp air into the mesh pocket on the tent's wall and fumbled for my watch. It was 6:30 A.M.

It was not raining, so I crawled barefoot from the tent, my boots in one hand and a pair of dry wool socks in the other. When I stood, my feet sank two inches into a damp mattress of moss and lichen; twigs poked at my feet, cushioned by the soft floor. Spruce needles stuck between my toes as I took a couple steps, then crouched to inspect the forest floor. In an area of two square feet, dozens of shoots of green moss and lichen tangled together to form a miniature jungle a few inches high. Prying it apart, I found needles, twigs, cones and bark in varying stages of decay, sinking into the ground. It was the first floor of the rain forest, and below it the engine of detritus worked full-time to feed the trees towering over our camp.

As I stood, a dead hemlock needle drifted from the canopy to rest on the mossy floor. Within days, big raindrops would pound it into the detritus, where fungus and bacteria would break it into organic compounds that would feed living matter from the understory to the canopy. In the forest's perfectly efficient system, organisms barely die before they are returned to the soil for recycling.

Throughout the Inside Passage, beaches form a thin line

between rain forest and ocean, much like the forest itself is a thin line between the Pacific and the continent's dry interior. Trees and understory crowd along the beaches, spilling over their rocks; high tide often laps only a few feet from the forest. Safety Cove was no exception. Four steps from our tent I pushed a few branches from my way, like opening a curtain, and stepped from forest floor to a cold, smooth boulder at the head of our beach. A crisp breeze carried the salty smell of marine air into the cove; I smiled up at pale blue sky.

The sky remained clear during the two hours it took to eat breakfast and pack our boats, but I refused to believe it would last. The steep forest surrounding our camp greatly limited our view of the sky, and I was sure when we paddled from camp we would see clouds and rain approaching from both ends of Fitz Hugh Sound. Such cynicism amounts to common sense in the Inside Passage and ensures rain gear is always close by.

We were on the water by eight-thirty. After paddling east for a few minutes our narrow cove opened into the wider Fitz Hugh Sound. The sound extended six miles to the south, where it yawned into South Passage, and five miles to the east, where it disintegrated into a train wreck of forested points and islands. To the north it narrowed gradually for twenty miles between two forested walls. In each direction the water was a flat pane blearily reflecting rain forest and blue sky, with no clouds in sight.

We leaned our kayaks to the right, so that our cockpit combings, the raised frame around the cockpit, almost touched the flat water. Extending our paddles far ahead and to the right, we made broad sweep strokes that turned our boats northward. By partially angling our blades against the water, we leaned on them for support, increasing the speed of our turn, and we faced northward after three strokes.

An incoming tide was filling Fitz Hugh Sound from South Passage, creating a current northward that would last a little more than six hours. In midafternoon it would reverse and we would fight an ebb for the rest of the day. To maximize our efficiency, we agreed to take only abbreviated breaks during the first part of the day, and although we paddled at a moderate pace throughout the morning, the forest on either side slid past quickly as the tide carried us northward.

"So, where are we?" I asked after an hour.

"Well," he stopped paddling and looked down at the plastic map case on his deck, "I'm not so sure."

I maneuvered my boat toward his and we rafted together, our paddles across our decks for stability. Bill moved the map case to his cockpit so we could both see it.

"Here's Safety Cove," he said, pointing at the map with a finger stained white with salt. His finger moved northward on the map and stopped at a small point on Calvert Island. "And I think this point is what we just passed. See how it doesn't stick out as far as the one to the north?" Keeping one finger on the map he pointed across my bow at a small knob covered in forest. It seemed to make sense.

"Looks like four miles. That's good speed," I said.

Throughout the morning we repeatedly pulled beside each other and looking down at the map case or pointing ahead at the coast tried to reconcile the three-dimensional landscape with the two-dimensional charts. With far more islands and peninsulas, Fitz Hugh Sound was more complicated than the coast along Queen Charlotte Strait, and the unbroken forest made everything look the same.

We traveled from point to point along the uneven coast, cross-ing the mouths of bays, inlets and lagoons, each bringing us one to two miles from shore for intervals of up to six miles. Away from shore the only sound was the wet slosh of paddle strokes. In the dis-tance, the endless forest was still and silent, and boats passed only occasionally. The walls of Fitz Hugh Sound narrowed and grew steeper as we traveled northward, always covered in thick conifer-ous forest with slightly varying shades of green. Lighter shades were the drooping branches of western red cedars and darker shades were Sitka spruces and western hemlocks. Occasionally, shorter alders and willows grew at the forest edge, deciduous trees that formed a bright green hem above the beaches.

There were occasional Douglas firs, too. As North America's third largest tree after sequoias and redwoods, they often form the highest portion of the rain forest canopy. Along southern Vancouver Island and the coasts of Washington, Oregon and northern California, they can tower to 250 feet with trunks more than ten feet in diameter and no branches below 100 feet. Smaller individuals grow in each western state and as far south as Mexico. It is likely some giant Douglas firs stood in the forest surrounding Fitz Hugh

Sound, but at latitude 51°30' we were nearing their northern limit on the coast. They were already a minority and would disappear altogether in another hundred miles. For me, such subtle changes would be a thrilling aspect of our trip. In the miles ahead, we would pass the northern-most red cedars and Pacific yews and North America's southern-most tidewater glacier. Although remaining in the same temperate rain forest ecosystem, our surroundings would change considerably in the coming weeks.

Streams formed narrow gaps in the steep forest, sometimes falling a thousand feet in less than a mile, tumbling between trees like veins carrying the lifeblood of the rain forest. Their small waterfalls turned the calm sea to white foam. Many standing dead trees formed slivers of gray on the green hillsides. Such frequent snags can indicate a healthy stand of old-growth forest or the presence of poor soils, both common in the Inside Passage. Either way, the snags can stand for a century after the tree dies, providing rich habitat for birds and small mammals and a constant supply of nutrition for the forest floor.

The shoreline was consistently rough and steep. From afar, it formed a thin, dark line between water and forest, but up close it varied between steep, loose boulders and steep, uneven bedrock. It only rose between five and ten feet above the water, but made landing our fully loaded sea kayaks difficult or impossible along much of the coast.

Late that morning we arrived at a point where low hills to the east provided our first view inland to the big peaks of the Coast Mountains. Fifteen miles away, they were huge, rounded mounds covered in deep snow that dwarfed the green hills in the foreground. Taking turns with binoculars, we saw fracture lines from recent avalanches, forbidding rock bands and blue wrinkles where glacial ice poked through the snow. Between 5,000 and 6,000 feet high, they likely received wet snow while we were stuck on Pine Island.

■ ■ ■

The Coast Mountains are long and rugged; they isolate the Inside Passage from the rest of North America and keep it cloaked in wet weather. They rise just north of the Fraser River in southern British Columbia and extend northwestward more than 1,000 miles to the

Yukon Territory, where their snowmelt feeds the southern headwaters of the Yukon River. They are an important link in a coastal mountain system that includes the Olympics and Cascades to the south and the Saint Elias, Wrangell and Chugach Mountains to the north. Their jumbled peaks are the result of ancient sedimentation and volcanism and more recent tectonic uplift, creating a complex array of metamorphic, igneous and sedimentary rock. The mix is perhaps most complicated along a coastal accretion zone, where northward movement of the Pacific plate smears fragments of crust along the coast. Some of the crust came from the west coast of North America, but geologists believe much of it originated farther south, bringing exotic geologic compositions to the Inside Passage. The mountains continue to grow today, especially in the north where rebound from recent glaciation compounds tectonic uplift.

Most of the Coast Mountains along coastal British Columbia are between 5,000 and 7,000 feet, although some, like 13,260-foot Mount Waddington, are much higher. The crest of the range is typically about fifty miles from the main channels north of Vancouver Island, often blocked from view by steep islands and forested hills along the water. However, many inlets reach far inland, bringing tidewater much closer to high peaks. And north of the Skeena River, where their crest forms the border between southeast Alaska and northern British Columbia, the mountains rise higher and the main channels are closer to their core. The result is increasingly dramatic scenery in northern British Columbia and particularly southeast Alaska, where mountainous islands rise more than 4,000 feet and mainland peaks reach 7,000 feet within a few miles of tidewater. Along the border many peaks reach between 8,000 and 10,000 feet less than twenty miles from shore.

Like many coastal mountain systems, the Coast Mountains have a split personality. On their east, they taper into the lesser mountain ranges, large river valleys and high plains of interior British Columbia, drained by large rivers such as the Fraser, Skeena, Stikine and Taku. The climate is dry, with as little as ten inches of annual precipitation in some places, resulting in sagebrush, lodgepole and, in the north, a hardy taiga of short black spruce and stunted willows. In the north, summer temperatures can stay in the eighties Fahrenheit for days while winter temperatures can sink to fifty below zero. But on the west side, the mountains plunge directly into sea, lacking significant flood plains except near a few large rivers. Most runoff is in steep streams less than ten miles long. The climate is also radically different, with cold ocean water and warm Pacific air creating a temperate climate of cool summers and mild winters. In addition, the steep mountains wring copious moisture from the marine air, blanketing the region in clouds and rain. From north to south it creates lush rain forest with huge trees above impenetrable understory.

But just 20,000 years ago, near the end of the Pleistocene epoch, the west side was very different. Coastal British Columbia was as much as 100 miles further west and included Vancouver Island and Haida Gwaii, with long valleys stretching from the crest of the mountains to the ocean. Immense glaciers filled most valleys, ending either at the ocean or in strong, braided rivers. The steep foothills of the Coast Mountains surrounded the valleys, most of them buried by glaciers, and only sparse forests of lodgepole pine and spruce grew in a dry, cold climate.

The Pleistocene glaciers melted rapidly in the following 10,000 years, receding high into the Coast Mountains. When melting ice caused the sea to rise 300 feet, reaching its current level 6,000 years ago, salt water swallowed long, deep valleys once covered in ice. The valleys became narrow ocean channels, and the tops of the foothills became the steep islands of today's coastal archipelago.

■ ■ ■

The nature and shape of the Coast Mountains played a major role in determining our route. First, for safety reasons we decided to paddle in channels closest to the mainland, where islands to our west would buffer the winds that create rough seas on the outer coast. Second, we knew the steepest, most dramatic topography would be along the mainland, where the foothills neared the crest of the range. And finally, although the time of year was also significant, the shape of the mountains influenced our decision to paddle from south to north. By beginning in the south, we used the more dramatic scenery of southeast Alaska as an incentive. Had we traveled in the other direction, the consistently poor weather might have convinced us to quit before reaching our goal.

But we couldn't complain about the weather this day. Late in the

74

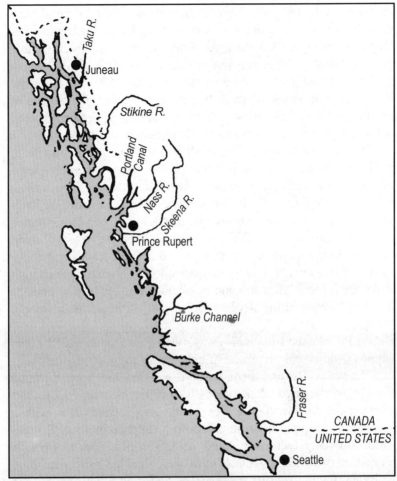

Map 4.1: Inside Passage, showing major rivers.

afternoon, after covering twenty-five miles in six hours, we steered into a glassy lagoon on the mainland. It was 200 yards in either direction and as still as a pond, with two tiny islets in its middle only large enough for a few trees each. Around its edges an unbroken knot of branches overhung rocky shores, and in its deepest corner a small stream splashed into the water, echoing slightly against a bluff. Ten harlequins paddled quickly from us as we neared shore, and a great blue heron watched us from a van-sized boulder, then extended its broad wings and flew overhead squawking loudly.

We paddled along a pale bluff in water ten feet deep, with bar-

75

nacles covering the rock at eye level, their shells closed tightly and snails moving slowly among them. Below, purple and gold foot-long sea stars sprawled along the bluff and rested on the floor in a garden of orange, blue, gray and red anemones that looked like fireworks. Two rock crabs and a hermit crab walked sideways along the floor; a translucent jellyfish drifted three feet below the surface of crystalline water that looked perfect for swimming. From high in an overhead snag, an eagle did its best impression of a rusty gate.

We paddled to one of the small islands, where a steep pile of boulders offered a reasonable landing below a flat, mossy area large enough for our tent. Thick forest surrounded the tent site, but a near-by slab of intertidal bedrock would make a decent kitchen. We landed one at a time on the narrow pile of boulders, then Bill emptied our boats as I carried armloads of gear over twenty-five feet of steep boulders to our campsite. Next, I piled our food, stoves and cookware in the kitchen as Bill looked around for a branch large enough to hang our food. After an hour, he climbed into his boat to go fishing, and I removed my fleece pullover and lay in sun on a smooth rock.

As Bill floated fifty yards away, tying a lure to his line, the harlequins paddled calmly ahead of him, frequently dipping their bills into the water. Beyond them, a kingfisher flew low sorties around the rim of the lagoon, occasionally tucking its wings close and piercing the flat water like a dart, emerging seconds later with a small fish struggling in its mouth. Before I slipped into a nap, a seal surfaced twenty feet away, loudly exhaling mist from its nose. It looked at me with big black eyes in a freckled face with long whiskers, then closed its nasal valves and sank quietly below the water.

I awoke after forty-five minutes to the sound of an outboard motor, and moments later saw a skiff speed past the entrance of our cove. Three young men without life jackets pointed their faces into the wind and yelled over the whine of the motor, but I couldn't distinguish their words. I assumed they were headed for Namu.

Before entering the lagoon we had seen Namu's small cluster of buildings on the mainland a little more than a mile to the north, remnants of a cannery town first established by whites in 1893. Canneries spread throughout the Inside Passage in the late nineteenth century. Like many of them, Namu had rows of two-story bunkhouses and cottages and a sawmill that produced lumber for construction supplies and salmon cases. Throughout much of the twentieth century, up to 400 seasonal workers and their families resided at Namu. The town had a power plant, dock, mess hall, school and recreation building, all linked by several kilometers of boardwalk. The employees came from all over the world and included Natives from nearby villages. But in the early 1980s the emphasis turned from canning to processing, and in the early nineties an unsuccessful attempt was made to turn Namu into a resort. Today it is only a small fishing lodge, and most buildings have been burned or torn down, while others are abandoned and in disrepair. Boaters still use its dock, and BC Ferries offers stops there for a tour of the original cannery. Surrounded by insatiable and ever-encroaching rain forest, its vacant buildings will not be visible much longer. But the old cannery represents only a brief part of Namu's history.

■ ■ ■

Beginning in the late 1960s, archaeologists unearthed tools, middens, labrets and human remains there that chronicle approximately 11,000 years of human activity. They are among the oldest findings in the region and make Namu one of the northwest coast's most significant archaeological sites.

The earliest artifacts from Namu, largely stone blades, probably belonged to small bands of seminomadic people who made recurring visits to the area. They likely camped there to take advantage of seasonal resources such as berries or fish, and eventually they wintered there surviving on stored foods. In *Peoples of the Northwest Coast*, Ames and Maschner called these groups "affluent hunter-gatherers," early people that remained stationary more than hunter-gatherers in other parts of the world, a result of temperate weather and abundant food.

Human burials at Namu from 6,000 years ago indicate an increasingly sedentary lifestyle. Labrets, jewelry worn in large piercings in the lip, found from the same period are among the oldest on the northwest coast and indicate a developed social hierarchy. The findings are concurrent with the evolution of the temperate rain forest in the Inside Passage, which occurred between 7,000 and

4,000 years ago. Its resources enabled early people even more free time, which they used to develop artwork, rudimentary social hierarchies and hunting and fishing technologies.

Throughout the Inside Passage, shell middens, the equivalent of garbage dumps, reveal an almost total reliance on fish, sea mammals and intertidal foods such as shellfish. Among other discoveries, a fish weir, used to trap salmon entering a stream, in southeast Alaska from the same period indicates advances in fishing and food storage. Each advance allowed early people more time to develop their culture.

A 4,000-year old human skeleton from Namu with a bone point imbedded in its backbone shows developments in warfare. The finding is similar to a piece of projectile found in 1996 in the approximately 9,000-year-old pelvis of Kennewick Man. Although Kennewick, Washington, is considerably farther south and inland from Namu, its closeness to the Columbia River salmon fishery resulted in very similar northwest coast culture. Throughout the region, archaeologists have also found daggers, spears, helmets and wooden armor that further document early warfare on the northwest coast.

Evidence from 3,000 years ago shows permanent villages with long plank houses similar to those found at the mouth of the Columbia River by Lewis and Clark in 1805. A thousand years later, houses were present as far north as Prince Rupert and as far south as Seaside, Oregon. It is likely they also existed throughout southeast Alaska. By 2,000 years ago, the unique artwork of the northwest coast existed from north of Yakutat to the Oregon coast. By that time, too, evidence of advanced fishing and food storage technologies was common throughout the region. The artwork and tools reveal an advanced culture that thrived in the Inside Passage until the arrival of whites in the 1700s.

Since the evidence found at Namu is among the oldest on the northwest coast, it is also important in explaining how and when humans first arrived in North and South America. And with recent evidence throwing once widely accepted theories about the peopling of these continents into controversy, Namu's archaeology remains relevant.

Until very recently, it was widely accepted that North America was first populated by Asians and Siberians approximately 15,000 years ago. The extensive glaciation of that period lowered sea levels, which created a land bridge between eastern Asia and Alaska. The Bering Land Bridge (also called Beringia, which includes the historically unglaciated portions of northern Alaska and the Yukon) was an ice-free, hilly land with a cold, dry climate. Its vast grasslands supported camels, giant bison, mastodons and scimitar cats— a cousin of saber-toothed cat with fangs three inches long. Humans also used this cold Serengeti, eventually migrating from eastern Asia and Siberia to Alaska. It has been thought that these early humans traveled south from Alaska through an ice-free corridor between the Coast Mountains and Rockies, populating much of North America and reaching southern South America within 4,000 or 5,000 years.

But recent evidence from thousands of miles away has created skepticism about parts of this theory. For example, stone tools found

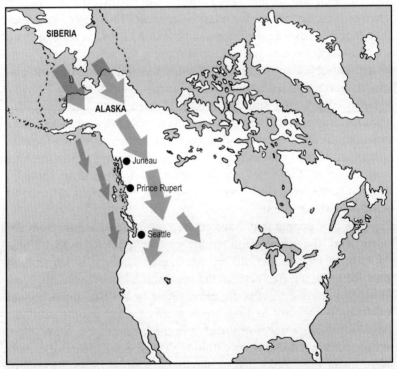

Map 4.2: Beringia is shown shaded between Siberia and Alaska. Arrows show possible migration routes between ice sheets in the Coast Mountains and Rocky Mountains.

in Clovis, New Mexico, and human bones found on the Channel Islands off southern California both date to at least 13,000 years ago. In addition, in 1997 archaeologists in Monte Verde, Chile, unearthed tools that indicate people lived there at least 14,500 years ago. Such early and widely dispersed evidence seriously challenges the once-accepted timeline for peopling of the New World. Recent studies of DNA and language evolution in the Americas have cast further doubt, indicating people could have lived here for 20,000 or 30,000 years. Based on similarities between early European tools and those found in the eastern United States, one theory proposes the first Americans crossed the Atlantic in primitive crafts as much as 20,000 years ago. The evidence does not mean that the Bering Land Bridge did not play a role in peopling the Americas, but it opens to debate the time when the first humans crossed from Asia and Siberia.

The timeline for the population of the northwest coast is also changing. In recent decades it has been generally accepted that massive glaciers covered the region until about 13,000 years ago, with an almost continuous wall of ice bordering the sea much like parts of present-day Greenland. While many recognized that minor glacial retreats could have created temporary refuges for early humans, a harsh climate and subsequent glacial advances seemed to make permanent habitation unlikely. However, recent discoveries of bear bones up to 40,000 years old in caves in southeast Alaska indicate that much larger refuges may have existed, making it possible that humans used the coast much earlier than previously thought. Human bones from the same caves suggest established usage by at least 10,000 years ago.

The first people may have entered the Inside Passage from the north and the south, following ice-free passes in the Coast Mountains such as the Stikine and Fraser. Other theories suggest they followed ice-free parts of the coast south from the Bering Land Bridge or crossed the Pacific in primitive boats. But archeological evidence is difficult to find; the shorelines early people used are now either under water or covered in thick rain forest. Sites under water today would be from within the Pleistocene, when sea levels were lower than today due to massive glaciation. Sites covered in forest today would be from a time immediately following the last glaciation, when sea levels were higher than today. But this lasted only briefly, before the land rebounded from the weight of the glaciers.

■ ■ ■

We awoke shortly before seven the next morning to a lone raven calling from somewhere above our tent. Evenly spaced and throaty, it echoed in the empty lagoon, *wha-oo...wha-oo...wha-oo.* Otherwise, our lagoon was still and silent under clear skies. With temperatures in the high forties Fahrenheit, we ate a quick breakfast beside our boats. As we broke camp a seal poked its head above water fifteen feet away and watched us quietly.

We paddled from the lagoon at nine, and by late morning the temperature rose to the low sixties; for the first time on the trip, we stripped down to T-shirts. Cormorants, eagles, gulls, mergansers and a kingfisher entertained us as we moved northward with a favorable current, enjoying several views inland to snowy mountains shining brightly above green forest and a background of rich blue sky. On a few peaks we could see the light blue crevasses of glacial ice. At noon, after covering ten miles, we ate lunch on a small sand beach facing the sun, then returned to the water after an hour.

Less than an hour later a sudden commotion erupted close behind my stern. *Pffff! Pffff! Pffff!* Then a rush of water. My arms froze in midstroke, my back straightened and I turned quickly, expecting to see the toothy maws of several orcas. They've never attacked kayakers before, but I wasn't thinking about statistics.

I turned just in time to see the glistening gray backs of two harbor porpoises slide below the water five feet behind me. A moment later, their obscured forms, both about six feet long, swam under my boat, then they surfaced again ten feet ahead. They exhaled small plumes of gray mist that dissipated quickly, then arched their backs and slipped below the surface. Within moments, the water returned to perfect flatness, stretching smoothly ahead and mirroring the rough coast, hills and sky. Paddling forward again, my bow divided the reflections into two small waves, leaving behind a wake two inches high that dissipated into the heavy flatness.

John Muir, the nineteenth-century naturalist and founder of the Sierra Club, first visited the Inside Passage aboard the steamboat *Dakota* in May, 1879. After spending several weeks in Puget Sound he traveled south to Portland, Oregon, where he boarded another steamer, a mail carrier called the *California* that took him to Wrangell, Alaska. While traveling the open ocean along the coast, he described widespread seasickness as the small steamer traveled "half-buried in spray." But upon entering the Inside Passage he provided a much different description: "Gazing from the deck of the steamer, one is borne smoothly over calm blue waters, through the midst of countless forest-clad islands. The ordinary discomforts of a sea voyage are not felt, for nearly all the whole long way is on inland waters that are about as waveless as rivers and lakes."

Throughout the year, the inland waterways of the Inside Passage offer far smoother seas than the outer coast. Even during calm weather, breezes and ocean swells can make the outer coast rough, but the half-drowned foothills of the Coast Mountains create sinuous channels with steep flanks and short reaches that provide little fetch. Especially in late spring and summer they offer consistently glassy conditions.

But as John Muir learned, the calm conditions cannot be taken for granted. During five months traveling the northern Inside Passage by steamboat and canoe in 1879, Muir had several harrowing experiences within protected channels. A few months after his arrival he described a rainy canoe trip north of Wrangell when his boat was "tossed like a bubble on the swells," and on another occasion he was so sure his canoe would capsize or smash into rocks that he untied his shoes so he could easily remove them when he fell into the water. Bill and I would soon learn the same lesson. Close to a week after leaving Namu high winds conspired with channel aspect to create terrifying conditions in a channel only a mile wide and surrounded by mountains.

■ ■ ■

The Inside Passage generally offers far smoother travel than the outer coast. Beginning in the mid-nineteenth century, as gold rushes brought increasing numbers of whites northward, steam ships established regular routes through the region, providing the only link to civilization. Steamers supplied small towns and lightkeepers, and provided cruises for tourists.

Now tagged a "marine highway" by the Alaska Department of

Transportation, the narrow channels still provide an important link to the world for residents of the Inside Passage. Ferries, freighters, fishing boats, pleasure boats, kayaks and cruise ships regularly ply its waters, converging in channels near large communities such as Ketchikan and Prince Rupert. In summers, boating near these communities is reminiscent of highway travel, with markers, buoys and lights serving as medians and exits.

With only six communities north of Vancouver Island accessible by automobile, the marine highway is an essential supply route for the region's residents. Large communities like Juneau and Prince Rupert have up to 30,000 people, with supermarkets, restaurants and car dealerships requiring regular supplies from barges, tankers and ferries. Smaller communities, some with fewer than 100 residents, rely on smaller vessels for mail and supplies. The protected waterways enable use of small ships and save fuel, which saves transportation costs on everything from oranges to ottomans.

Ferries provide essential transportation between communities. In 2002, BC Ferries operated forty boats covering twenty-five summertime routes, most of them near southern Vancouver Island. Only four routes served nine small communities north of Port Hardy, two of them running between the mainland and Haida Gwaii. The same year, the Alaska Department of Transportation operated nine ferries serving fourteen communities. Like British Columbia ferries, they are large, sea-going vessels with several passenger decks, lounges, solariums and car decks. They travel at roughly sixteen knots and carry up to 625 passengers. Once a week, the largest ship sails between Skagway and Bellingham, Washington, covering nearly the entire Inside Passage in roughly sixty-two hours. The one-way cost for an adult and vehicle is about $900.

Residents of remote communities use the ferries to visit friends and family, and merchants use them to move limited goods. In close to twenty trips, I've seen high school football teams, church groups, loggers and legislators commuting aboard the ferries. But in summers, when their schedules expand, tourists outnumber residents. They can visit most of the region's communities, staying in hotels, hostels, campgrounds or staterooms aboard the ferries, with their RVs, cars, bicycles and kayaks on the car decks. "Better than a cruise ship," one retiree from Maryland once told me. "We make our own schedule and can stay in towns for as long as we want. It's cheaper, too."

Each spring, hundreds of young men and women from all over take ferries north for summer jobs in bars, resorts, hotels, fishing boats and canneries. Many have pre-arranged jobs, some including housing, while others rely on rumors and luck and carry tents. At night, they lie in sleeping bags on the ferry's floors, pointing their headlamps at *Into the Wild, Coming into the Country* or *Travels in Alaska*. They include college graduates and young drifters following dreams of raw nature or fast money. In the fall, they ride southbound ferries with modest sums of money in their pockets and mountains and glaciers in their eyes.

Tourism is the most rapidly growing industry in the Inside Passage and relies heavily on the marine highway. By far, cruise ships drive the business, bringing close to 700,000 visitors in 2001. In Juneau and Ketchikan, up to five ships can arrive in one day, bringing as many as 10,000 visitors to small downtown areas. The ships dwarf most other vessels on the marine highway, weighing 100,000 tons, standing up to twenty stories tall and exceeding 700 feet long. Their draft, the amount of hull under water, can exceed thirty feet, and they can carry more than 3,000 people, one-third of them crew. Crews include personnel for onboard bars, casinos, hair salons, tennis courts, pools and movie theaters. Traveling at more than twenty knots, an impressive speed for any floating city, most cruise ships run roundtrip excursions from Vancouver or Seattle to Skagway, with average itineraries of eight days. Popular stops include Ketchikan, Petersburg, Sitka, Juneau and Glacier Bay. At each port, small businesses offer flight-seeing tours, salmon bakes, raft trips, fishing excursions and city tours.

While few disagree about the economic benefits, many are concerned about the industry's massive growth. The boats produce significant air and water pollution, including ozone and raw sewage. And although Alaska recently passed stricter guidelines, British Columbia has few environmental regulations for them. But the industry shows no sign of slowing. Prince Rupert plans completion of cruise ship docks in the summer of 2004 that could bring hundreds of thousands of visitors to the city, and Princess Cruise Lines recently added one more ship to its Alaska itinerary, the massive *Star Princess*, which carries 3,600 people.

Smaller boats also contribute to traffic and tourism in the Inside Passage, including small tour boats, luxury yachts and sailboats, carrying anywhere from a few to a few dozen to a few hundred people. Like the larger boats, they have itineraries of about eight days, but boast far greater flexibility and intimacy with the surroundings, with excursions including kayaking and nature hikes. In addition, the marine highway is popular with private yachters, sailboaters and pleasure cruisers. Each summer, thousands travel between Vancouver Island and Skagway. In eight seasons working and traveling in the area, I've met retirees, schoolteachers, millionaires and families traveling on private boats. Kayakers also belong in this category, with guide companies throughout the area offering extended trips or day trips, and thousands of private kayakers visiting each year.

Although most marine traffic is now related to tourism, commercial fishing is still a major industry. In addition to one of the richest salmon fisheries in the world, there are commercial seasons for herring, halibut and various species of crab. Overfishing has led to heated conflicts between the U.S. and Canada and tight restrictions in both countries. Nonetheless, commercial fishing contributes tens of millions of dollars annually to the U.S. and Canadian economies.

Obviously, the marine highway can be crowded, particularly during summers. But it's a big archipelago, and its labyrinthine nature can belie its popularity, making many passages seem empty. In spring, before the busy season, we saw an average of three to five boats per day, and some days we saw none. Considering that we spent all day and night either on or beside the water, we regarded this as light traffic. But along the busiest channels, we found rope, buoys, netting, line and even pieces of boats; if the Inside Passage is a marine highway, these were the hubcaps, blinker lenses and bits of rubber one would find hiking along I-5. Sometimes the amount of traffic and garbage was frustrating, but we rarely saw signs that people came ashore and took solace knowing that the land beyond the channels was largely wilderness.

■ ■ ■

The clear weather held for the afternoon and evening. Seals, birdlife and two humpback whales less than half a mile away provided entertainment as we paddled. We set our camp on moss bordering a steep shore of jagged bedrock and enjoyed a big pasta meal with our backs against a giant piece of bleached driftwood. Above the near-by forest seven ravens performed aerial stunts as we ate. In pairs, they flew almost vertically upward, touched talons, then separated to free-fall toward the forest, their wings folded against their bodies. They pulled out of rapid descents at the last possible moment, and a couple of them corkscrewed in flight, momentarily flying upside down. When the aerials were done, they settled out of sight in tall trees behind camp. For the next hour, as we cleaned dishes and hung the food, they performed a strange concert from within the forest. It consisted of loud calls, throaty gurgles and eerie impressions of crying babies, mewing cats and even a dripping faucet from unseen in the dim forest.

At nightfall, which did not fully arrive until after nine, bright stars flickered above our narrow channel, and the green hills turned to black silhouettes hulking above camp. Around midnight I stepped out of the tent to urinate and saw faint green flickers of northern lights above the forest. The only sound was the gently lapping sea near camp.

The next morning we emerged from the tent to thick clouds covering the sky like molten lead. They shifted slowly throughout the morning but never rifted, creating a dense ceiling atop steep fiord walls, enclosing the narrow channels. By late afternoon, as light rain developed, we arrived more than forty miles from Namu. Fitz Hugh Sound had tapered into Fischer Channel, which averaged three miles in width. After ten miles we turned west into Lama Passage, which varied between one and two miles wide. Twelve miles later, we turned north into an even narrower channel. Each turn felt like paddling in a green-walled maze of narrowing channels. Bays and inlets along the sides grew smaller, making the walls more uniform, and the walls grew steeper and higher, averaging close to 1,000 feet a mile from shore. With the exception of a few small clear-cuts, the walls remained densely forested.

Civilization receded with each paddle stroke. The 700,000 residents of Vancouver Island, which we had not seen since turning our sterns on Safety Cove, steadily withdrew to the south. To the east, the nearest highway was BC Route 1, a two-lane road with small towns 110 miles away and growing further. A remote archipelago filled the distances to our west and north, with logging roads and small villages the only exceptions in a seemingly empty landscape.

Near five, during a break between cool showers, we began a three-mile crossing to a mountainous island ten miles long and five miles wide. I reached far ahead to grab the flat sea with my paddle blade as reflections of the cloudy sky sped along my beam. The island's trees gained detail with each stroke, and before long I could see individual branches, then cracks in the rocky shore. Ten yards from the island a flock of fifty gulls flew in unison from an offshore rock.

We landed on a pebble beach fifty yards long with a gentle grade. At its head, a level area of gravel would provide comfortable camping below the branches of a tall Sitka spruce. It was one of the nicest beaches we would find during the entire trip, but it had no water. As Bill set camp, I walked a quarter mile south to a small stream splashing over broken bedrock, clambering over rough coast once past the edge of our beach. Crouching over the stream I filtered water into four quart-size bottles, then climbed upstream over rocks and pushed through alder and spruce branches to return to camp through the woods.

Once inside the dim forest I stood among wet blueberry bushes under a dense canopy of tall spruce, hemlock and cedar, with the only sound the angry chattering of a red squirrel. Almost immediately, I found a game trail that paralleled the beach—a brown strip twelve inches wide running through the forest's green upholstery of moss and lichen. Game trails almost always follow the forest edge along the Inside Passage. They are narrow paths forming thoroughfares through dense understory for deer, otter, porcupine and wolves. They are usually the creation of bears, which run their daily routines under cover of forest but near enough the water to graze on sedges, feed in the rich intertidal zone or fish for salmon at the mouths of streams.

When I returned to camp Bill had used the last of our water for hot chocolate, which we drank from thermoses under the tangled branches of a hemlock leaning over our beach. Afterward we made big burritos, then hung the food above the kitchen. Darkness came early and the cool rain drove us into the tent before nine, where we quickly fell asleep.

I awoke in the middle of the night to the sound of nearby water

4.1: Giardia and Kayakers

Giardia lamblia is a single-celled cyst that lives in the intestines of some people and animals. It is spread when victims ingest food or water contaminated with feces and is one of the most common causes of waterborne disease in the United States. Ingestion of just a single cyst can cause *giardia*, a painfully diarrheic disease.

Giardia usually becomes obvious seven to ten days after infection, with rank flatulence, abdominal distention and cramping preceding prolonged diarrhea. Some victims also experience nausea, headaches, loss of appetite or low-grade fever. The condition usually lasts up to two weeks, but if untreated it can become chronic, relapsing persistently.

Bears, beavers, goats and more than twenty other species carry the *giardia* cyst, but aside from humans only domestic dogs appear susceptible to the disease. Often, those humans that carry the cyst are immune to the disease. The *giardia* cyst has long been present in North American fresh water systems, but in recent decades it has increased significantly, largely due to careless campers. Today, few streams are not

lapping gently on our pebble beach, like the side of a big river. It was soothing for a few moments, but when I remembered our beach lacked water I sat up quickly and fumbled for my headlamp. Once I found it in the corner of the tent, I unzipped our door and shone the beam into our front yard. Ten feet away it reflected from the inky surface of the sea. The tide had consumed almost our entire beach.

I leaned over Bill for our tide book, then pulled my watch from the pocket on the tent wall. It was one-fifteen, but high tide was not for almost another hour. Although the water was ten feet away horizontally, it was only two vertical feet below us, and I worried it would flood our tent by high tide. I sat thinking for a moment, then did a mental inventory of the gear on the beach. I knew the stoves and cookware were piled at the base of the tree we had used to hang our food, safely distant from the tide, and I knew the boats were securely tied to big pieces of driftwood. But what about the paddles, life jackets and skirts?

For a few minutes I tried to convince myself I didn't need to leave the tent, but I kept imagining our gear lying on the beach and floating away in the advancing tide. Finally, I slipped on my sandals and unzipped the door, then crawled from the tent and shone my headlamp in all directions, half expecting to see it reflected in bear eyes near the forest edge. Then, wearing only boxers, I scurried twenty yards to our boats, with cold mist tingling my skin. I quickly located our skirts, life jackets and paddles inside our cockpits, panned the beach for dry bags or other gear and then returned to the tent.

I climbed back inside my sleeping bag and waited. Bill was still asleep, and I decided that if the water came within four feet in the next half hour I would wake him and we would move the tent. Shining my headlamp through the door, I could tell the water was already closer than when I awoke. On the level beach it would not need to rise much more to flood the tent. On the other hand, tides move slowest during the hour before a peak tide. With less than an hour before high tide, it was going to be close.

As I waited I recalled a few misfortunes regarding the big tides of the Inside Passage. A few years earlier a friend on an extended kayak trip in southeast Alaska camped on a beach fifty miles from civilization. Before going to bed, she pulled her kayak above what she thought was the high tide line, but did not tie it to anything. When she awoke the next morning the kayak was gone, quietly stolen by the overnight high tide. She broadcast an embarrassing distress on her marine radio, and three hours later a couple in a skiff towed her boat to her camp. Another time, I left my kayak on a

contaminated.

Fresh water sources are contaminated when animal or human carriers defecate near or in streams, where the cysts last for several months and seem particularly hardy in cold water. Although most campers realize that defecating in streams is harmful, many are unaware that defecation must occur well away from streams, where rain or snow melt will not lead to contamination. Backcountry waste management varies between ecosystems, and it is important that campers check with local officials to determine the best method. (See Sidebar 14.1.)

Polar Pure, a crystalline iodine treatment, is perhaps the easiest way to purify water in the backcountry. Each small bottle can treat 2,000 quarts of water and costs only about $10. Because it uses small quantities of iodine for each treatment, many users never notice the iodine taste, which is the major drawback of standard iodine treatment. Boiling water for about a minute is another way to purify water, but it consumes significant time and fuel. Water filters are also popular and effective and are what Bill and I used on our trip. Although we filtered our water most days, in remote areas we drank freely and never got sick. We also drank from steep streams, those where we could see the snowfields or glaciers that supplied their headwaters.

small southeast Alaskan island connected to land at low tide. I walked across the intertidal and onto the mainland, then explored a nearby muskeg for thirty minutes. When I returned to the beach, the incoming tide had created a channel fifty yards across and up to four feet deep. Wading back to the boat, which contained all my food and survival and camping equipment, was painfully cold.

Tidal exchanges, the distance in vertical feet between high and low tides, can reach twenty-six feet in the Inside Passage and occur roughly every six hours. Their large size is due to the constrictions of narrow channels, which magnify and accelerate the movement of tidal swells. They create powerful currents and drastically change the shape of the steep coastline. For instance, a smooth, sandy beach at high tide can turn to bedrock too steep for landing at low tide, or a mudflat only twenty feet long at high tide can reach a half mile six hours later. Some beaches present at one peak disappear entirely at the next. The changes are most dramatic in southeast Alaska, where shores are steepest.

The extreme tides affected our lives daily. Each morning and evening they determined how long we had to carry our gear while loading or unloading our boats, and each night they determined where we set our tent and cooked our food. Sometimes they forced us from lunchtime beaches, either by swallowing small landings or uncovering ledges or mud that made carrying our kayaks back to the water difficult. While paddling, their strong currents, commonly between two and four knots, accelerated or hampered our speed. Throughout the region, extreme currents create whirlpools and strong eddies, and in the last weeks of the trip we found one channel where they created challenging whitewater conditions with 12-foot standing waves and powerful holes.

Thirty minutes before high tide the water covered pebbles five feet away and less than one vertical foot below us. I knew it would not rise the remaining foot necessary to flood the tent in the next half hour, but the thought of a passing vessel kept me awake for another hour. The wake from a tanker or ferry would easily swamp our tent.

The time and size of tides vary daily, dependent upon the moon's position and phase. For instance, larger than normal tides, called spring tides, occur roughly every two weeks, flooding beaches ordinarily safe for camping and creating strong currents. The time and size also varies within each day, with four peak tides (two highs and two lows) of varying sizes occurring daily in the Inside Passage. To understand the complicated process we regarded our tide books, produced by the Canadian Hydrographic Service and the U.S. National Oceanic and Atmospheric Administration (NOAA), among our most important tools. They provided times and sizes of each peak tide. We consulted them daily to predict direction and strength of currents and to determine which beaches were suitable for camping.

The water was about five feet from our door at high tide, and lying on my stomach I looked straight across its smooth surface from inside the tent. For the next half hour I watched it slip away as silently as it had approached, and finally, near three in the morning, I fell asleep as rain began crackling at the tent.

Most people who live or work in the Inside Passage have stories of misfortune or inconvenience—lost gear, beached boats, soaked tents—from misjudging the tides. As much as rain forest, mountain, salmon or bear, they define the nature of the Inside Passage. Our lives were governed by a steady, albeit ever-changing, system. They determined our speed and comfort and on a few occasions led to dangerous situations. We quickly learned that understanding the tides in the Inside Passage is as important as keeping warm and dry.

CHAPTER FIVE

Cold Rain and Snow— Weather in the Inside Passage

Shortly before seven I crawled from the tent to a dim morning with damp, chilly air. Across the channel, a thick layer of white cloud concealed everything above 500 feet, leaving a forested hill rising steeply into clouds. Above, the gray ceiling spit scattered raindrops. The tide had receded 100 feet from our tent, revealing large black rocks scattered across our beach.

"Looks like yesterday...only darker," said Bill, sitting on a bald piece of driftwood and pulling on a pair of light nylon rain pants.

"Man," he said, "I had this crazy dream we were paddling through downtown Manhattan. Second Avenue was a kayak park and we were stopping at stores and bars. We were tying our bow lines to old hitching posts in front of the buildings."

I laughed and asked him if he missed the city.

"Sometimes I do," he said after a moment, "But this is all so completely different...sometimes I think I'll leave New York when this is over."

We walked across the beach to where our food dangled fifteen feet above the ground in a tall snag. Six days after leaving Pine Island, there was still enough food to fill a large mesh sack and three dry bags. Untying the rope from a nearby hemlock, Bill slowly lowered the bags to the ground, and we carried them back to the drift log near our tent. As I emptied the breakfast bag, Bill retrieved our stoves and cookware from the base of a nearby tree. He set them on a bare log more than three feet in diameter, and when he lit them steam panicked into moist air. Ten minutes later, we were eating hot oatmeal with brown sugar, raisins and cinnamon. With nowhere dry to sit, we paced the beach.

"I'll get the food together if you do the tent," Bill said when we finished eating.

"Sounds good. What's for lunch?"

"How about soup, apples and crackers and cheese?"

"Perfect. Will you pull out two granola bars and a Clif Bar, too?" Kept in the pocket of my fleece, these bars were usually enough to get me through the morning.

Inside the tent I packed our sleeping bags and sleeping pads into dry bags and put our books and journals into large zip-sealed bags, which I stuffed into dry bags with our clothes. Then I disassembled the tent. Its inside remained dry, but cold raindrops covered its outside, which I shook off in the light rain. My hands ached with cold after rolling the wet tent into a dry bag, and I knew it would remain wet for days. Meanwhile, Bill boiled the rest of our water for soup, which he poured into thermoses, and filled a small dry bag with snacks and lunches. Then he organized the rest of our food into dry bags and cleaned our dishes in the salt water. When I rejoined him we put the stoves and cookware into dry bags.

We walked to the forest edge and untied our bow lines from a large piece of driftwood. Empty, the boats weighed sixty pounds each, and with Bill at the sterns and me at the bows, we carried them together. The ebbing tide had revealed wet rocks ranging in size from basketballs to microwaves, all covered with barnacles, big clusters of mussels and a layer of slippery, orange rockweed three inches thick. We put the boats at the water's edge, then returned to the pile of gear at the head of the beach. Skidding clumsily in our rubber boots, we made three trips each to get everything to the boats.

As I stuffed my first dry bag far into my bow, the low sky collapsed suddenly into heavy rain, and we quickly slapped our hatch covers back in place and retreated up the beach to the protection of a broad cedar. Standing close to its trunk, we watched rain hammer at our beach, splash from the decks of our boats and gather in puddles in our cockpits. It hissed around our small shelter. A dark cloud erased the other side of the channel, and ghostly fragments of mist blew past our beach along the surface of the sea.

We silently wished we could go back to bed, but our tent and sleeping bags were already inside dry bags, lying on rocks by the water with rain splattering off of them. In addition, the tide was still receding; the longer we waited, the farther we would have to carry the boats to the water. After ten minutes, we hurried down the beach and fished rain gear from our cockpits. I pulled my hood over my head, which eliminated my peripheral vision, and with rain beating loudly against me resumed packing. I had to move my head around to survey the pile of gear at my feet, and occasional raindrops ran down my shirt. Impatiently, I crammed the stove into my stern, cutting my finger.

Although kayaks are roomy, the amount of gear we carried required careful packing; simply shoving everything into the holds like they were bottomless only resulted in leftover bags. We also had to pack for stability and performance, with equal weight in the bows and sterns and the heaviest objects close to the bulkheads to prevent listing. We used deck rigging, shock cords on the forward and aft decks, to secure light, bulky gear such as tarps and fishing poles atop the boats. However, too much gear on the decks could impede progress by catching wind, and heavy objects on the decks could reduce stability, making us top heavy. Further complicating the process, certain items needed to be accessible while paddling. We kept spare paddles, paddle floats and bilge pumps on the decks with the map case and a small dry bag containing lunches, binoculars, cameras and the marine radio. Our water bottles, gloves and sunscreen, which could tolerate wetness, were tucked behind our seats, and extra clothing was stuffed atop gear in one of the holds, where it was easily reached if we rafted together.

But with rain gathering in my cockpit and storage compartments I cursed quietly and tried to hurry the packing process. Twice I had to remove the large bag that contained our tent to more efficiently pack smaller bags around it. Finally, after nearly forty minutes, I closed my hatch covers and slogged back up the beach to look for litter or forgotten gear. In the busy process of dismantling camp and loading boats, it is easy to miss a knife left on a drift log or a water filter lying beside a stream.

I walked to our kitchen and slowly circled it, looking for wrappers, silverware or lighters, then inspected the area near our food-hang. In the meantime, Bill inspected our tent site and the area where we had tied the boats. After a couple minutes, we simultaneously started back toward the kayaks.

"Find anything?" I shouted through my hood and the driving rain.

"Nope. You?"

"Nope."

At the boats we stood twenty feet apart facing the sea and urinated in the pouring rain, then helped each other carry the boats to the water, which had receded ten feet. We put our spray skirts and life jackets over our rain gear, pushed our boats into eight inches of water, then climbed into the cockpits nearly three hours after leaving the tent. But my mood improved after only a few paddle strokes. My spray skirt provided improved protection from the rain, and I realized that some exercise would be a nice way to warm up. Although the storm had swallowed the scenery, the low, blowing mist and cloud-obscured forests had turned the Inside Passage into an enchanted place.

Our next passage was slightly more than a mile wide and seven miles long, although its disappearance into low clouds made it appear endless. Gauzy clouds clung to its steeply forested sides like cobwebs, and small bands of white mist rose from between trees like Hollywood poltergeists. They followed breezes northward through pouring rain, dragging along the top of the forest. Five hundred feet up, they joined gray tendrils of moisture that oozed downward from dense clouds. Big raindrops hissed loudly around us, their impact standing two inches on the water's surface, an army of pawns. They drummed noisily on our hoods and decks, and we had to speak loudly to communicate.

Late in the morning the rain decreased to showers, then light mist. Eventually, it stopped completely and the ceiling rose to 800 feet. We went ashore at a sand beach only fifteen feet wide, an idyllic nook between steep, forested walls, and ate candy bars, drank water, then fell asleep with our backs against wet boulders. But twenty minutes later we awoke to cold raindrops on our faces and hurried back to the boats. For the rest of the day we paddled in showers ranging from light sprinkles to hard downpours and separated by dry spells. The thick ceiling remained low, and the temperature never reached fifty.

We had an arsenal of rain gear to contend with the intermittent weather. We kept gloves, hats and pogies (capiline mittens designed for paddling) behind our seats, and extra fleece layers were dry but accessible in our holds. We stuffed our rain gear just beyond our feet, where it was easily reached during sudden downpours. Our gear consisted of loose-fitting bibs and rain jackets made of sixteenth-inch rubberized material, the type used by commercial fishermen. It's heavy and baggy—not exactly designed for paddle sports—but effective for long hours in miserable weather. Although a dry suit would have provided much better protection from hypothermia in a capsize, possibly meaning the difference between life and death, its lack of breathability combined with long hours in the boats made it an uncomfortable option. Our rain gear, on the other hand, could easily be removed while inside the boats.

For footwear, we practically lived in sixteen-inch capiline boots, commonly called gumboots. We also had sandals, but the numbing coldness of the ocean and streams and the jagged rocks and barnacles on the beaches required boots. They were great for walking in the woods, too, which required trudging through mud, puddles and streams. However, they provided almost no ankle support, making twisted ankles a constant threat. They also retained the moisture from sweaty feet, rarely drying completely in the cool, wet climate. Even with wool inserts and socks, our feet were always damp—slipping the boots on in the morning was often gruesome.

We landed at five that afternoon on a narrow pile of cobbles surrounded by a lonesome slab of bare bedrock angling sharply from the water. The rock extended unevenly 100 feet to a meadow of tall grass, still yellow from winter, with a dark forest 100 yards beyond it. The forest was level for a quarter mile, then rose steeply into low clouds. On either side of a narrow channel, hills were gray apparitions, their trees smudged together by blowing mist.

It was a poor place to camp, but the best available landing within more than a mile of steep shore. The meadow was saturated, so we set our tent on relatively flat rock at its edge, but with no trees beside the water we had nowhere to set a kitchen tarp. After dinner, we would have to carry our food through soaked grass two feet high to hang it in the nearest trees almost a football field away.

We sat on life jackets by the water and cooked rice and bags of pre-made Indian food, with fine mist dancing in the dim air. But hard rain began after half an hour, and we ate dinner cloaked in wet rain gear, pacing in circles to stay warm. Chilled and staring down at rain striking flat water, I tried to imagine what I would be doing

An unnamed glacier spills from the alpine deep in southeast Alaska's backcountry.

Above: The Inside Passage is comprised of narrow waterways and thousands of islands, both large and small.
Photo: Mark Johnson

Left: Many glaciers flow like giant rivers of ice from the Coast Mountains of British Columbia and southeast Alaska.

Below: Sunlight breaks through thick clouds to illuminate a rocky intertidal. The temperate rain forest grows almost to tide line in the Inside Passage and even colonizes small rock outcroppings.

Old growth temperate rain forest consists of trees of all ages, thick understory and much dead timber.

Background: A cave leads into the blue ice of a glacier.

Top, left: A buried mountain range. From about 5,000 feet and higher, snow falls nearly year-round in southeast Alaska's Coast Mountains, contributing to ice fields more than 4,000 feet deep in places.

Below, top inset: Kayaking through calm water and icebergs in LeConte Bay.

Below, bottom inset: Low tide has grounded this iceberg on a shallow bar, revealing its true size. While floating, only a fraction of the berg was visible above the water.

Background: Morning stretch. Low clouds veil waterfalls swollen by days of heavy rain.

Top, left: Kayakers unpack their gear on one of the Inside Passage's many rocky beaches.

Top, right: Some kayakers use bear-proof canisters to secure their food. While the canisters are very effective, they occupy valuable space in a kayak's hold.

Left: A fellow Forest Service backcountry ranger takes a break during a hike through thick woods and heavy rain.

These even-aged spruce trees cover a valley floor about 200 years after a glacier's recession. Their dense canopy blocks sunlight and inhibits understory growth.

The steep terrain surrounding glaciers offers kayakers few places to land and camp, and falling rock is often a concern.

Water and ice splash 150 feet into the air as a tidewater glacier near Juneau calves.

Background:
**These unnamed peaks in
the Coast Mountains of southeast
Alaska are close to 10,000 feet high and
only ten miles from the ocean.**

**Bundle up. Cold rain is common in the Inside Passage
and requires sturdy rain gear. A sense of humor
helps, too.**

Sometimes you get lucky. Relaxing in warm sun and flat water near the face of a tidewater glacier in northern southeast Alaska.

Above: Slow go—kayakers slowly force their way through crushed ice two miles from a tidewater glacier.

Left: Mountains near Juneau on a warm summer night.

Below: A mother seal and pup on an iceberg.

Above: A large valley glacier winds down from the Coast Mountains in northern British Columbia.

Right: A giant iceberg dwarfs a kayaker on a lake near the Stikine River. Many valley glaciers calve icebergs into lakes.

Below: Lots of dry bags and efficient packing are essential for an extended kayak trip.

Background: Steep mountains surrounding narrow fjords are typical of the Inside Passage and often create calm ocean water.

Inset: Stunted shore pines are common in the saturated soils of muskegs.

Calm water mirrors icebergs and mountains near one of southeast Alaska's tidewater glaciers

When glaciers recede they leave behind barren valleys of broken rock. Unless the glacier makes another advance, lush rain forest will cover this valley in a couple of centuries.

back in Colorado. Reading in warm sunshine on my deck? Having dinner at a restaurant? Napping after backcountry skiing under blue skies? The heavy rain and low clouds made everything dreary and lonely.

The rain was torrential as we hung the food, falling in thick, unbroken streams that hissed loudly in the forest and ran steadily from our hoods. A gray cloud engulfed everything within a half mile as we returned to the tent, bringing early darkness. Soaked and tired, we climbed inside the tent near seven. After stripping from wet clothes and climbing inside our sleeping bags, Bill fell asleep quickly, but I stayed awake reading. Moisture condensed on the tent walls, and I could see my breath in the beam of my headlamp. The rain beat against the tent and smacked the surrounding bedrock.

We awoke the next morning to steady rain crackling at the tent. We put on our driest socks, unzipped the door, and pulled on our damp boots, then crawled from the tent into cold rain. Reluctantly we put on our rain gear, piled in a wet wad under the tent vestibule, and walked across the meadow to our food. The sky was a gray watercolor smudge that erased the top half of the surrounding hills.

We stood under the shelter of a big spruce eating cereal with soy milk kept in a plastic container. Afterward, we discussed the possibility of resting for the day. We had paddled seven days in a row since leaving Pine Island, covering more than thirty miles on some days and battling rough seas on others. Between packing, unpacking and paddling, we had worked an average of ten hours per day, but we had not yet taken a day to rest, and the heavy workload was wearing on our spirits. The consistently gray weather didn't help, and we had less to say each morning. In eleven days, we had enjoyed only three days of sun.

We deserved a rest, but what would we do with the time? Climbing a nearby hill would only provide disappointing views of the inside of a cloud. Although the rain forest is always a dynamic place to investigate, on a rainy day it would have meant getting soaked, and we were already wet. We considered reading and relaxing in camp, but the rain would have kept us lying next to each other in the damp tent all day. Already growing chilly, we agreed to wait for better weather to rest and to concentrate on reaching our food delivery, still ninety miles away.

For ninety minutes we packed camp and loaded the boats, slip-

5.1: PREVENTING AND TREATING HYPOTHERMIA

The following is a list of essentials for hypothermia prevention and treatment in the Inside Passage:

- A marine radio
- Fleece, capiline and other synthetic clothes-avoid cotton
- Carry an easily accessed dry bag with layers of warm clothes in case of capsize or heavy rain
- Sleeping bags packed in durable dry bags
- Gloves and hats
- Strong rain gear
- Keep food and fluids close-by and snack regularly-food and water are the fuel the body needs to retain and produce heat
- Listen to weather reports, recognize personal limitations and know poor judgment is a symptom of hypothermia

Early treatment is important for mild hypothermia, which left untreated can lead to severe hypothermia. A victim showing early signs of hypothermia needs immediate removal from the cooling agent, whether cold water, wet clothes or cool,

ping over cobbles covered in rockweed and slick algae, then entered the water near ten. Steady rain persisted throughout the morning and inevitably seeped through my rain gear and spray skirt, dampening my crotch and thighs and badly wrinkling the skin on my fingers. My sleeves moistened as water ran up my arm with each paddle stroke, and occasional drops coursed frigid streams down my neck. The ceiling sank to about 300 feet, and on either side of our narrow channel, forest, shoreline, and sky surrounded us in shades of gray and green. The sea contributed to the monotony with a featureless green reflection of the forest. A passing barge and sailboat provided the only variations in scenery, and we paddled quietly, seeking shelter deep inside our minds.

For the first hour I tried to relax with memories. I recalled the sunny beaches of Baja one hot May and hikes in Arizona, bringing to life saguaros, organ pipes and ocotillo. For a few fleeting moments I left the Inside Passage entirely: I was with a seamstress I'd once known in Albuquerque, relaxing on her couch as warm sun filled her studio apartment. Her window was open above a busy street, and she mixed margaritas as we planned a camping trip to the desert. But the memories only lasted a little while; soon the rain seeped back into my psyche. What kind of vacation is this that I need to pretend I'm somewhere else? I changed tack and started thinking of plans and listed resolutions for when I rejoined civilization, which led to thoughts about finances, and I became lost in mathematical equations. But with consistently small sums, I realized that thinking about my lack of money while paddling in rain would not make me feel better.

I thought about music. I had been lucky enough to discover the Beatles as a child and had all their music on vinyl, but I hadn't seen the albums since I put them in storage after college. As I envisioned all the old record jackets, my arms went on autopilot, the rain disappeared and a flood of old songs came to me. I decided I would sing as much as I could remember of the White Album, in order. With Bill fifty yards ahead, probably lost in his own mind games, I didn't feel self-conscious about belting them out. I'm pretty sure I listed all thirty songs. I didn't always get the words right, but enjoyed trying to remember them.

An hour later the passage of an eighty-foot cabin cruiser brought me back to the Inside Passage. The boat passed within 200 yards and sent an eighteen-inch wake toward us. A man and woman inside the cabin didn't wave; they simply stared at us through binoculars, as though watching wildlife. Bill stopped paddling, and I pulled alongside him. We floated next to each other as the rain ran from our hoods and beat against the flat sea.

wet weather. Next, the victim needs warmth. Although fire is a great source of heat, it is often difficult to light in wet weather. In the Inside Passage, setting the tent, dressing in warm clothes and climbing into a dry sleeping bag is often the quickest source of heat. Food and warm fluids speed recovery. In more serious cases, heated water bottles placed at the victim's armpits, neck, groin and along the chest will help warm the body's core; sharing body warmth by climbing into a sleeping bag with a victim is also helpful, as long as it does not risk cooling the rescuer.

If symptoms are advanced, with confusion, apathy, depressed vital signs or unconsciousness, the victim needs immediate and professional help. Getting the victim out of wet clothes and into a sleeping bag is important, but jarring the body or shocking it with warm fluids can cause ventricular fibrillation and death.

The boat was from Seattle, and the couple was probably on vacation, enjoying the Inside Passage from the dry confines of a $100,000 pleasure boat.

As they took turns with the binoculars, Bill exclaimed, "Look at those crazy bastards! What are they doing *inside a boat* on a day like today? Why aren't they out here kayaking!" He looked at me bewildered, beads of water hanging from his nose and chin.

At midday we steered into a small indentation and pulled our boats onto round rocks at the mouth of a stream. It spilled over boulders and filled a tight valley that wound inland, disappearing into thick clouds a quarter mile away. Tall cedars, spruces and hemlocks leaned haphazardly on either side, their uppermost branches obscured in clouds. Thick understory overhung the stream's banks. Erosion from the steady rain turned the water golden brown. As we climbed from our cockpits, a mature bald eagle flew inland from the channel, only thirty feet overhead. Its heavy wings beat the air. I watched it follow the stream, quickly disappearing into clouds and forest, and wondered what the scenery looked like behind the clouds. For all I knew, there were magnificent peaks towering over the stream.

Carrying a dry bag full of snacks, we climbed over slick rocks and a treacherous pile of loose drift logs to the edge of the forest, where we sat on wet boulders close to the trunk of a broad cedar. Although out of the rain, large drops and streamlets of cold water ran from branches, landing all around us. They ran along our coats and splattered inside an open bag of trail mix we were sharing. Eating moistened trail mix was joyless, but we knew high caloric intake was the only way to stay warm.

"Well, this wet trail mix may taste like shit, but at least it's raining," joked Bill.

"Yeah, and at least we don't have to worry about sleeping indoors tonight."

"Right. Or putting on dry socks in the morning!"

"Goddamn. Whose idea was this anyway? Y'know, with the money we saved all winter we could've just gone to Mexico or something." I was only half joking.

We felt chilly after only thirty minutes on shore and relaxing no longer felt very relaxing. We stuffed granola bars in our pockets and with our hoods over our heads emerged from the cedar into rain pouring in straight lines. As we sponged puddles from our seats, a soaked mink, its rusty coat bedraggled, stared at us from between drift logs.

But the rain diminished to sprinkles, then mist early in the afternoon, and the ceiling lifted to 800 feet, then a thousand. Ragged clouds of varying sizes hung everywhere, stuck to the trees like cotton candy. Creeks spilled dirty water into the calm sea, and the surrounding conifers seemed to sag, as though waterlogged. For the rest of the afternoon clouds of all sizes, colored from white through gray, coursed the sky busily. They obscured, then revealed parts of the surrounding hillsides. The clouds raced, collided and tore apart, changing form constantly. Sometimes they gathered in dense masses that promised rain; other times they separated to reveal patches of blue sky. The swirling cloudscape created a softened mixture of sea, forest, mountain and cloud. Water-streams, sea, fog, light showers-blurred the boundaries between land and ocean.

We landed our boats in a small bay that evening. After unloading, we set the kitchen tarp at the base of a cliff and put the tent fifty yards away on gently sloping gravel. The temperature was in the low forties with sprinkling rain. An hour later, we added Parmesan cheese and pesto sauce to a steaming heap of pasta. Afterward, with rain increasing slightly, we cleaned our dishes, hung the food from the cliff above the kitchen and crawled into the tent before dark. Climbing into our sleeping bags was the only way to be warm and dry, but at seven it left a long time to read, write or stare.

■ ■ ■

The intermittent rain and dynamic cloudscape we experienced are common in the Inside Passage. Even in areas receiving more than 200 inches of annual precipitation, intermittent rain is frequent, and fog and mist contribute significantly to annual precipitation. Of course, heavy rain is also common, particularly in autumn and winter. This wet, temperate climate results from a combination of ocean currents, atmospheric pressure and mountains, creating perfect conditions for glaciers and rain forest.

A critical element is the Huroshio Current, an ocean current flowing to the northwest coast from near Japan. Warm, moist air masses following the current keep winters surprisingly mild, with mean January temperatures between northern Vancouver Island and Juneau hovering right around freezing at sea level. However, an eddy from the Huroshio Current also brings cold water from the Gulf of Alaska, keeping summers cool. Between northern Vancouver Island and Juneau, the mean July temperature is only fifty-seven degrees Fahrenheit. The temperate climate gives the Inside Passage the longest frost-free seasons in Alaska and British Columbia.

Air masses following the Huroshio Current absorb copious Pacific moisture. When they reach the Inside Passage, the flooded foothills and icy peaks of the Coast Mountains force them upward, where they cool. Because cool air cannot retain moisture, it condenses, bringing fog, mist, low clouds, and rain to the Inside Passage. But the Huroshio Current is only part of the story. The Inside Passage also benefits from a stationary low pressure system in the northwestern Gulf of Alaska called the Aleutian Low. In part it is a storm-maker; in part it strengthens existing storms rolling down from northeastern Siberia. It swells in late summer, and westerly winds point its storms southeastward across the Gulf of Alaska. By mid-October, it directs windy, wet weather as far south as Washington, Oregon, and northern California. It is strongest in autumn and early winter, the wettest months in the Inside Passage. Although it weakens in mid-winter, it continues to send nasty weather to the region well into spring.

	Jan	Feb	Mar	Apr	May	Jun	Jul	Aug	Sep	Oct	Nov	Dec
Port Hardy	9.5	6.6	5.8	4.4	2.9	2.9	2.2	2.2	5.1	10.2	10.2	10.2
Prince Rupert	10	8	7	7	6	5	4	6	10	15	11	11
Juneau	4.5	3.8	3.3	2.8	3.4	3.2	4.2	5.3	6.7	7.8	4.9	4.4

Chart 5.1: Average monthly precipitation in inches for Port Hardy, Prince Rupert, Juneau.

The Aleutian Low is weakest in late spring and early summer. As it recedes northwestward, a high pressure center near southern California, called the California High, strengthens, and by mid-summer its influence extends well into the Pacific Northwest, bringing annual droughts to Oregon, Washington, and southern British Columbia. Although the northern portion of the Inside Passage still receives much wet weather during summers, the California High is sometimes strong enough to extend periods of sunshine across the entire coast. Brief periods of high pressure also extend to the northern Inside Passage from the Canadian interior.

The Coast Mountains are very efficient at tapping moisture arriving in the Inside Passage. Precipitation levels vary widely throughout the region, but typically average between 100 and 200 inches annually, almost all of it rain at sea level. Below an average elevation of 2,000 feet, the abundant rain and moderate temperatures combine to create tall trees and thick understory. However, between 2,000 and 3,000 feet, consistently high winds and heavy snows create a sub-alpine zone of short, gnarled trees that eventually diminish to the treeless alpine environment.

Even higher, beginning around 5,000 feet, almost all precipitation falls as snow, especially in the north, bringing more than 100 feet of annual snowfall to some areas. Snow occurs at any time of year at these elevations, where cool summer temperatures prevent much melting, and glacial ice forms as each year's snowpack compresses the snow of previous years. Because temperatures steadily grow cooler traveling northward, glacial ice is present at lower elevations in the northern Inside Passage. For instance, it is as low as 3,800 feet on Mount Olympus in Washington, within a few hundred feet of sea level in the Coast Mountains of British Columbia, and all the way to sea level in southeast Alaska.

The next morning was terrible, with rain simply pissing from the sky in cold streams. It battered loudly against our rain fly and smacked the rocky beach outside our tent door, sending fine mist through the screen like shrapnel. Lying on my stomach, I stared bleakly through the screen at my boots, which had been wet for days, and I dreaded the thought of slipping them on my dry feet. Then I envisioned the hundreds of raindrops that would fall on my head and run down my back as I let the food down from its tree. I saw myself shivering and pacing as I ate my lame breakfast.

Very little of what we owned was dry. The tent was soaked from being rolled up in the kayak each day and set up in the rain each night, our sleeping bags were damp, and our rain gear was wet inside and out. Our gloves and hats were drenched, and our socks, fleece pants, and fleece pullovers all ranged from damp to soaked. The sun four days earlier seemed very distant.

119

"At least it's raining," said Bill, lying on his back and staring at the ceiling.

The fact that we were only twelve miles from Klemtu, a native village of roughly 200 people, provided the sole motivation for getting out of the tent that morning. By mid-afternoon, we could be eating candy bars, interacting with people other than each other, and making phone calls to friends and family. They were great luxuries twelve days after leaving Port Hardy.

The rain fell heavily, and we hardly spoke as we ate breakfast, broke camp, and loaded our boats. Like the days before, the light was dim, and our surroundings consisted of low clouds wrapped around green hills. But the rain stopped at mid-morning, and during the next hour the clouds rose quickly, lifting our moods with them. Patches of blue sky opened, and sunlight sparkled on the water. I took off my wet fleece hat, laid it on the deck of my boat, and felt warm sun drying my damp hair. Having long ago buried my sunglasses somewhere deep inside my boat, I squinted in the brightness.

The cloudscape became complicated and restless, with clouds of varying shapes clinging low to the forested hillsides and squatting on the ridgetops. Giant cumuli billowed above distant mountains like atom bombs from the 1950s. Narrow bands of fog hovered just above the water, stretching the entire distance of our view. For the first time in four days we could see inland to bright snowy peaks where the recent rains probably fell as snow. Endless forest carpeted the dozens of lower hills and long valleys below the higher mountains, and I wondered if our views would have been as spectacular if the clouds had lifted in previous days. Looking miles from shore, I imagined a wilderness of bears, tall trees, secret hollows, and unnamed gorges.

The temperature rose into the high fifties, the most promising weather since Namu, and I dared to hope it was the beginning of a stretch of good conditions. I allowed myself to imagine putting the tent, our socks, boots, tarps—everything—on rocks to dry.

We made a three-mile crossing of Mathieson Channel and turned west into Jackson Passage, its entrance only a quarter mile wide between tall, forested flanks. The narrow gateway led us to a channel eight miles long and only a half mile wide, and the low, rolling hills that had surrounded us for 140 miles turned suddenly to steep fiord walls. The shore became a steep foundation of barnacle-covered bedrock, providing very few places to land. The forested walls rose sharply from the water, with several places reaching 1,000 feet within a quarter mile. Smoothly rounded mountain tops rose to 2,000 feet within a mile, lining the channel like a row of knuckles. They were separated by deep U-shaped valleys that plunged half way to sea level, dumping waterfalls from gaps in the forest. The water gushed downward in silver streams, some flowing 1,500 feet to sea level in seconds. Their sound rolled down the hills and echoed in the fiord.

Several slide paths scarred the new landscape. Some had swept soil, trees, and rocks from several hundred feet above; others had merely sloughed a fifty-foot section of trees. Willow and alder had reclaimed the older paths, forming swaths of bright green amid the dark conifers, but the more recent ones were still barren. Looking upward we tried to imagine the sight and sound of a hundred trees and a rush of saturated soil slipping into the sea. Small waves and dark trees would have filled the calm fiord.

Jackson Passage boosted our morale. Its mountains were tall proof we had made progress and a reminder that if we endured the impending challenges we would soon be paddling below enormous mountains and the faces of tidewater glaciers. They softened our disappointment when we saw rain clouds scraping along the water ahead of us, like we were paddling toward a gray abyss. Within thirty minutes the sun disappeared, and thick clouds swallowed the mountains. Soon, light rain hissed softly on the water and tapped at our decks. It harmonized with the slosh of our paddle strokes, and the surrounding streams and waterfalls provided a soaked rhythm.

Early in the afternoon we approached Klemtu, where a neat row of houses lined a one-lane dirt road less than a mile long. Thick forest surrounded the town on three sides, poised to engulf it, and light clouds rose like smoke from green hills. From a quarter mile away, the community was strangely quiet, with no automobiles, machinery, or voices, and as we drew closer we heard only barking dogs and squawking ravens.

We approached town from below, paddling past tarry pilings covered in seaweed and mussels. Light rain leaked from a dock above and echoed against the sea, and a naked baby doll stared from below two feet of water. A man and woman waved shyly from the dock, then walked away. On the ferry to Vancouver Island, someone had warned us against stopping in native villages, claiming anti-white sentiment was strong and theft was common. It stuck in our minds, and as we landed in smelly intertidal we were apprehensive about leaving our boats and nervous about the reception we would receive.

We tied our boats to pilings, clawed up a steep embankment, then climbed over boulders at the edge of Klemtu's street. The band store, or village co-op, was a couple houses away with a pay phone beside it. We bought sodas, then I used the phone as Bill kept an eye on the boats. With rain beating against the phone booth and big ravens squawking from a nearby roof, I talked to friends in Colorado about skiing and roadtrips to the desert and family on the east coast about a wedding on Long Island and the season opener at Fenway Park. Sandstone arches and Red Sox baseball seemed worlds away.

As Bill took a turn at the phone, I chatted with a twelve-year-old native boy named Patrick in the foyer of the band store. Like everyone I encountered in Klemtu, he was friendly and curious about our trip. He asked questions about the kayaks, then changing the subject, told me that he was actually Patrick the Third.

"My Dad's name is Patrick," he told me, "and then before that his Dad's name was Patrick. But he died."

"Your Dad's dad?"

"Yut. Sea got'm. He drownt." The sea has always been both benefactor and killer for people of the Inside Passage.

As a new meteorological twist, sleet mixed with rain as Bill returned from the phone. It splashed in muddy puddles and popped loudly on the dirt street. Patrick wished us luck and watched from the street as we descended to our boats through low-tide muck.

"My Dad had a quadruple bypass," Bill said kind of matter-of-factly as we untied our boats.

"Is he okay?" I asked, startled.

"He got home from the hospital the day before yesterday and he and my Mom took a walk today. I guess he's okay…He had a heart attack when we were on Pine Island."

"Wow…What should we do?"

"Try to make it past Sarah Island, like we planned. There's

nothing I can do from here. I'll call from Hartley Bay and see how things are."

"We must be getting close to that beach, right?" Bill asked.

"Well, I can't quite figure it out. Want to have a look?"

We were two hours past Klemtu. Shortly after leaving, the rain decreased to intermittent showers, and the ceiling lifted to 1,000 feet, with tattered clouds speeding overhead and colliding with the steep forest. An incoming tide created a strong current northward, and the green hills ahead unfolded steadily into detailed trees and rocky shores, then disappeared behind us. It was the fastest any current had moved us.

Bill rafted alongside me and looked at the chart. We had planned to camp on a small beach seven miles north of Klemtu, one of few places that offered decent camping along the east side of Tolmie Channel. Past it, our charts showed several miles of shores too steep for camping.

"Huh," said Bill, "it's pretty hard to tell where we are."

The clouds concealed all peaks useful for navigation, leaving nearly uniform walls of green around a mile-wide channel with no outlets or deep bays that would show up on our charts. We knew we were in Tolmie Channel, but couldn't figure out where, or how far from decent camping. With limited daylight remaining, we hailed a fishing boat two miles to our north. After laughing at our apparent incompetence, the captain provided his coordinates, adding, "You're probably about two miles south of me."

We had paddled at five knots in strong current, much faster than we had expected, and were now four miles past our intended camp. We were disoriented because we had been looking for our location on a section of map we had already passed. Although happy for the progress, we realized we might have difficulty finding a decent place to camp.

The Inside Passage can be a confusing place, with islands, mainland points, and hills blending together under a monotonous layer of forest. Low clouds frequently conceal mountains useful for navigation, and mist obscures the boundaries between landforms. Low points in the foreground blend with higher ones in the distance, even from less than a mile away, and narrow channels look like small bays until viewed from a specific angle, which might require looking back after passing them. All these factors are compounded by the low vantage of a sea kayak.

We chatted with the captain for a few minutes, who sounded impressed when we listed Juneau as our destination, although perhaps he was simply astounded that people with our poor map skills would attempt such a feat. As he signed off the air, he left us with an ominous warning: "Big storm coming tomorrow. Keep dry out there!"

Forty minutes later we landed on a steep shore of crumbled bedrock, the best available, and after emptying our boats balanced them precariously on a narrow bench ten feet above the high tide line. The hills rose steeply from the water, and we barely fit our tent on uneven ground between two mammoth spruces that towered into the clouds. We ate dinner at the edge of the intertidal in cool rain and retreated to the tent by eight.

I lay on my stomach facing the tent door, tucked deep inside my sleeping bag and warm and nearly dry. My rubber boots were under the rainfly, their tops folded over. Beyond, through a break in the forest, distant hills turned dark over Tolmie Channel. The sounds of water surrounded us: a nearby stream rumbled and splashed into the channel, fat drops of water smacked the forest floor from the canopy, fine rain hissed on the understory and crackled on the tent like interception on an old television.

"What's up, Bill?" I asked. He lay on his back, staring at the ceiling. It was odd for him not to be reading or writing.

"Just thinking," he said.

"You worried about your dad?"

"It sounds like he's okay, so I don't think I'm worried. It's weird, though, not being there. I've been writing him this long letter in my head all day."

"Hey," he said, changing the subject, "what do you suppose that fisherman meant about a big storm coming? I mean, this whole frigging place is one big storm. What's it gonna do, rain again?"

I found a weather station on the marine radio, its reception broken by the mountains above camp. It was difficult to hear, but we got the essentials: Heavy rains starting tomorrow afternoon and hurricane-force gusts on the outer coast by evening.

"My sister said it was 68 and sunny in Manhattan today," said Bill.

Hurricane-force is over seventy-four miles per hour. The forecast called for such gusts on the outer coast, only thirty miles away. We knew the steep archipelago would harbor us from the strongest winds, but we expected no respite from the rain, which tapped lightly on our coats as we ate breakfast and studied our charts. We would continue north in Tolmie Channel for only a short distance, then enter Princess Royal Channel, one mile wide and stretching generally northward for thirty-five miles. Most of its shoreline was too steep for camping, but we marked a broad beach ten miles away where we could rest and assess the weather.

Light to moderate rain fell from a leaden sky throughout the morning, and by lunch a southeasterly breeze with occasional gusts pushed the rain at an angle. Waves one foot high urged our boats northward. We went ashore at a small cobble beach and ate in a damp hollow in the woods with the rain hissing around us, but with temperatures only in the forties, we quickly grew cold.

"What do you think?" I asked Bill.

"It's the same as the last few days. If we set camp now, what's there to do for the rest of the day? Let's get some miles out of the way."

Our maps showed ten miles of steep coastline interrupted on the east by three large inlets, each requiring crossings of roughly a mile. Although the maps indicated shores too steep for camping, we were confident we could find somewhere to go ashore if the weather grew dangerous. Waves near our beach were still only one foot high when we began paddling.

But soon the rain turned heavy, then became a deluge. It came in streams rather than drops, as though poured from a strainer, and shattered the surface of the choppy water. Simultaneously, the wind quickly increased from the southeast, at first arriving in bullying gusts, but quickly developing into a steady blow. The north-south axis of the channel allowed good fetch, and the seas grew to two, then three feet. They were closely spaced, and I tightened my grip on my paddle.

The sky sagged almost to the water, sometimes less than 100 feet above us, eclipsing all but the lowest trees. Only occasionally we discerned faint fragments of ridges high above, featureless lines appearing briefly in the clouds, like ghosts. Visibility decreased to less than a mile, and the wind shook large branches near shore, indicating speeds of about twenty-five miles per hour, with stronger gusts. Streams swelled to violent torrents, erupting from the low clouds and racing down what little of the mountainsides we could see. Ahead, they were thick silver, but close-by they foamed yellow and brown with soil. The largest exploded from V-shaped notches and sent plumes of mist into the rainy air, boulders knocking around in their turbulent depths.

After an hour, we reached the mouth of a mile-wide inlet stretching northeast. Forested walls on either side rose steeply into a 300-foot ceiling, but disappeared abruptly two miles away in a low cloud the color of a deep bruise. Crossing the inlet, strong winds blew three-foot waves from the northeast, which collided with the northbound waves of Princess Royal, creating confused seas and occasional nausea. The strongest gusts surprised me and felt powerful enough to knock me over. We leaned hard into them and paddled close to each other.

We finished the crossing in thirty minutes and returned to northbound waves of three and four feet. They lifted our sterns before the waves in front fully released our bows, which made surfing difficult and required frequent braces. Paddling close to shore, we had to shout over the roar of wind and waves, which still increased. Soon whole trees beside the water were in motion, their largest branches appearing ready to tear free. Twigs and small branches blew to the sea, and the thrashing trees added to the roar. Brutal gusts slammed into our backs, soaking us with rain and spray that crackled against our hoods. The spray shot past with violent speed and disappeared into fog 100 yards ahead. With each gust, now between thirty-five and forty miles per hour, I ducked my head toward my deck and grit my teeth. The wind yanked hard at my paddle, like it could rip it away, and I held it tightly with white knuckles.

After an hour we passed a small meadow where we should have camped, but neither of us said anything. Thoroughly drenched and dreading the thought of setting camp and hanging the food, staying in the boats seemed easier. Within moments the waves carried us past the meadow and along shores too steep for landing, and fifteen minutes later we were beside bare rock rising almost vertically 100 feet into fog. It was dark gray under a film of running rain, with the sea splashing against it. Across the channel I thought I glimpsed snow covering a high peak above the sea, but the pelting rain forced me to look away. When I looked up again, dense clouds covered everything.

We reached the edge of an inlet one and a half miles wide and stopped for a rest on a lee-side beach with one-foot waves breaking against it in quick succession. The nearby hills rose at a forty-degree angle, leaving no place for camping, and we crept under the branches of a recently fallen tree for shelter. My soaked clothes pressed against my legs and torso with each movement, chilling my whole body.

We ate moistened granola bars without saying a word as gusts lashed trees overhead. I felt absolutely miserable and wanted to quit. I wanted to hail a boat, a helicopter, the Coast Guard, and simply go home. But I knew we were stuck. At the time, the closest ferry service was in Prince Rupert, more than 100 miles away, and we had no real excuse to hassle boaters or the Coast Guard. I knew the rain could continue for days and wondered when my clothes would be dry again.

Then Bill announced that he was done. When I looked up at him, several drops of rain ran cold down my chest. He was looking down at the rocks.

"I don't think we can camp here," I said, knowing he meant something else.

"No. I mean I'm done with this trip."

I was miserable, trembling with cold, and nervous about the upcoming crossing. Each time I wiped a drop of water from the end of my nose, another immediately replaced it. My hair was plastered to my forehead and cheeks, and my soaked rain gear drooped heavily from my body. I felt and looked savage.

"What the hell am I supposed to do with that?" I asked angrily. "I mean, what good can that possibly do? You know we can't get out of this. What're we gonna do, call the Coast Guard because we're wet?" He only expressed what I had just thought, but it filled me with anger.

"I know. I know. It's not just the rain, though…It's my father, too. I need to see my family."

I was angry at Bill, then the rain, then myself, and I felt guilty for yelling at him. Who was I to say he shouldn't want to leave this miserable trip? Who was I to say he shouldn't feel intensity about his father? But I didn't apologize.

We exchanged sarcastic comments, then separated as best we could on the small beach. Unfortunately, the tide didn't give us time to regain composure. It floated our boats, leaving no room on the beach and forcing us to help each other. I sat on Bill's stern to steady his boat as he got in, then gave it a shove. In turn, he paddled to my bow and leaned on it as I fumbled into my cockpit. We were soaked and cold.

The wind blew fiercely from the inlet, clashing with the rest of the storm, whipping the rain in circles, and creating confused seas. Strong gusts wrestled for control of our paddles, and unexpected waves forced us to brace quickly and splashed against our soaked rain gear. The sea was a jumble of green and white with waves exploding against a rocky, south-facing shore ahead, spray shooting a dozen feet into the air.

"You okay?" we asked each other after each strong gust. I trembled from cold and fear, and my heart pounded, pressing against my life jacket.

The sea turned brown as we finished the crossing and gave wide berth to surf on the rocky shore. During the next half hour, we passed six live trees floating in murky water, victims of a landslide somewhere nearby. We may have passed right by it, but with our heads tucked deep inside our hoods we never saw it. After another hour, we finally reached a short beach near a valley where we could camp. Although only four in the afternoon, it was dark enough to be evening.

Exhausted and soaked, we slowly unpacked the boats and carried gear into the woods, where a damp hollow provided the only place to camp. The skin on my hands was saturated and peeled as I hung the food, and my fingers fumbled numbly as I helped Bill tie a tarp over the tent. Shivering, we tied it too loosely and had to start over, and the few words we spoke came slowly.

"So, this is what hypothermia feels like," said Bill.

He was right. Our shivering, grogginess, slowed speech, and loss of dexterity indicated mild hypothermia, and without warming up soon we risked sinking into severe hypothermia. I realized the first sign had occurred a couple hours earlier, when we foolishly paddled past a small meadow where we could have camped.

We crawled into the tent and removed our wet clothes, then put on dry fleece and climbed deep inside our sleeping bags. We thought that after a couple hours we would cook dinner, but I didn't wake up until five hours later. I opened my eyes but could not see anything in the dark tent. I was warm, but damp and exhausted, and rain still rapped hard at our tarp. The sea heaped itself onto the nearby beach in quickly spaced waves, like it was chomping at the land. I fell back to sleep, but awoke several more times feeling dazed. Each time a strong gust rushed through the woods overhead I pictured loose branches crashing down on our tent.

By eight-thirty the next morning we had been inside the tent for close to sixteen hours. We forced ourselves out of our warm sleeping bags and walked to the beach in steady rain. The air was saturated and cold, with the temperature near forty, but the wind was gone. Work Island, a low, forested slab, was about a half mile away, and the ceiling had lifted to 1,000 feet, revealing wet snow on tree branches across the channel. It formed a straight line across the hillside about 700 feet above the sea. The sea was flat and brown, with swollen streams running into it from the fiord walls. The brush with hypothermia and skipped dinner left us drained, and we agreed to take a much-needed day of rest. Unfortunately, the rain would keep us confined to the tent, which was soaked and sagging, with puddles in its corners.

Hours later, when the rain finally

5.2: Personal Survival Kit

A good personal survival kit, a waterproof kit containing essentials for survival, can mean the difference between life and death in the Inside Passage. It is intended for the rare but possible event that paddlers become separated from their boats and gear, which can result from capsizing, becoming injured while hiking or misjudging an overnight high tide. Some companies make personal survival kits that attach to the back of PFDs so they are always with a paddler. They are easily removed and kept in a tent at night or in a backpack during a hike. Personal survival kits should contain the following:

- Two lighters in vacuum-sealed plastic
- Magnesium striker, which can be used to start a fire without matches or lighter
- Compact space blanket
- A few energy bars in vacuum-sealed plastic
- Three personal flares
- A Leatherman-type tool with saw and knives
- Three candles (A victim can huddle over a candle to keep warm.)

The kit should be vacuum-sealed and kept inside a durable sack, and paddlers should know how to use each of its items.

stopped and the ceiling rose to 3,000 feet, I walked back to the beach. Three thin, U-shaped valleys separated the mountains across from camp. Their bottoms were barely above sea level, while the mountains they separated reached 2,500 feet within a mile of shore. For the first time, we saw deep snow covering alpine meadows above tree line, which demonstrated our progress northward. But we were too discouraged by the weather of the past six days and the harsh words between us to become excited. That evening, we quietly ate veggie burgers and dehydrated potatoes in fine rain. Looking across the channel, I wondered if Bill would take a ferry south from Prince Rupert, but I felt it was too soon to ask. If he did go home, I wondered if I would have the courage to complete the trip myself.

CHAPTER SIX

Legacies—Human History in the Inside Passage

By the middle of the eighteenth century, the unique northwest coast Native culture existed from the Copper River, near present-day Cordova, Alaska, to the Columbia River. Although mostly confined to the coast, the culture reached hundreds of miles inland on major salmon rivers such as the Columbia, Fraser, Nass, Skeena, Stikine and Taku. Cultural similarities extended southward into northern California, but that area is not always considered part of the northwest coast culture. The culture was defined by similarities in art style, house construction, language, tools, social hierarchy and a heavy reliance upon salmon. However, significant variations were common across the region and resulted in at least twenty distinct groups, including the Tlingit, Haida, Tsimsian, Heiltsuk and Salish.

Exactly how many distinct groups existed on the northwest coast is a topic of debate in both academic and Native circles. Other areas of uncertainty regard the time the first people arrived on the coast and when their unique culture became fully developed. Archaeologists have difficulty answering these and other questions due to both natural and social causes.

One of the most frustrating challenges facing archaeologists is the region's history of varying sea levels. From 20,000 to approximately 6,000 years ago, melting glaciers raised sea levels along the northwest coast up to 300 feet, burying evidence of its earliest humans. But by a process called isostatic rebound, the land also rose, rebounding when the great weight of the glaciers disappeared. The land rose at a much slower rate and continues to rise today in the northern Inside Passage. As a result, many shorelines used by prehistoric people are now a short distance inland and covered by thick forest. Thus, today's archaeologists must look both beneath the water and inland from the coast for prehistoric evidence.

Archaeologists face other challenges, too, such as the glacial advances and retreats of the past ten thousand years, which have intensified local sea level variations and erased all signs of human presence in some areas. The fact that much of the culture's tools and artifacts were made of quickly decomposing wood presents a further challenge. In addition, American and Canadian efforts to obliterate the culture in the nineteenth and early twentieth centuries destroyed countless artifacts and a rich oral history. For these reasons, significant gaps exist in our knowledge of pre-European northwest coast culture.

But there is also much that archaeologists agree upon. For instance, it is universally accepted that the northwest coast culture was generally advanced in comparison to other prehistoric cultures. Although its people subsisted by hunting and gathering, they showed advances that are more commonly associated with agricultural groups, including a developed social hierarchy, permanent villages and a wide-ranging trade network. These advances occurred because reliable and abundant food resources such as salmon enabled people to remain stationary rather than migrate in search of food. The time they would have spent traveling was instead devoted to developing their culture.

One indication of the culture's advancement was its dense population in comparison to other North American prehistoric peoples. Most estimates of the region's population in the mid-eighteenth century are between 200,000 and 300,000, although some estimates are as high as 500,000. According to even the lowest numbers, the northwest coast was probably the most populated region in pre-European North America, and parts of the coast were more populated in the eighteenth century than they are today.

The crews of the *Chatham* and *Discovery* were well aware of the population density along the northwest coast. During three summers in the region, they regularly encountered Natives from Puget Sound to Cook Inlet, and Vancouver often traded with them. In his journals, he referred to the Natives as "well behaved," "civil" and "obedient," but despite his obvious condescension only one encounter led to violence, although on a few occasions violence was only narrowly averted.

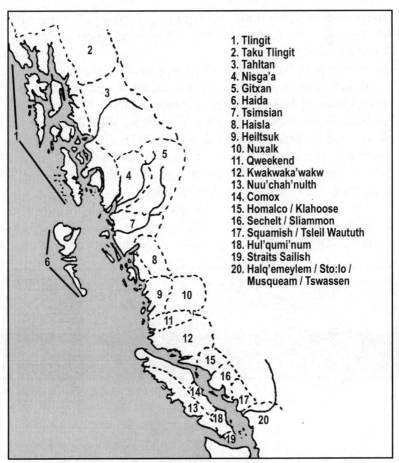

1. Tlingit
2. Taku Tlingit
3. Tahltan
4. Nisga'a
5. Gitxan
6. Haida
7. Tsimsian
8. Haisla
9. Heiltsuk
10. Nuxalk
11. Qweekend
12. Kwakwaka'wakw
13. Nuu'chah'nulth
14. Comox
15. Homalco / Klahoose
16. Sechelt / Sliammon
17. Squamish / Tsleil Waututh
18. Hul'qumi'num
19. Straits Sailish
20. Halq'emeylem / Sto:lo / Musqueam / Tswassen

Map 6.1: map of the Inside Passage showing names and general boundaries of twenty known cultural groups.

A series of contacts between Vancouver's crew and Native people in late June, 1793, were typical. The *Chatham* and *Discovery* had reached northern California on May 2, 1793, after wintering in the Hawaiian Islands, and sailed past Safety Cove later that month. They resumed their meticulous surveys at nearby Burke Channel, where work had concluded the previous August. Shortly after Burke Channel, Vancouver investigated Dean Channel, where he reached Elcho Harbor on June 5, 1793. Forty-seven days later, Alexander Mackenzie reached the same harbor by land, becoming the first white man to cross North America north of Mexico and providing strong evidence against the existence of a Northwest Passage. By late June they had surveyed Tolmie Channel and most of Princess Royal Channel.

Not far from Work Island, where Bill and I spent a day recovering from hypothermia, Vancouver dispatched Joseph Whidbey and several men in two small boats to explore northern Princess Royal Channel. Within two days they reached a series of fiords Vancouver would soon name Verney Passage and Douglas and Ursula Channels. The channels were several miles wide and stretched inland approximately forty miles; they surrounded dozens of islands and included scores of bays and small inlets.

On June 28, six days into Whidbey's outing, eight Natives in two cedar canoes approached and presented two salmon reported to weigh seventy pounds each. The crew traded a small piece of iron

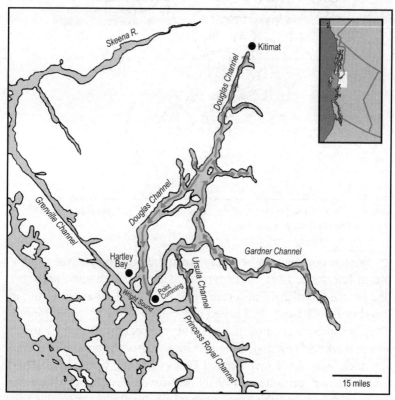

Map 6.2: Whidbey's fourteen day exploration of Princess Royal Channel, Ursula Channel, Gardner Channel, Douglas Channel and Wright Sound.

for the fish, and the Natives departed "very well pleased with the exchange." Vancouver's crew knew that iron, copper and other metals were regarded highly by the Natives, who used them for woodcarving and signs of status such as jewelry. Such signs were extremely important in the hierarchical culture of the northwest coast.

The crew encountered the same Natives the following day; they traveled together in a dead-end fiord ten miles long. The group ate dinner at the end of the fiord, where sixty more Natives in ten canoes soon joined them. Whidbey reported that the largest canoe, which carried a chief and his family, was elaborately decorated with carvings similar to those he had seen in other villages. The art style described was the same that could be found at the time throughout the entire Inside Passage. It decorated wooden boxes, tools, utensils, jewelry, weapons, houses, canoes and ceremonial masks, blankets and shields.

After dinner, the crew traded pieces of copper, blue cloth and blankets for sea otter pelts and shared their grog, sugar and bread. Then the entire group traveled out of the inlet to an area suitable for camping. On the way, the Natives sang songs, which the crew described as "by no means unmelodious or unpleasing." At camp, Whidbey expressed his desire to sleep. The Natives traveled to a nearby bay where they "remained perfectly quiet" for the remainder of the night.

The following day the group traveled together to present-day Kitimat, the furthest point inland in the area. From there, the Natives departed up the Kitimat River in their canoes, and Whidbey and his crew began their return to the *Discovery* and *Chatham*. The canoes were not seen again. On July 2, nine days after beginning his surveys, Whidbey exited Douglas Channel and rejoined the rest of the expedition in Wright Sound. They met near a spot that Vancouver named Point Cumming.

Vancouver's journals are full of anecdotes of peaceful interactions like those reported by Joseph Whidbey. Many of the Natives he encountered offered sea otter and beaver pelts for trade, and a few even had muskets, demonstrating regular contact with white traders before Vancouver's arrival.

■ ■ ■

Bill and I arrived in Wright Sound the afternoon after our rest near Work Island. Our spirits were not much revived since the storm; our clothes, sleeping bags and tent remained wet. Intermittent rain continued as we paddled the last stretch of Princess Royal Channel, but large breaks in the clouds developed as we approached Point Cumming. Bright sunshine illuminated a sandy beach on its south shore. A double rainbow filled the sky to our east.

With strong paddle strokes we drove our bows onto the sandy beach, then climbed from our cockpits and stretched in the sun. Although billowy clouds encircled the blue sky, promising to block it before long, we pulled dry bags from our holds and emptied our wet clothes and gear onto the beach. We laid the clothes on black boulders facing the sun and hung our sleeping bags and soaked tent from a dead spruce branch. The beach looked like a yard sale as we dug into the boats for our lunch.

Seventeen days after leaving Port Hardy we were nearly out of food, and the little that remained was soggy and bland. We split the last bagel and lathered it with unappealing peanut butter, then plopped down in the sand to share the last of our trail mix. The temperature rose into the high fifties. Our faces warmed in the sun for what felt like the first time in weeks. After lunch, we napped and read, giving our clothes and gear time to dry before clouds and rain returned.

After relaxing quietly for ninety minutes, we packed away our moist gear and began the final push for Hartley Bay, eight miles across Wright Sound. We would be three miles from shore for much of the crossing, but in calm conditions estimated less than three hours of paddling. We added a high-protein drink mix to our water bottles, stuffed trail mix into our pockets and then entered the water, hoping our food delivery would still be at the Hartley Bay post office.

We departed Point Cumming near two in the afternoon, with cottony clouds clinging to the surrounding mountains and soon gained views of Douglas Channel and Verney Passage. They varied between one and three miles wide and had steeper walls than any we had yet seen. Several miles up the channel, dark cliffs rose 2,000 feet above the sea, too steep for much forest; one snow-capped peak reached over 3,500 feet less than two miles from shore. Big alpine meadows with abundant snowfields rolled above the walls.

The forbidding mountains and deep snows livened my mood, and I wanted to detour into the channels for a week or more of exploration. With no signs of civilization, I knew I had the same view Whidbey did more than 200 years earlier. I envied his opportunity to explore far beyond what I could see. He had reported miles of sheer cliffs, towering mountains, abundant waterfalls and avalanche paths that brought snow all the way to sea level. Camping each night was difficult on a "rugged rocky shore that scarcely afforded...horizontal space to land and remain upon."

The fiords were similar to what I had seen years earlier in Alaska. I regretted passing them without exploration. I was frustrated about losing so many days to poor weather and disappointed that a quarter of our expedition had passed without climbing a mountain or venturing very far into the forest. As we continued paddling and the views disappeared behind ridges, I made a resolution that we would hike more, regardless of how much poor weather remained ahead of us.

We were quiet through much of the crossing. We had apologized to each other for rudeness and sarcasm but had not yet talked about how much longer Bill would continue the trip. I assumed he was trying to decide that for himself and gave him space on the issue. After all, neither of us could do anything about it until we reached Prince Rupert. In the meantime, I tried to prepare myself for the prospect of finishing the trip alone but shuddered each time I thought about Queen Charlotte Strait or Work Island. I didn't want to handle such situations alone.

A light southeasterly skimmed the water and helped us make decent speed across the sound. Gulls and scoters flew overhead, and we saw our first marbled murrelets. These small birds have short wings that enable them to dive more than 100 feet below the water, but they are poor fliers. Each time we approached them, they made clumsy attempts to fly away, speeding from us by beating their wings against the water and running with their small legs. Their plump bellies bounced on the water for 100 feet, then they either gained low flight or gave up trying and dove below the water. Surprisingly, marbled murrelets nest high in the canopy of old-growth forests.

We reached land one mile from Hartley Bay at close to six. An hour earlier, the sun had disappeared behind high clouds, and only

6.1: Dugout Canoe Use and Construction in the Inside Passage

James Cook, George Vancouver and other early explorers reported encountering scores and sometimes hundreds of dugout canoes in the Inside Passage, some up to sixty feet long, seven feet high and capable of carrying dozens of passengers. Although they varied throughout the region in style and size, they were usually made from a single western red cedar log and were essential for early life in the Inside Passage, where mountains, ice and thick forest isolated most villages.

In most cases building a canoe was an important and even spiritual event reserved for specialist canoe-makers, with help from spirit guides and assistants, although individuals also made smaller, personal canoes. They were considered among the most valuable objects in a village and were often used to display wealth.

Canoe-makers usually selected straight cedars growing close to the water. After felling, they used hammers, chisels and sometimes hot rocks to carve or burn a basic V-shape in the log and round its bottom, then they often left it in the woods for a winter to season the wood. Next, they dragged the log to the water

a small patch of blue sky remained to the south. With nowhere in town to stay, we set camp at the head of a beach near some fire rings, a cut tree and some crumpled tin cans. That night's meal, a bland pile of rice and beans, was the dregs of our first food supply. Afterward, we crawled into the tent as light rain began falling.

"Is tomorrow Sunday?" I asked.

"I think so."

"I wonder if we'll have trouble getting into the post office for our food."

Hartley Bay sits beside calm water between the mainland and an island four miles across. It is less than a mile long, with several rows of houses set upon a gradual hill leading up from the water. The houses are small and well maintained and separated by streets of dirt and wood planks one vehicle in width. As we paddled toward town in light rain, we counted a tractor, two ATVs and one old pickup parked throughout town. Behind the houses, wet forest stretched upward into low, white clouds.

Like Hartley Bay and Klemtu, prehistoric villages along the northwest coast often sat beside calm shores, protected from winter's high winds. But they always had easy access to the water, which far more than the forest represented hunting grounds and trade routes. Food gathering also occurred at the water's edge, where the intertidal provided seaweed and shellfish. Even the cedars used for canoe and house construction came from the forest's edge, where they were felled into the water and towed to town with canoes.

Northwest coast villages were highly organized according to a strict code of social hierarchy and usually consisted of a single row of houses, although some larger villages had multiple rows. The wealthiest and most powerful villagers occupied houses in the middle of the first row; people of lower class lived either at the edges or in the second row of houses, furthest from the sea. The compact villages enabled strong defense against enemies and made efficient use of limited space along the steep coast.

By 2,000 years ago, most permanent villages consisted of longhouses made of cedar planks with sand and shells covering their earthen floors, which facilitated drainage. The houses were rectangular and sheltered between ten and fifty people, usually part of the same extended family. The structures varied between 100 and 400 feet long and were commonly fifty feet wide, although one exceptionally large example was 600 feet long and sixty feet wide. Household densities were highest in the northern part of the region, where village populations were greater.

Houses included one or more hearths with wooden racks above them used to dry salmon. Shelves

and towed it to the village, where they used adzes to more precisely carve the shape and make the hull even throughout. Although most consisted of one log, in some places separate bow and stern pieces were carved, then attached. After carving, builders partially filled the canoe with water, then used red-hot stones to produce steam to stretch the wood, sometimes lodging logs or sticks between the gunwales to facilitate spreading. Afterward, they inserted thwarts and treated the wood inside and out with fish oil. Finally, sacred carvings and paintings were added.

The boats served varied purposes, including moving people, equipment and cedar planks for seasonal camps and hunting, fishing and gathering each season's food resources. Haida Gwaii Natives used canoes to cross open water to the mainland and even Vancouver Island to trade or gather eulachon or other foods unavailable on their islands. Others traveled hundreds of miles for potlatches, trade or war. Styles varied throughout the region in answer to different purposes such as whaling, hunting seals and traveling on big rivers like the Fraser.

Men, women and children paddled canoes and paddles were typically made from yew or yellow cedar. Canoes lasted many years and splits or holes could be repaired with pitch and new wood.

lined the walls; intricately carved cedar boxes containing personal belongings filled the shelves. Many houses included areas where specialists such as toolmakers and carvers worked. Like the villages, the houses communicated social hierarchy, with wealthy and powerful people residing in the far corners and lower classes and slaves by the front door.

■ ■ ■

We landed on a beach below Hartley Bay shortly before nine on a soggy morning. Ravens squawked from atop telephone poles and trees, dogs barked from in front of houses and a few children played on bicycles at a nearby intersection of wooden streets. Like Klemtu, the absence of mechanical noise seemed uncharacteristic for a human settlement.

Although everyone in Klemtu had been friendly, we remained wary about vandalism and theft and decided Bill would watch the boats as I went to find the post office. But before I could walk up the beach, a man in blue jeans and an old black coat approached us. He was in his early thirties with a dark goatee and thick stubble on his cheeks. Shaking our hands, he quietly introduced himself as Ian.

"My Mom sent me down," he said, pointing 100 yards up the hill at a blue house. "She said you should come up for coffee."

We looked at the house, which had a picture window facing our boats, then accepted Ian's invitation and followed him up the short hill. Inside the house, Ian watched quietly as we removed our boots on a small rug by the door. His mother, Belle Eaton, walked toward us from the kitchen. She was tan-skinned and heavyset with black hair streaked gray hanging in tangled shocks over her furrowed forehead. She wore green slacks, a bright yellow shirt and big, octagonal glasses on her giant face. She greeted us warmly with a firm handshake and a broad smile, then led us to the kitchen.

"You boys drink coffee?" she asked after offering us seats at a small table by a window. The window looked over a small back yard that rose quickly into a knot of alders and berry bushes. Hills beyond the yard rose into dark forest and smoky clouds.

"Sure," said Bill.

"It'll warm you up good. Must've been chilly in your canoes this morning."

Ian carried another chair from the living room and joined us at the table. Belle poured four cups of coffee, then served peanut butter, jelly, muffins and bread.

"Eat up," she said, "and tell us about your trip."

The kitchen was small and crowded but neat. Plants hung from the ceiling in its corners and beside the window. Several pieces of northwest coast Native artwork hung on the walls among pictures of family and friends. Photos and personalized magnets showing four generations of loved-ones covered the refrigerator.

Herbie, Belle's youngest son, entered the kitchen as we told Belle and Ian about our trip. He poured himself some coffee and joined us at the table. He was a stocky thirty-year-old with a mustache, thick black hair and tan skin. He explained that he had just returned from a few weeks on a fishing boat "down south." Of course, "down south" is relative; as I pictured the Gulf of Mexico, Herbie explained that he had been off the west coast of Vancouver Island. Like many young men in Hartley Bay, he often left town for a few weeks or months to make money.

Then Tony appeared, a large man with black hair and a big smile. At thirty-eight, he was Belle's oldest son. He shook our hands, grabbed an apple from the refrigerator and, with no room left at the table, leaned against the stove. He and Belle asked us questions about our trip as Herbie and Ian listened quietly.

After fifteen minutes the front door flew open, and a neighbor named Stan walked into the room. He was slender and full of energy, and after shaking our hands began talking with Herbie about fishing in some nearby lakes. Meanwhile, Bill and I asked Belle questions about the area while Tony and Ian discussed a boat they needed to move into the water at the next high tide. Suddenly the kitchen was busy with conversation, with our hosts occasionally slipping into the Tsimsian language. Jokes and laughter peppered each discussion. Bill and I relaxed about our gear and felt welcome.

During a lull in the conversations, Tony pointed out the window at the "harbormaster" walking in the rain. He looked about thirty, was hunched inside a leather jacket and walked slowly through the backyard as if looking for something. Had he looked up, he would have seen everyone at the table laughing. Belle looked at Bill and I and explained that he was not an actual harbormaster.

"He steals anything," she said laughing, "especially the gas. He sells it."

With the attention back on Bill and I, Stan asked us where we lived. When I said I was from Colorado, Belle slapped both palms on the table and gave a big whoop that revealed two gold teeth. The guys cracked several simultaneous jokes I couldn't understand, and everyone but Bill and I laughed. Without explanation Belle reached up to a VHF radio above the table.

"Hey everyone!" she laughed into the microphone, "We've got a hockey player in town tonight! He's from Colorado. There'll be a game at the gym at seven!" She gave another big whoop and everyone laughed.

It was April 28, 1996, and the Colorado Avalanche had shut the Vancouver Canucks out of the Stanley Cup playoffs the previous night. As Bill and I ate rice and beans and read in our tent on the outskirts of Hartley Bay, much of Canada's population had watched the game on television.

The radio crackled to life for a few minutes, as half a dozen Hartley Bay residents joked about the presence of a Coloradoan in their small village. They requested autographs, called for a rematch and one woman proposed kidnapping me. Everyone at the table laughed.

After coffee, Tony, Stan and Herbie left the house to move a motor from one boat to another, and Ian walked to the living room and turned on the satellite television. After Bill and I helped Belle clear the table, she called Meryl, Hartley Bay's postmaster, on the VHF. Meryl confirmed there were two big boxes at the post office marked "HOLD FOR KAYAKERS" and said she could meet us there in fifteen minutes.

"Ian," Belle called from the kitchen, "you get off that couch and show the boys where the post office is. They've got two big boxes of food over there and need help carrying them back here to the house." Turning to us, she said, "And you better get those boats up here by the house. You leave them down by the water all day and the kids will do something to them." She shook her head disapprovingly. "These kids will do anything. They'll steal 'em, go through 'em. They'll just shove 'em into the water. Ian, give the boys a hand getting their kayaks up by the house."

We tried to tell Ian that he could stay inside, but Belle insisted that he help us.

"You help these boys, Ian," she said, leading the three of us to the front door.

"And after you get your food you can shower here, and tonight we'll all have a big dinner, okay?"

Cold rain fell steadily as we walked across the small town, our boots making hollow thuds on the wooden streets. Dogs barked at us, ravens squawked from telephone poles and rooftops and five children on bicycles sped past going one way, then returned going the other way. They looked at Bill and I curiously.

Inside the post office, which was a small brown house in the middle of town, Ian introduced us to Meryl Smith. She was short with thick black hair and glasses and greeted us with a smile. As she led us into a small, windowless room lined with aluminum shelves, she asked about our trip and joked about the playoffs. In the corner of the room, I recognized Patti's handwriting on two big boxes. Ian and Meryl held the doors open as Bill and I carried the boxes outside, each weighing more than thirty pounds.

"You're lucky to be staying with Belle," said Meryl as she locked the door behind us. "She's a good host."

Ian borrowed a nearby wheelbarrow, and Bill and I took turns pushing it the quarter mile to Belle's house. On the way, rain quickly moistened the cardboard boxes. They ruptured as we carried them up the stairs to Belle's door. Ian followed us into the house, picking up granola bars and bags of bagels.

"You going to be able to fit all that food in those little boats?" Belle asked with a laugh when we returned to the house. Then she led us to her basement, where she said we could organize our supplies.

We sat on a concrete floor next to a water heater with a bare bulb hanging from the ceiling and tore into the wet boxes like children, elated to find bags of homemade brownies and cookies. Although they were a little hard after being mailed across the continent and stored for a week in the post office, we consumed them greedily as we emptied the boxes.

We created a large pile on the floor consisting of dozens of granola bars, candy bars, crackers, apples and bagels. There were two dozen small juice boxes, two pounds of cheese and several large pieces of hard salami. Patti had removed most packaging and filled bags with trail mix, cereal, pasta, rice, dehydrated black beans and veggie burger mix. Smaller bags contained dried potatoes, dried fruit, sun-dried tomatoes, dried shitake mushrooms and pasta sauces such as pesto and alfredo. After several nights of bland meals, we were excited about fresh garlic and small doses of lemon pepper and cayenne pepper. There were also two boxes of rice milk, a bottle of honey and a new supply of olive oil. The pita bread was moldy and one of the trail mix bags had spilled, but overall our plan had worked. We now had food for two more weeks.

We spent the next hour cleaning dry bags, throwing away old food and organizing new food. Then we went upstairs and shared our treats with Belle, who was cooking in the kitchen. Afterward, I enjoyed my first shower in what smelled like a very long time while Bill walked back to the post office to phone his family.

■ ■ ■

The elaborate art style of the northwest coast was a significant achievement for a people who subsisted by hunting and gathering. Its complexity and degree of uniformity across well over 1,000 miles of coastline is unique among prehistoric artwork, as was its importance in symbolizing wealth and status. It is still prevalent today throughout the region and remains very much alive in the hearts, lives and spirits of Native people, whose culture continues to flourish throughout the Inside Passage. Called *at óow* in Tlingit, what outsiders might consider mere art is more accurately described as highly revered spiritual property, unique to each clan, and it reveals much about the beliefs and activities of the region's original inhabitants.

Although it varied significantly within the region, the artwork followed the same basic style and portrayed the same subject matter from the Copper River to the Columbia River. It commonly represented human and animal characters with emphasis on their prominent features. For instance, a long, straight beak represented the raven, while a curved beak with its top turned downward represented the eagle. A set of teeth, two large forepaws and a protruding tongue represented the bear. These motifs were similar throughout the region, as were the wolf, salmon, beaver, frog, hawk and thunderbird.

Illustrations 6.1 and 6.2, below: Two examples of northwest coast artwork: the Killer Whale and the Eagle.
Illustrations: Robert E. Stanley Sr., Northwest Native Arts: Basic Forms.

In addition, characters usually had rounded features within thick black outlines, or formlines, with ovoid shapes. Narrower formlines separated features and sometimes wound continuously throughout the work. Several rounded characters were commonly adjacent to each other within a single piece and blank spaces were rare. Rounded claws, feathers, ovoids, eyes or circles filled the areas between characters, creating a collage that blended fluidly. Symmetry was also extensive, with characters often shown from two angles. For instance, all four appendages might be shown outstretched or both sides of a head depicted symmetrically.

Before contact with Europeans, coastal artists carved with adzes made of stone, shell and bone. Bark, fungus, moss, berries, charcoal, lignite and ocher are some of the materials used to provide pigment. Common colors included red, black and yellow. Copper, the only metal used before European contact, was corroded in urine to produce a blue-green color that was also common. The guard hairs of porcupines were sometimes used as paintbrushes.

In *Passage to Juneau*, Jonathan Raban suggests that northwest coast Natives developed their art style "directly from their observation of the play of light on the sea." Raban suggests that the amount of time people spent either on or alongside the water influenced their emphasis on prominent features and use of ovoids and symmetry. He points out that the calm inlets of the Inside Passage produce many mirrored reflections, creating split images of mountains, forests, floating loons, bears feeding in the intertidal zone. Light breezes or tidal currents move the water just enough to distort reflections, blending features and rounding their edges. Without modern distractions, these images surrounded early residents of the northwest coast.

Among the earliest examples of artwork along the northwest coast are a carved stone in southeast Alaska and several antler tools found in southern British Columbia, all between 4,000 and 5,000 years old. Although these items include ovals and rounded features, most archeologists agree that northwest coast art did not fully develop until 2,000 years ago. Stone, antler, shell and bone carvings occurred at that time, but the primary material was wood from western red cedars, yellow cedars, spruce and hemlock. Unfortunately, wood decomposes quickly in the rain forest, and archaeologists cannot say exactly how early the art developed or when wood became the preferred material.

Art was abundant and adorned houses, canoes, paddles, tools, blankets, chests, mats and baskets. Carved jewelry was also common and included labrets, earrings and bracelets shaped from copper or the teeth of seals, bears and beavers. Totem poles were common, too, along with decorated posts by the entrances of houses in the north and memorial poles marking the graves of important figures throughout the region.

The purpose of art varied significantly from north to south, but its ceremonial and spiritual importance were consistent throughout the region. Ceremonies were most common during winter, when limited daylight and bleak weather drove people indoors. In longhouses smelling of cedar and salmon and lit by torches, they used song, dance and stories—each revered property of the clan—for highly spiritualized ceremonies that honored important events and powerful spirits and sustained the mythology that defined their world. As rain drummed on the roofs and wind rushed through tall trees overhead, dancers in elaborately decorated costumes and intricately carved masks assumed the personalities of animal spirits. While singing in the guttural languages of the northwest coast, they hunched over and stamped their feet to represent the bear or screeched with outstretched arms within feathered robes to represent the eagle. Artwork also adorned rattles, drums and specially carved ceremonial dishes, often sacred items that were only used for specific ceremonies.

The most important ceremonies were potlatches, great gatherings that occurred throughout the year. Their purpose varied between groups, but often honored marriages, deaths, treaties, ascensions to power or even the completion of a longhouse. Multiple clans attended, sometimes traveling hundreds of miles by canoe; ceremonies lasted for days. Although trade, dancing and great feasts occurred at potlatches, distribution of wealth and acknowledgment of power were often their most important purposes. Guests and hosts demonstrated their wealth and power through lavish gift giving; a gift's artwork often determined its value. Potlatches were also important in exchanging information and technology between groups from different parts of the coast.

■ ■ ■

"How's your dad, Bill?" It was late in the afternoon, and I was sitting on a couch in Belle's living room. Bill had just walked into the room after chatting with Belle in the kitchen.

"He's OK. He's sleeping a lot, but he's going for walks each morning. My mother talks like it's really no big deal." He plopped down into an armchair beside the couch. "It was good to talk with them today. It has been on my mind a lot these last days, and I've been wishing I'd been there when it happened. You know, the whole family was by his side except for me."

"I guess that felt pretty weird," I said.

"Yeah, it did. It still does. But, hell, there's not much I could have done...I'm still feeling cautious, y'know? Maybe I'll relax more when I talk to them from Prince Rupert. That'll be another week, right?"

"Yeah. It could be even less."

Simultaneously, we looked out the picture window. Strong

breezes drove heavy rain against the glass. Foggy clouds obscured the tops of conifers on a nearby island. Half a mile from shore, Wright Sound disappeared into a smudge of low, gray clouds. We could estimate the day of our arrival in Prince Rupert all we wanted, but it was ultimately up to the weather.

Ian and Tony stepped in the front door, stripped their soaked rain gear and rubber boots and walked to the kitchen. Tony soon returned and sat beside me on the couch. I asked him what they had been doing in the rain.

"We're getting gear ready for camp," he said. "In a few weeks we'll head to one of the islands south of here to camp for a month."

Tony described the upcoming subsistence trip, when several families from the village would relocate for a month to collect seaweed, abalone and clams and fish for salmon and halibut. Others would travel to nearby mainland rivers to take advantage of eulachon runs. Coastal Natives have long valued these anadromous smelts for their oil, which is used for cooking and preserving salmon. Later in the summer and fall, residents would travel to other areas to fish for salmon, collect berries and hunt deer. Food gathered in the summer would supplement winter diets.

These modern residents of the northwest coast stayed in cabins while away from Hartley Bay. They fished with modern gear, hunted with rifles and traveled by motorboat. With the aid of kerosene heaters, gas stoves and generators they continued a subsistence tradition that dates back thousands of years. Their ancestors hunted and gathered the same foods on the same islands, but used fishing lines of cedar bark and hooks made of wood. They cooked in earthen ovens and used hot stones to boil water inside watertight baskets made of cedar and spruce root. They hunted seals with harpoons attached to floats made of inflated seal bladders. The floats exhausted and forced the animals to the surface.

Their ancestors traveled from permanent winter villages to summer subsistence grounds in cedar canoes, their bows decorated with colorful artwork. Some were large enough to carry sixty people, while smaller ones hauled supplies such as cedar planks removed from winter houses. The planks were laid across canoe gunwales on the way to subsistence camps, then attached to wooden frames left standing the previous summer. They used cordage made of cedar bark and spruce root to make the attachments. Based from these temporary structures, they gathered food that would feed them during the rough winters.

As Tony told us about the upcoming summer, the delicious smell of baking turkey filled the house. Increasingly, hard rain blew against the window, intensifying my appreciation of the hospitality. A little after six, Belle poked her head into the living room and invited us to eat.

The wind shook alder branches outside the window as Bill and I crowded around the small table with Belle's three sons. She placed the big turkey in the middle of the table and brought over bowls of salad, mashed potatoes, rice, string beans and rolls. Then she sat at the head of the table. Several conversations began as we reached across our plates for salad dressing, butter, gravy and pitchers of juice.

"When do you get to Juneau?" Ian asked us as Herbie and Tony talked about fishing.

"We're hoping for early June. Maybe the second week."

"It'll be Celebration," he said. "Our cousins will be there, too."

"That's right!" Belle said excitedly. "They'll be in town for the whole week. You can come see our cousins dance!"

Celebration is a cultural gathering of northwest coast Native groups that has occurred every two years in Juneau since 1982. It has recently attracted more than 5,000 guests per day and over 1,800 dancers from forty-seven groups. It occurs over a weekend in early June and includes a parade through town, a grand entrance by all the dancers at a convention center and dance performances every thirty minutes for three days. The dancers range from preschoolers to elders and take the stage in colorful masks, costumes and blankets to perform centuries-old songs and stories from all over the coast. Late into the night, traditional drums and singing bring alive a culture that developed with the nature of the northwest coast.

After dinner Ian went to the living room to watch television, and Tony and Herbie went to visit a neighbor. Bill and I helped Belle clean the kitchen, and she told us about life in Hartley Bay. She said only about 200 people lived there, but that at any time a quarter of the population might be out of town either working or visiting relatives. Drying her hands, she leaned on the sink and shook her head with disappointment.

"Some of the kids here are mixed up," she said, "they leave town too much and get into alcohol and drugs. Hartley Bay is dry, but still some of the kids get mixed up."

Belle took us into the living room when the kitchen was clean.

"This is our crest," she said, handing us a wooden plaque carved with an intricate design. "I'm Tsimsian, but my clan is Blackfish."

Belle explained that lineages along the coast are associated with animal spirits, which original people believed were their ancestors. Each village consisted of several houses, each representing a specific clan. Most people in a house were part of an extended family, and families were parts of clans such as Eagle, Raven, Wolf and Dog Salmon. Each clan had family members in villages throughout the region.

"I have Blackfish relatives in Metlakatla, Nass River, Rupert and Klemtu," said Belle. "Just like here, those places have Raven and Eagle and other clans, too."

In the northern Inside Passage, in the territory of the Tsimsian, Haida and Tlingit nations, crests were important in clan identity. Often, a large carved motif of a clan's animal spirit decorated the entrance of each house. However, along the southern half of the coast, crests were not used to indicate lineage.

A matrilineal determination of lineage was also unique to the northern part of the region. If a person's mother was Blackfish, that person could not marry someone within the Blackfish clan, no matter their village. Even today, members of the same clan are called cousins, even if they are not blood related. This strict system prevented incest and fostered peace by linking villages through clan relations. Along the southern half of the coast, where many more different groups occupied smaller areas, lineage was usually determined patrilineally.

After talking for another hour, I joined Ian in the living room as Bill and Belle began a marathon gin-rummy game that would last until well after midnight. I sat on the couch as Ian surfed channels from the armchair, switching between CNN, movie channels and network television. It was the first television I had watched since Seattle.

I looked to the window when strong gusts rattled the door or drove sheets of rain against the house. Water ran down the glass, distorting spotlights above the wooden streets, and Wright Sound was invisible in the blackness. Knowing I would have to paddle into that miserable weather in the morning, I sunk deep into the couch, pulled my sleeping bag up to my chin and savored each moment of television. The cheaper, the better, I thought as Ian came across a movie about a giant squid that torments a coastal community.

Meanwhile, the gin-rummy game in the kitchen got off to a slow start. Bill was new to the game and forgot the wild card six times during the first hour. Belle responded with exasperation, slapping her cards on the table and calling him a "fart-head." Eventually, Bill grasped the game and even won several hands. Each time, Belle slapped her cards on the table, called him a name, and demanded a rematch.

I sat motionless on the couch, absorbing the sounds of rain, wind, card game and the movie. I looked around the room at Belle's family photos and her rattles, drums and blankets covered in northwest coast artwork. I knew it was a night I would long remember.

Belle was up early the following morning and cooked scrambled eggs for breakfast. Afterward, she gave us a big bag of bannock, then hugged us goodbye at her front door. Ian helped us carry our gear down to the water, and for thirty minutes we packed our boats with steady rain running from our coats and beating on the kayaks. By the time we slid our boats into the water, ten villagers stood above us on a wooden dock, waving, joking and wishing us well. As we made our first paddle strokes, the rain turned to sleet.

"At least it's bouncing off of us!" Bill said.

We soon arrived at a rocky point, and I looked back for a final glimpse of Hartley Bay. As my boat continued moving forward, the rocky shore behind us and a nearby forested island overlapped the village from either side, drawing together like a curtain. Within seconds, dark trees hid the village and an almost silent forest surrounded us—it was like Hartley Bay had never existed. The only sound was a lone raven gurgling from high in a nearby tree. We floated quietly as low clouds blew across the tops of trees and rain and sleet popped against our rain gear. We were back on the border between land and water.

CHAPTER SEVEN

A Walk in the Woods— Getting to Know the Rain Forest

Something was being attacked in the woods. I could hear raspy screams and twigs snapping on the forest floor as I paddled fifty feet to shore and rested my hand on a submerged boulder. Above, the ragged edge of a mossy carpet and a few root ends overhung a rocky bluff ten feet high. I could see some alder branches with young leaves, but not much more of the nearby forest.

"What is that?" Bill whispered as he paddled alongside me, the loud screams continuing.

At the time, I had no idea what could have made such agonized sounds, but several years later I heard them again while walking in the rain forest not far from shore. I looked to a shaded hollow twenty feet below and saw two mink wrestling, screaming loudly as they tumbled across moss and small branches. These slim, muscular members of the weasel family are generally solitary creatures who will often fight upon contact, sometimes until death.

We had seen three mink since leaving Hartley Bay the previous day, each about eighteen inches long with a rusty brown coat of smooth fur. While eating lunch on a rocky beach, one peeked curiously at us with shiny black eyes from behind a drift log. It approached to within ten feet and sniffed the air in our direction before scurrying away. Mink are common in the Inside Passage and spend most of their time in the intertidal, where they feed on shellfish. They also hunt rodents and small birds in the forest.

Since leaving Hartley Bay we had also seen our first river otter. It emerged from the water less than fifteen feet from my boat with a foot-long fish struggling in its mouth. After taking a few steps onto a nearby beach, it put the fish below its front feet. Then it suddenly noticed us and eyed us intently, the fish writhing under its feet. After a long moment, it grabbed the fish in its teeth and took a step back toward the water, then stared at us like it had just completed a chess move. A moment later, a big bald eagle landed with outstretched wings and a loud whoosh on a branch overhead and glared at the otter. Bill, the otter and I simultaneously looked up at the eagle, then back at each other. Then the otter ran quickly into the water and disappeared. I looked up at the eagle, which stared back with intense yellow eyes.

We also saw creatures that had become common to us. Seals rose behind our boats or watched us curiously from safe distances; ravens and eagles flew overhead or perched high in trees near shore; mergansers, scoters, murrelets and loons floated on the water. But we had yet to see a bear. I saw them frequently in Alaska, often watching them feed in the intertidal as I floated close by in my kayak. Since Safety Cove I had anxiously awaited our first sighting. Each night, we took precautions against surprise encounters by hanging our food and sleeping with a loaded rifle between us. At several camps we saw their tracks and scat in the woods. There were a few nights when I awoke suddenly because I thought I heard something moving in the woods near our tent. But by the third week of our trip, my anxiousness had turned to disappointment. A person camping in the Inside Passage for that long should expect to see bears.

Both black and brown bears inhabit the Inside Passage north of Vancouver Island, where they enjoy prime habitat. Sedges along shore, shellfish in the intertidal and tubers, carcasses and insects in the forest provide abundant food in spring. A prolific berry season begins in midsummer and lasts into autumn. And for most coastal bears, abundant salmon contribute significantly to summer diets. Beginning in early summer and continuing well into autumn, all five species of Pacific salmon enter coastal streams to spawn in huge numbers. They die within days of spawning, their carcasses littering streamsides and the intertidal. Those bears not swift enough to catch live fish pick through thousands of dead ones. A few weeks after consuming the last salmon and berries, bears head inland to find winter dens. Some climb high into the alpine where deep snows will quickly insulate them. Others use root wads or caves in the forest as their winter home.

But near Hartley Bay it was neither black nor brown bears that I most hoped to see. It was white bears. The central coast of British Columbia is home to the extremely rare Kermode bear. Also known as the spirit bear, this subspecies of black bear is born with a white coat that it maintains its entire life. It is most prevalent near Princess Royal Channel and Wright Sound, but has also been found near Terrace, Kitimat and Prince Rupert and as far inland as Hazelton, British Columbia.

Spirit bears are the result of a double recessive gene, which means that both mating bears must carry the gene in order to produce a white cub. But when two such bears mate, the resulting cubs are not necessarily white, and a mother can produce both white and black cubs from the same pregnancy. On Princess Royal and Gribbel Islands, where spirit bears are most common, biologists estimate that only 10 to 30 percent of cubs are born white. In the entire region, they estimate a population of 800 to 1,200 bears, with as few as 120 having white coats. However, because not all spirit bears are white, no one knows for certain how many exist.

Beginning in the late 1980s environmental groups, sometimes joined by Native organizations, fought to protect the spirit bear's habitat from logging. The area's pristine old-growth forests also contain abundant salmon streams and populations of Sitka black-tailed deer, otter, wolves and both brown and black bears. At first the government proposed roughly 100,000 acres as a "study area," but agreed to renegotiate in the late 1990s after increased public pressure and a successful boycott of British Columbia lumber led by Greenpeace. Negotiations included sixty-five environmental, Native, industry, recreation and government groups and lasted more than two years. In April, 2001, they ended with an agreement that delighted environmentalists by setting aside 3,000,000 acres of the rain forest along the northern British Columbia coast, some of it protected permanently, some of it where logging will be deferred for ten years.

■ ■ ■

Grenville Channel is a narrow lane pointing northwestward for forty-five miles and connecting Wright Sound to the waters south of Dixon Entrance. Its southern end is seven miles west of Hartley Bay. Its northern end is thirty miles south of Prince Rupert and only sixty miles from the Alaskan border. The southern portion of the channel is one mile wide and edged by forested hills only a few hundred feet high, but within ten miles the hills on both sides turn to steep walls closely bordering the water. Thickly forested, they rise between 1,500 and 2,000 feet less than a mile from shore, occasionally interrupted by narrow valleys reaching almost to sea level. Twenty miles from the entrance, the walls grow even steeper and the fiord narrows considerably.

We entered Grenville Channel in cold rain, with a powerful ebb pushing against us. Gray clouds stained the surrounding hills, and the midday light was dim. Near three, with our fingers pruned and rain soaking through our coats, we set camp after covering only twelve miles. We dried ourselves and napped and only left the tent for about an hour for dinner.

We awoke the next morning to broken clouds, light rain and temperatures around fifty Fahrenheit. Knowing that incoming tides create strong northward currents in the area and that high tide was shortly before noon, we packed quickly and entered the water by eight. We made swift progress in light rain and covered twelve miles in only a few hours. The clouds varied wildly, with some filling valleys down to sea level and others tearing apart to reveal large sections of blue sky.

By midafternoon, after another eight miles, the fiord walls rose to more than 2,000 feet; we saw peaks almost 3,000 feet high just one mile from shore. Near their tops, the green forest that had surrounded us for weeks diminished to low alpine vegetation colored yellow and rusty orange at the edge of big snowfields. Avalanches had filled alpine basins with filthy snow, which was marked with runnels from recent rains. They were the beginnings of streams that fell thousands of feet to the steep shores beside the channel. Sheer bands of rock protruded from the snowy alpine and led upward to craggy summits, but sharp peaks were rare as almost each mountaintop was a rounded dome.

Deep, U-shaped valleys and narrow inlets separated the mountains, their sides rising 2,000 feet in less than half a mile. Rich forest clung to the walls, and large streams poured from the valleys in loud waterfalls. The streams sliced narrow gaps through the forest and wound sinuously between the mountains. There, deer, bear and wolves rarely saw humans; centuries-old spruce trees towered over

155

salmon streams. Green moss carpeted nearly everything. I longed to explore each valley.

Late in the day the channel narrowed to less than half a mile. The water was perfectly calm, and on either side areas of bare rock too steep for vegetation interrupted the forest. But the channel's impressive steepness also lay below us. Our nautical chart showed depths approaching 1,200 feet in parts of the channel less than half a mile wide. Emptied of its water, the channel would have been a slim valley with walls more than 4,000 feet high. More than any of the fiords we had paddled, it revealed the Inside Passage's glacial history.

Nearly every marine waterway in the Inside Passage, whether termed a canal, passage, inlet, arm, reach or strait, is a fiord. These narrow, deep seaways are the work of glaciers and are typically U-shaped, with high, steep walls and rounded floors. While this shape is not always characteristic of Puget Sound, the fiords north of the Strait of Juan de Fuca are increasingly steep-sided. The trend culminates in southeast Alaska, where mountains more than 6,000 feet high border some of the deepest fiords in the world.

Before the ice ages of the Pleistocene epoch, Grenville Channel was an already existing valley created by rivers or previous glaciers. During the Pleistocene, a glacier flowed into the channel on its way to the sea from immense ice fields covering the Coast Mountains. The river of ice filled Grenville Channel because glaciers, like water, follow paths of least resistance. Confined between valley walls, the ice dug downward with immense pressure, widening, deepening and straightening the valley. In periods of severe glaciation, when ice a mile or more thick blanketed the whole Inside Passage, the glacier spilled over the tops of the surrounding mountains. Its constant motion seaward and the rocky debris trapped within it smoothed the mountaintops into rounded domes.

All the fiords in the Inside Passage have histories similar to Grenville Channel. Today they act as a map showing the routes of the deepest Pleistocene glaciers. The U-shaped valleys extending inland from the fiords show where smaller tributary glaciers flowed into main trunks.

■ ■ ■

156

We gained our views of the surrounding mountains through a dynamic and broken cloudscape that ranged from dark gray to bright white. Some clouds rested heavily on the water and turned to light rain as we paddled into them, while others squatted atop high peaks or oozed down fiord walls. We passed valleys and inlets stuffed with soggy clouds or haunted with bands of drifting mist. The clouds constantly shifted, one moment hiding the scenery entirely and the next lifting to let sunlight onto the water. They turned our surroundings into a kaleidoscope of rock bands, snow-fields, waterfalls, forest and sea.

After paddling about twenty miles, we landed on a cobble beach in a small lagoon with a smooth bedrock peninsula reaching into its center. Although most of the peninsula was bare, a patch of scraggly forest crowded its highest point. Like a microcosm of the surrounding woods, small saplings and tangled understory grew around taller trees and dead snags. It was a climax forest for the thin soil base of the peninsula. Beyond it, mature forest rose steeply into a dark gray cloud.

A long and narrow mound of bedrock separated the lagoon from Grenville Channel. It was ten feet above the water and without vegetation. I piled our food and kitchen gear onto it as Bill set our tent at the head of the cobble beach. A half mile across the water, an enormous waterfall thundered into the sea, roaring like a freight train. It was the terminus of several streams that ran down the face of a mountain nearly 3,000 feet high. From our kitchen, we could see several such mountains lining the other side of the channel, with deep snow fields and broad alpine summits rolling along their upper reaches.

After dinner, we picked bits of rice from grooves in our bedrock kitchen. Keeping a clean camp was in our interest and that of local bears. The grooves were up to half an inch deep and ran parallel to the fiord, carved by rocks trapped in glacial ice more than 10,000 years gone. Bill commented that similar striations line exposed rocks in New York's Central Park, carved by the ice sheet that covered the northeastern United States during the Pleistocene.

As Bill spread his sleeping bag across level bedrock and began reading, I took a short walk into the woods, following a game trail for a few hundred yards along a rumbling stream. It was well worn, as though made by hikers, and enabled quick travel, a rarity in the thick forests of the Inside Passage. After ten minutes a glimpse of white on the predominantly mossy floor attracted me to the side of the stream, where I found a dead eagle upside down in the duff. Its white feathers, scattered with twigs and needles, were stained yellow, and its eyes were gone, most likely scavenged by ravens. Its yellow talons were frozen in a tight grasp; its body appeared deflated. Sprigs of moss reached upward along its sides, slowly pulling it into the forest floor where its nutrients would feed everything from salmon fry to red cedars. Recycling begins immediately in the rain forest and spreads resources widely.

Bill was still reading when I returned to camp. The skies had become mostly clear. An alpen glow illuminated the mountaintops, turning their snowfields dull white and faintly pink. At almost nine, it was still light enough to read without a headlamp. Since leaving Port Hardy, we had gained almost two hours of daily sunlight, a result of both time and distance, as we were a few weeks closer to summer solstice and nearly 200 miles closer to the Arctic Circle. We gained several more hours of daylight in the following weeks. By the end of our trip the nights were less than four hours long and only slightly darker than twilight.

"Let's hike tomorrow," I said.

"You read my mind. I've been thinking about the lakes up behind these hills." Earlier, we had noticed the lakes a few miles inland on our nautical charts.

"Yeah. And if we can get up high maybe we'll get some views of the mountains around here," I said.

"Either way, it'll be nice not to paddle tomorrow."

We awoke the next morning to blue skies and temperatures in the fifties, one of only four such mornings in the previous three weeks. By teetering along a narrow strip of bare rock between thick forest and a ten-foot drop to the sea, we found a smooth shelf facing the sun a short distance south of camp, where we sat on our PFDs and cooked pancakes. Looking at our maps, we chose a lake less than two miles away and approximately 800 feet above sea level as our destination. We could reach it by following the stream emptying into our lagoon.

After breakfast we stuffed a backpack with lunch, snacks, rain gear and cameras, then hung our food in a big spruce by the forest's edge. Only three days from Hartley Bay, our food filled two mesh sacks and four dry bags and weighed sixty pounds. Hanging it required two ropes 100 feet long with several carabiners tied to their ends and took up to thirty minutes.

We pried through branches at the head of the beach and entered the forest, where tree trunks and thick understory quickly replaced our views of the sea and mountains. Under the canopy, the air was cool and moist and we removed our sunglasses in the dim light. After crossing a spongy carpet of moss we stood at the bases of several tall Sitka spruces growing beside the stream. The largest was almost three feet in diameter and, like many mature spruces, appeared to grow perfectly straight without tapering. Its bark was gray and scaly, and I could have chipped it off with my fingers. Its lowest branch was fifty feet from the forest floor, draped with thick moss, and its crown was lost in a canopy well overhead. It was probably between one and two centuries old, which is not much for a coastal Sitka spruce.

Two enormous stumps, four feet high and more than three feet in diameter, stood among the spruces. Moss covered them almost entirely, and several young trees grew from their tops and sides. One of the saplings grew twenty feet high from the center of a stump and embraced its sides with roots running to the ground. It appeared to guard the stump's nutrition to itself.

Several decades earlier, the stumps were the bases of spruces much larger than those left standing, possibly 200 feet tall and six or seven centuries old. Had they fallen by wind or disease, as most Sitka spruces do, their logs would have remained on the forest floor for as much as two centuries. Such nurse logs provide habitat for termites, beetles and other insects and rich nutrition for a carpet of moss, lichen, mushrooms and dozens of saplings. Woodpeckers and bears open their softened wood searching for insects, creating habitat for more insects and spreading nutrition to the forest floor. Generations of mice, voles, squirrels and foxes, among others, find shelter and breeding habitat in the logs. Occasionally black bears hibernate in hollows beneath their root wads. When such trees fall over streams, they create check-dams that keep sediment out of salmon spawning beds; their rotting wood supplies nutrients for young fish. However, the conspicuous absence of nurse logs beside our big stumps meant the trees had fallen unnaturally.

■ ■ ■

In 1820, Virginia representative John Floyd argued that Congress should provide economic incentives for American settlement of the Oregon Country. Listing timber as one possible advantage, he was among the first American officials to acknowledge the northwest's vast timber resources. But Floyd's recommendations did not pass, and within ten years it was British subjects at Fort Vancouver, along the Columbia River, that built the Pacific Northwest's first sawmill and began exporting timber to California and Hawaii. Further north, in the Inside Passage, only small-scale logging for construction occurred near the region's few white settlements such as Sitka and Vancouver.

More sawmills appeared in the 1830s and 1840s as Americans settled the Columbia and Willamette Valleys, but timber did not become a significant part of the northwest's economy until the California gold rushes of the midcentury. The search for gold created a building boom in California and made San Francisco the largest city on the West Coast, with close to 60,000 residents by 1860. Timber surrounding San Francisco Bay quickly disappeared. With no roads or railroads to get inland logs to the coast, the building boom increasingly relied upon timber from the north.

The rough coasts of California and Oregon had few harbors for loading logs, but sawmills along the calm waters of the Willamette, Columbia and Puget Sound prospered. In the following decades, as the coastal population grew and gold rushes drew prospectors further north into British Columbia, logging towns spread west along the Olympic Peninsula and north along eastern Vancouver Island and the British Columbia mainland. Entrepreneurs and speculators soon purchased vast forest lands in California, Oregon and Washington.

Pacific Northwest logging was slow and arduous work during the middle of the nineteenth century. Handloggers used axes and crosscut saws to fall trees as much as eighteen feet in diameter and over 250 feet tall. In pairs, they stood on planks called springboards hammered into massive tree trunks. By placing the springboards as much as fifteen feet above the ground, they avoided cutting through the widest part of the tree. Nonetheless, it could take hours to fall a single tree. The thick forests required precise cuts to ensure falling

160

trees did not hang on others. Once a tree was down, limbing and bucking it took many additional hours.

Crews reduced each tree to logs that teams of up to a dozen oxen could pull from the woods over skid roads. The roads consisted of peeled logs half buried facing the direction of travel and greased regularly with whale oil, kerosene or water. They ran from hillside logging camps to rivers or seaways where men rafted logs to steam-powered sawmills. Thus, between fallers, buckers, road builders and those who cared for oxen, each tree brought to mill represented significant investments of time and labor.

But in the 1880s, the steam donkey greatly improved the efficiency of northwest logging. These large steam engines powered spools with hundreds of feet of cable that could tow bigger logs than teams of oxen. Donkeys could be placed farther inland near long wooden flumes leading to mills. Soon after, spar trees reaching 100 feet tall with their tops removed supported thousands of feet of cable that carried logs from steep hills; large clear-cuts soon appeared.

Even with the advent of the steam donkey, vast inland forests remained inaccessible, but the 1880s also brought railroads to the northwest. Logging increased to supply wooden tracks and ties and to fire steam engines. Soon locomotives reached farther inland than was previously imaginable. Small rail lines extended into the forest from logging camps to bring timber to rivers and ocean ports. They also connected to transcontinental rail systems, which reached Portland, Tacoma, Seattle and Vancouver by the early 1890s. Timber production boomed in Oregon and Washington, and logging camps spread northward well into the Inside Passage.

In addition to technological advances, events far to the east influenced timber production in the Pacific Northwest. Until the middle of the nineteenth century, America relied upon the white pine forests of the northeast for its timber, but centuries of ungoverned logging eventually decimated the region's forests. Although timber companies began logging the Great Lakes region in the late 1830s, it was at the end of the Civil War, thirty years later, that the pine forests of the east finally disappeared and the Great Lakes region became America's primary source of timber. But lessons of sustainability were still more than a century away, and by the late 1890s the timber of the Great Lakes was nearly exhausted. Once again, timber interests looked west. For years, rumors had filled Great Lakes logging camps about endless forests of huge trees in Oregon and Washington.

As timber companies and lumberjacks headed west in the late nineteenth century, new technologies replaced steam donkeys and rails and made logging big trees even more economical. Loggers used adapted farm tractors, with tracks instead of wheels and gas and diesel instead of steam, to tow multiple wagonloads of logs along roads built far into the forest. The roads cost much less than rails and could access farther and steeper land. This period also brought the first pneumatic saws, which were powered by large engines, but practical chainsaws were still several decades away.

Concerns of a "timber famine" arose in the late nineteenth century as the forests of the Midwest disappeared and northwest forests fell with increasing speed. Many feared that America would run out of wood and become dependent upon imports. In response, Congress passed legislation in 1891 that created America's first forest reserves; the Forest Management Act of 1897 outlined the nation's first forest management policy. Between 1905 and 1907, on advice from his Forestry Chief, Gifford Pinchot, Teddy Roosevelt greatly expanded the forest reserves, renamed them national forests and created the U.S. Forest Service. He put the new agency under the Department of Agriculture, which demonstrated the early-century view of forest ecosystems as crops. By that time, speculators and entrepreneurs had bought much of the coastal forests of Oregon and Washington, but the Olympics, Cascades and a majority of southeast Alaska became national forest. In British Columbia, similar concerns and a lack of comprehensive forest management policy led to the Forest Act of 1912, which created the British Columbia Forest Branch, later the B.C. Forest Service. Canadian forest experts and U.S. officials such as Gifford Pinchot helped organize the agency, which today manages about 95 percent of British Columbia's coastal forests.

World War I brought the next significant rise in northwest logging. Demand increased for Douglas firs, which were used to make chests for soldiers and temporary battleground camps. In addition, aircraft engineers began using the light, straight-grained wood of Sitka spruces in warplane construction. Its strength-to-weight ratio was greater than early metals, it was cheaper and easier to repair and, unlike metal, it did not crack when struck with bullets. By the

162

end of World War I almost all the big Sitka spruces in Oregon and Washington were gone, which increased logging in coastal British Columbia and southeast Alaska.

Even as advanced logging technology in Oregon and Washington helped the Allies win World War I, handloggers still worked the more remote Inside Passage north of Vancouver Island. They established small logging camps and cruised shorelines in skiffs, gathering drift logs and removing the biggest trees (nicknamed "pumpkins") growing by the water. They rafted their timber to small mills in the Inside Passage or to larger ones in Vancouver and Prince Rupert. Perhaps that was the origin of the big stumps Bill and I saw at the beginning of our hike.

■ ■ ■

We followed the game trail inland along the stream. Like others we had come across, it was a thin strip of bare soil surrounded by moss, understory and debris. It wove around big trees, formed canyons through berry thickets and traveled under large logs hung a few feet above the floor. In one spot, it created a tunnel three feet high through thick brush. Rather than fighting the surrounding vegetation, we crawled along it on hands and knees.

We found much evidence of bears. Their prints were preserved perfectly in muddy areas by the stream, with several larger than our hands. We found claw marks left on large logs across the trail and scraggly hairs hanging from the undersides of logs suspended above the ground. We also stepped over numerous heaps of grassy scat left in the middle of the trail. In addition, we found deer tracks and a few salmon bones from the previous summer, but no sign of humans.

Steep hills closed around the stream after half a mile, and the trail disintegrated amid fallen trees, tangled berry bushes and devil's club. We struggled through chest-high understory while sidestepping along the increasingly steep slope, our ankles twisting frequently in our rubber boots and wet soil eroding easily beneath our feet. We tripped over downed branches when the tangled understory hid the ground below us.

"Let's top out on this hill and follow the stream from above," I called from the forest floor. I had just fallen for the second time, snarling the rifle in a nest of wiry blueberry branches. Bill had

7.1: To Arm or Not to Arm— Carrying a Firearm in Bear Country

Whether to carry a firearm in bear habitat is a difficult decision for some paddlers: a weapon occupies valuable room in a kayak and requires maintenance, yet in a real emergency it could save a life. Ultimately, understanding bear behavior and responsible camping and travel techniques are by far the best defense against a violent encounter (sidebar 9.2), and carrying a firearm is a matter of personal preference.

Although bears will almost always avoid humans, they occasionally act aggressively, usually when provoked or previously conditioned to associate humans with food. Understanding how to react to an angry bear will usually prevent an attack. However, real attacks sometimes occur.

Bear mace, a highly concentrated pepper spray that can shoot up to thirty feet, is one popular alternative to carrying a firearm. Although it has proved an effective deterrent

paused a few feet ahead to pick devil's club prickers from his hand. The prickers are barbed so that removing them often requires tweezers.

With the rifle slung across my back, where it would do little good if I surprised a mother bear with cubs, I clawed up the steep hill. At the steepest points, I grabbed berry bushes and young hemlocks to pull myself upward or crawled uphill by digging my fingers into the wet ground. Once, I had to quickly wrap my arm around a young tree to prevent myself from falling backward. Toward the top of the hill, I climbed atop a downed spruce three feet in diameter. It was tall enough to get me above the understory, and I walked up it like a ramp.

After 200 feet at a thirty-degree angle, the hill flattened into a forested plateau. Below us, the creek rumbled through a ravine.

"Fun, huh?" I asked Bill.

"I thought you said we were going hiking. This is more like a wrestling match!" He was out of breath, and mud stained one of his cheeks.

We leaned against a fallen spruce and drank from our water bottles. Through thick forest, we glimpsed only fractured views of the mountains across the channel and the water below. The only sounds were the stream and a varied thrush somewhere above our heads. It sounded like a telephone ringing in the distance.

164

Some trees were enormous, with the base of one cedar close to eight feet across. Its bark peeled outward in papery strips and drooping branches hung to the level of our heads. A knotty hemlock three feet across leaned on a nearby cedar at a seventy-degree angle. Another thick hemlock was broken in half 100 feet up. Fat spruces reached straight upward, their branches disappearing in thick canopy, and a downed spruce had a root structure standing thirty feet tall. It held a large rock twenty feet above the ground and trapped enough soil to support a few young trees growing from its top. By falling, the tree had tilled part of the forest floor; young herbs grew beneath its upended roots. Fifty hemlock seedlings stood in a line along its trunk. Moss carpeted the forest floor. Downed timber and dense understory filled the gaps between trees.

All ages of trees were present, from seedlings a few inches tall to enormous individuals many centuries old. There was much dead timber, too, both standing and downed. The larger downed trees had taken several others with them and opened big holes in the canopy. Under the uneven awning, patches of sunlight reached the ordinarily dim forest floor, creating a rich mosaic of understory herbs and shrubs. Berries and ferns grew where sunlight hit the floor, and devil's club and hemlock saplings grew in the shade.

Diversity, in the form of an uneven-aged stand, an understory

to aggressive bears, it is limited by wind direction. In addition, some bears have proven tolerant to pepper spray in field tests.

If paddlers choose to carry a firearm in the Inside Passage, they need a powerful rifle such as a .338 or stronger or a shotgun with slugs, and synthetic stocks and stainless steel barrels will resist rust much better than other materials. These are big weapons, but anything smaller may only injure and possibly anger a large bear. Powerful handguns such as a .44 can also be effective, but they are illegal in Canada and require much more training and accuracy than a rifle.

Carrying a firearm is a big responsibility and requires training, practice and frequent maintenance in a wet marine climate. Travelers should treat it as a last line of defense against an aggressive bear-after camping and traveling responsibly-and should be knowledgeable about bear behavior. For instance, bears frequently bluff charge, and a weapon should only be used if a bear is within extremely close range and showing sure signs of attack.

mosaic and a varied canopy, is the key characteristic of an old-growth forest and provides abundant habitat. Squirrels and wood-peckers live in snags, murrelets nest high in the mossy canopy and small birds nest in shrubs. Over fifty species of songbirds feed on a variety of seeds and berries and are occasional prey to ravens, eagles and hawks. Small mammals burrow or breed below downed wood and provide food for martens, foxes, mink and bear. The downed wood also keeps hillside soils in place, preventing erosion into salmon streams. Where the canopy is dense, the forest floor remains free of snow in winter, providing forage for deer and mountain goats. Lichen falling from tree branches during winter storms enriches the soil with nitrogen and provides nutrition for foragers. Wolves hunt these animals or feed on their carcasses. In this way, old-growth forests provide crucial niches to most wildlife of the Inside Passage.

Of course, these forests are also valuable economically, as timber companies can turn a single acre into tens of thousands of board feet of lumber. A single Douglas fir or western hemlock from this area can contain enough wood to frame an entire house, while a big red cedar can provide more than enough shingles, or perhaps enough caskets, for the whole neighborhood. One mature Sitka spruce can provide thousands of dollars worth of guitars, crates, doors, boat finishings or plywood. Since the end of World War II, when house construction boomed and the gas-powered chainsaw was introduced, about 94 percent of old-growth forests from California through southeast Alaska have been clearcut.

■ ■ ■

We climbed hills for more than an hour with the stream rumbling an average of 100 feet below us. We crossed several tributaries of the stream so that our progress upward included scrambling down into a few valleys, where we splashed through small streams and mud puddles. Sometimes we found game trails leading out of the valleys, but more often we clambered uphill through dense understory, branches slapping against our chests and faces.

Wherever we could, we hopped atop mossy logs that formed elevated walkways above the forest floor. Carefully negotiating around their dead limbs and saplings was easier than fighting the understory. On one occasion, a big log formed a bridge across a ravine thirty feet deep, filled with a jumbled mess of downed limbs, young trees and thick brush. Although the log was two feet in diameter, it bounced under our weight as we crossed it with small steps, bits of bark falling to the ground.

Pieces of blue sky appeared between the trees as we approached the crest of a steep hill. At the top we finally spotted fragments of the lake. It was 300 feet down a steep slope with dozens of bald logs floating near its outlet. Descending the slope was a combination of falling and awkward side-stepping through chest-high understory that concealed limbs and logs on the ground. Sometimes we walked slowly, patiently picking through the knot of vegetation, but other times we crashed through it, forcing the branches apart with our legs, arms and chests. I fell twice, hitting the soft floor with a muffled thud. Sticks poked my face and hands; wiry bushes wrapped around my arms and legs.

Halfway down we arrived at a big clearing where dozens of trees had fallen into a pile 500 feet long, 100 feet across and up to thirty feet high. Only a few trees remained standing, and the pile consisted of logs of all sizes. Along its edges, many trees leaned against others, their branches broken and trunks scarred. Most downed trees faced northward and still had green needles on their branches, signs that a recent storm with strong winds from the south had knocked them down.

The clearing provided our first unobstructed view of the lake, which was dark blue and sparkling in the sun. It was only half a mile wide, but wound sinuously between steep mountains for several miles. Its shape was similar to Grenville Channel, with a comparable glacial history. Forest covered the slopes surrounding it, and the mountaintops consisted of alpine vegetation and bare rock.

I reached up and balanced the rifle on a big hemlock lying even with my head. Using both hands, I grabbed a sturdy limb and pulled myself upward, then swung my leg around the trunk to straddle it. I rose slowly to my feet, slung the rifle over my shoulder and surveyed the pile. Some trees were broken in half while others were bent under great pressure. A tangle of understory grew from the bottom. Limbs of all sizes stuck into the air, which would provide nice handholds but complicate balancing along the trunks.

Bill climbed onto the hemlock and went ahead of me. He

jumped down six feet to a big spruce trunk, walked southward along it for fifteen feet and then ducked under two smaller trees lying over it. He emerged from the other end on hands and knees, and then stepped onto a spruce that formed a ten-foot ramp back to the top of the pile. He followed that for a short distance, then turned north on a rotten hemlock. Next, he turned southeast and carefully balanced across a hemlock only eight inches wide. It bounced under his weight and he almost fell. Spooked, he straddled the log for the remaining ten feet, then stepped onto a cedar and slowly negotiated around its vertical limbs.

I watched Bill for a minute, then chose my own route through the pile, zigzagging across hemlocks, cedars and spruces. One moment I was high atop the pile looking down at crisscrossed logs and broken branches, the next I was deep inside climbing through thick brush and uneven trees. I found giant spruces with splintered trunks, loose logs that rolled under my feet and a few hemlock saplings already winding upward through the mess. In most places, the pile completely hid the forest floor. After five minutes, I met Bill on the other side.

"It's like nature's monkey bars," he said.

While fire is the agent of renewal in most western forests, opening the forest floor for new life by thinning crowded stands, wind plays that role through much of the Inside Passage, especially in the north. In the south, summers droughts occasionally lead to forest fires. And archaeological evidence as far north as Prince Rupert shows that early people used fire to stimulate berry growth. But in the wetter north, where lightning is uncommon, fire is rare and plays almost no role in forest renewal.

The climate of the Inside Passage is so conducive to growth that almost all of the forest's nutrients are locked inside living or dead organic matter; only thin soil supports often massive trees. Because water and nutrients are close to the surface, tree roots are usually shallow, and a tree 200 feet tall may have roots only two feet deep. Thus, big trees in the Inside Passage are highly susceptible to wind throw, especially during autumn and early winter storms, when their broad crowns sail in the wind and heavy rains saturate the soil. Each falling tree takes a few others with it. Falling trees also hit others without knocking them down, scraping bark from their trunks and exposing them to disease and rot. This eventually makes trees along the edge more susceptible to wind, which slowly but constantly renews the forest.

Clearings do not last long in the rain forest. Increased sunlight enables previously shaded trees to grow tall and extend their branches outward. Shade intolerant seeds that may have lay dormant for years, such as red cedar, quickly become seedlings and saplings. Other shade intolerant species like elderberry and huckleberry fill the understory, and herbs and ferns grow where uprooted trees tilled the soil. Thus, old-growth forests develop their multi-aged stands and uneven canopies largely as a result of wind and thin soils.

In contrast, such diversity cannot be found in clearcuts, which remove most organic material from the forest floor. Without downed timber, soils lose nutrition and erode easily into streams, where they bury salmon spawning beds. If replanted, especially with only one species, clearcuts develop crowded, even-aged stands that shade the forest floor and lack diversity. A healthy understory and varied habitat are not likely to develop for at least a century, possibly more, which could be too long to save old-growth-dependent species threatened with extinction.

■ ■ ■

After hiking for more than two hours and covering less than two miles, we stepped from the forest onto boulders beside the lake. It was about a quarter mile wide at its end but stretched southward several miles beyond our view. A raft of more than 100 bald logs and a few big root wads clogged the lake's outflow, with hundreds of bare branches sticking between one and six feet into the air. Each log was bleached gray with only its top third above the water. Beyond, a light breeze skimmed the blue water. Thick forest bordered the lake, leaving little room between woods and water, and rose steeply along the mountains. Some mountains had domed peaks with rusty alpine vegetation that would be lush green in another month. In the distance, several avalanche paths interrupted the forest with narrow strips of light green, where young alder and willow leaves provided important spring nutrition for bears.

We stepped carefully onto the logs, testing each with one foot before trusting it with our full weight. Some bobbed, their water-logged corpses surfacing slowly, but most remained steady atop hundreds of sunken logs that appeared golden brown through the water. Zigzagging along the largest logs, we reached the middle of the raft and gained an unobstructed view across the lake. We found a log broad enough for sitting and pulled the last of Belle's bannock, some trail mix and two peanut butter and jelly sandwiches from our backpack. As we ate, Bill rested his back against a bare limb, and I sat cross-legged on a wide trunk. Behind us, the stream's outflow gurgled quietly as water began its short trip to the lagoon by our camp. Otherwise, our surroundings were perfectly quiet. We were away from the boats of the marine highway and at the edge of an enormous wilderness.

"This lake has no name, right?" Bill asked.

"I don't think so."

"Lake Solitude," he said after a moment.

Bill moved to another log where he lay comfortably on his back. I found a limb to lean against and extended my legs toward the lake. I imagined the hollows, hiding places, ravines and cliffs we would find if we hiked the surrounding mountains. I knew we would find enormous trees, eagle nests and cascading streams. If we hiked long enough, perhaps we would find a bear den or the mossy bones of a dead wolf. I lamented that I would only see the lake for a few short hours and not explore its surroundings. I knew I would never be there again.

I grew up in suburbs in New England, with no outdoor skills and little knowledge of the natural world. In my early twenties, after a few extended vacations to the west, I started spending time in Alaska and moved to Colorado. For the following five years, I worked seasonally throughout the west, guiding adventure trips or working for the Forest Service, rarely living more than six consecutive months in one location. I discovered glaciers, big trees, deserts and high mountains, learned to backpack, mountain bike, ski and kayak, and became fascinated with the west's natural history. Each spring and fall, I explored the region with a fervor slowed only by periodic destitution or the rare failings of my 1966 Dodge Dart.

While the lifestyle provided a great sense of geography and knowledge of fascinating regions, it prevented intimacy with any one place. I learned statistics about wildlife, precipitation and topography in each location, but never saw one place change between seasons. Finally, during the previous winter, I began longing for a better sense of place. I wanted to remain stationary long enough to watch winter snow pile up, then rush away in summer streams or note the arrival of birds in spring and hear elk bugle in the fall. I wanted nearby forests and lakes I could investigate repeatedly and come to know deeply. Looking around Lake Solitude and realizing I would never truly know it, never see its seasons change or spot the elusive creatures that used it, I made a resolution that after the trip I would settle down. I just had to figure out where.

Our return to camp took a little more than an hour. In addition to having gravity on our side, we found a good game trail that led almost directly to our lagoon. Once there, we napped in the sun, cooked dinner, then relaxed in our sleeping bags on the rock peninsula. Below, the channel was as calm as a lake.

The sun sank behind mountains to our northwest around eight, and a little before nine turned the snowy peaks across the channel red and pink. Darkness arrived slowly, especially in the north, where the sun would skim below the horizon for much of the following four months. It turned the northern sky a light blue and turquoise above snowy mountains. To the south, steep, forested ridges slowly turned to black silhouettes against a purple sky. After ten, a giant yellow moon peeked over a black ridge to our southeast and climbed slowly into the sky. It stained the shimmering sea yellow and cast dull shadows on the mossy forest floor. Rising, it turned bright white so that only a few stars shone faintly in the southern sky.

The moonlight sharpened the shadows in the nearby forest, making sprigs of moss, spruce needles and cones on the floor clearly visible. I could see shadows in the glacial striations beside my sleeping bag. It turned the snow atop the nearby mountains creamy white against a dark purple sky, illuminating cornices, rock bands and narrow chutes. It lit up a small cloud atop a snowy peak, turning its edges white and silver and its center light brown. It looked like blurred water flowing over the peak to a small basin above treeline, following alpine contours with gentle curves. Below, moonlight streaked white across inky water.

To the north, the sky was still light blue and neon green at eleven, marking the position of the sun over the Arctic. No boats passed—the only sounds were the waterfall across the channel and occasional light breezes quietly rustling the sedges a few feet from my head. All else was perfectly still. I lay in my sleeping bag, looking at the same pristine landscape John Muir had seen 100 years earlier and Vancouver had seen in July of 1793. With no clearcuts, roads or boat traffic, I knew I saw the same world that surrounded Tsimsian villagers a thousand years earlier. I watched the mountains and moonlight for a long time and, when I finally grew tired, walked quietly to the tent.

CHAPTER EIGHT

The Big Tease—Hard Lessons About Winds and Tides

From half a mile away we could hear the low rumble of diesel engines on a small tanker motoring south in Grenville Channel. It was pale black and 200 feet long, with a large cabin lined with windows above its deck. Piles of white water surfed a third of the way up its high bow and boiled behind its stern. It sent a two-foot wake toward us, a wrinkle on flat water.

"I think I just saw an orca," said Bill, looking toward the boat.

"Yeah, there's four of them!" he said a moment later.

I stopped paddling and squinted at the water.

"Six!" Bill said, pointing at the tanker.

Finally I saw an arched back cut the surface of the water about 100 feet behind the tanker, rising high enough to show the perfect contrast of its black back and white belly. With a six-foot dorsal fin, it could have been a male about thirty feet long and weighing eight tons. It swam powerfully, rising three times in quick succession in the tanker's wake, then disappeared. But a few moments later four smaller orcas surfaced only fifty feet from the stern, rising and diving quickly like porpoises. Then two larger ones rose behind them, and the big male appeared again. For a few seconds, all seven were visible as they confidently kept pace with the tanker. From our kayaks, we took turns with the binoculars and angled our bows toward the approaching wake.

A widely distributed population of roughly 1,000 orcas spends time in the waters between Puget Sound and Skagway, with maybe 200 more passing most of their time further offshore. Commonly called killer whales, they are actually the largest members of the dolphin family and at the top of the marine food chain in the Inside Passage. They can swim up to seven knots (about 8 m.p.h.) and have approximately forty sharp teeth two inches tall and curved inward that enable them to devour up to 100 pounds of fish daily. Although most feed on salmon, herring and other fish, some hunt sea mammals such as seals, porpoises, sea lions and even other whales.

With a gestation period of seventeen months and a nursing period of a year, females often give birth only once every four years. This slow reproductive rate makes them sensitive to changes in the marine environment such as overfishing and increased vessel traffic. They are also more susceptible to dangerous pollutants such as PCBs, which gather in greatest densities at the top of the food chain.

Orcas usually travel in pods of five to a dozen, including several adults and several young dominated by a single female. Pods are matrilineal, with females mating outside the group so that the big males seen in each pod are usually brothers or uncles of the young. They are highly intelligent, with complex languages of up to sixty distinct vocalizations, and commonly cooperate in hunting. Most pods travel and feed together for their entire lives and are part of larger extended families of up to fifty animals. Occasionally, two extended families join together for a few days, especially near big salmon runs, forming a "superpod" of more than 100 individuals. Such groups have been seen from Puget Sound to near Glacier Bay.

■ ■ ■

The skies were clear again with temperatures near 60°F the morning following our hike. While paddling from our lagoon, we gazed around at the flat water reflecting slightly distorted images of the green and white mountains surrounding us. Unfortunately, full moons create tidal exchanges up to sixteen feet, so we began the day fighting a powerful ebb accelerated by Grenville Channel's narrow walls. With our chart showing ebbing currents could reach four knots—a force we could make little progress against—we paddled only twenty feet from shore, hoping to catch a few eddies and avoid the strongest current.

We paddled strenuously and inched northward at under two knots, slowly approaching the half-way point in Grenville Channel. Our boats quickly reversed each time we paused; needles, foam and small branches floated past us in the opposite direction like we were paddling against a wide river. Whirlpools several inches deep and a

174

few feet across spun downstream from rocky points, and at one point a long log sped past us heading south. The tanker and its trailing orcas were catching a nice ride.

Ordinarily, battling such a strong current would have been senseless, but because Grenville Channel links two large bodies of water, Wright and Chatham Sounds, its tides ebb and flood from both directions. If we reached its halfway point quickly enough, the ebbing tide would travel north rather than south, rewarding our struggle with a strong boost toward Prince Rupert. Of course, if our progress was not swift enough, we would reach halfway only to battle the flood tide.

We worked hard for the first two hours, covering less than four miles, but felt the current weaken shortly before lunch. We went ashore on a pile of slippery boulders and ate crackers, humus and cheese, then resumed paddling a little after noon. Re-energized, we made swifter progress and within a short time reached an area of disturbed water where the ebbing tide ran both south and north. The water swelled in circles a few inches high and a yard or two in diameter, like the channel was at a slow boil, and turned suddenly to inexplicable whirlpools a few inches deep that trapped piles of brown foam. Small eddy lines appeared and faded quickly, and we crossed several microcurrents that yanked our bows one way then the other within a few feet. I gripped my paddle tightly, unsure what to expect from the moving water.

The water calmed after twenty minutes, and the resistance we felt all morning disappeared. With the ebbing tide now flowing north, we steered to the middle of the channel to make a more direct course and take advantage of the current's full strength. Soon, the forest on either side slid past swiftly.

The walls diminished throughout the afternoon, and the channel widened to two miles near its end. The mountains decreased to low hills like those we had seen near the entrance of the channel, so that Grenville Channel began and ended with low hills surrounding a crescendo of snowy mountains. Large bays opened on either side, surrounded by low but steep hills covered in forest. They rose and fell quickly in uneven shapes, like waves on a rough sea. Taller mountains covered in snow stood inland.

The current slowed as the channel widened, but we still found occasional evidence of its power. Late in the afternoon we arrived at

175

another area of disrupted water at the mouth of an inlet more than a mile wide. In addition to whirlpools and strong microcurrents, standing waves to two feet covered an area 100 yards wide. They collided from all angles, forming steep pyramids that rushed loudly. Paddling through them felt like crossing a rough river.

A shallow bar formed when a Pleistocene glacier deposited debris at the mouth of the bay created the small rapid. Thousands of years earlier, glacial ice flowing from the Coast Mountains filled the U-shaped inlet, and instead of mature rain forest, bare rock and hardy pines surrounded the glacier, which calved big icebergs into Grenville Channel. Each calving deposited debris ranging from silt to boulders. And when the glacier receded it left a moraine that would disrupt tidal currents daily for millennia.

We left Grenville Channel late in the afternoon, and shortly after six arrived on a small island in Chatham Sound. The sound was several miles across with half a dozen islands dotting its blue water like orphaned bits of green forest. Far to the north, the sound opened even wider to meet Dixon Entrance. After close to three weeks, we were almost to Alaska. An hour after landing, we sat in pulverized shells and sand as we ate pasta. The sun slowly drifted across the sky to the northwest, almost skimming the tops of the highest islands, and two ravens chased a bald eagle across our view. They maneuvered sharply behind the eagle and dove at it as though trying to pull its white tail feathers. The eagle maintained a straight course with steady wing beats, but frequently turned its head toward the ravens and screeched loudly. The three eventually disappeared into forest on one of the nearby islands; for ten minutes we heard them arguing from inside the canopy.

"I'm going to sleep on the beach tonight," said Bill as we relaxed after dinner.

"You know that'll make it rain, right?" I said.

"Yeah, well I miss the rain. What's it been…two days?"

"At least."

"Hey, you think we could get away with not hanging the food tonight?"

"Yeah, I do."

The island was small and several miles from shore, and the chance of encountering a bear was remote. We were happy not to hang our heavy food supply and, as the sun dipped below a forest-

176

ed island to our northwest, cleaned our cook set in salt water with pebbles and sand. After tying the kayaks to a tree at the head of the beach, we set our sleeping bags on flat sand not far from the sedges. I crawled inside, propped my head against a dry bag full of clothes and waited for the moon.

The sky turned turquoise to the north. To the south Grenville Channel tapered into a collision of lumpy hills. Steep-sided like big camel humps, they turned to black silhouettes against a purple sky. At ten, a big yellow moon climbed above the dark hills and colored the sea gold. At midnight it shone brightly, illuminating snowy mountains on the mainland and grains of sand and broken shells beside my sleeping bag. Prince Rupert was behind some islands to the north, but we saw lights from boats traveling in and out of its harbor. Their slow, silent motion in the distance made our beach seem more remote.

"We're just thirty miles from Prince Rupert," I told Bill the next morning, looking at the map.

"Let's get there today," he said, "we've done thirty miles in one day before, no problem."

"Steaks and ice cream," I said. "And beer."

"You think two days will be enough time there," he asked. "Maybe we should spend a third day before hitting the water again."

It was another sunny day with a light breeze from the north. We expected little resistance from the tides in the wider sound. Reaching Prince Rupert seemed an attainable goal, and I started looking forward to a break from the trip. I pictured a hotel room with television, a telephone and hospital corners on crisp bed sheets. After three weeks dominated by stress and rain, I was very ready for a rest.

Standing on sand at the edge of the water, we ate bagels with honey and studied our maps. The most direct route to Prince Rupert was through Chatham Sound on the west side of Kennedy Island, which was about six miles long from north to south. However, we chose a slightly longer route along the east side of Kennedy through Telegraph Passage, a channel twenty miles long and three miles wide that veered toward the mouth of the Skeena River. Although not the most direct route, the narrower channel would likely be calmer than the larger Chatham Sound. Unfortunately, we did not anticipate the influence of the Skeena.

177

■ ■ ■

After the Fraser, the Skeena is the second largest river entirely within British Columbia. It begins as small alpine streams high in the Skeena Mountains more than 150 miles north-northeast of Prince Rupert and only 100 miles from tidewater, then winds an arcing course 360 miles to Telegraph Passage. With its major tributaries, the Bulkley and Babine, along with hundreds of small mountain streams, it drains approximately 15,000 square miles of northwestern British Columbia. Whereas most streams entering the Inside Passage north of Vancouver Island flow less than twenty miles from mountainous islands or the Coast Mountains, the Skeena divides the Coast Mountains with a low, broad valley. This gap in ordinarily impenetrable mountains has enabled ecological and cultural exchange between the coast and the interior for thousands of years.

The Skeena, as well as the Fraser, Nass, Stikine and a very few other big rivers, offered the first ice-free passes to the Inside Passage during the late Pleistocene. Plants, animals and eventually humans used these routes to reach the coast, populating the region as the glaciers receded. Eventually, with Pacific air masses bringing moisture inland and dry winds from the interior of the province blowing cold air to the coast, a hybrid ecosystem of temperate rain forest and interior montane forest developed along the rivers. Sitka spruces, western red cedars and western hemlocks from the coast mixed with aspen, blue spruce and lodgepole pine from the Interior.

"Skeena" is the corruption of a Tsimsian word that means "water from the clouds." By 3,000 years ago the river's mouth was the center of Tsimsian territory, with permanent and temporary villages along its rich estuary. Each spring, summer and fall millions of salmon from all five Pacific species, as well as steelhead, swam upriver to spawn, some traveling hundreds of miles inland. Each autumn, coastal and interior groups gathered to fish and trade as far inland as the confluence of the Bulkley and Skeena, roughly 180 miles from the ocean, near present-day Hazelton, British Columbia. Thus, food, materials and information traveled between the coast and the Interior along the river.

The Skeena proved an important way around the Coast Mountains for whites, too. The first white person to write about the Skeena was probably James Duncan, captain of the trading

178

schooner *Princess Royal* in 1788. Traveling past the river's estuary, he named it Ayton's River, a name that did not last long. Five years later, shortly after exploring Grenville Channel, George Vancouver sent Joseph Whidbey and Peter Puget in small boats to investigate Telegraph Passage. At the mouth of the Skeena they found extensive shallows and what they thought was a swift current ebbing from another ocean channel. The men traveled about nine miles upriver, where they camped one night. Finding more shallows and many logs half buried in muddy banks, they observed two low tides before determining that the channel ended in a small stream. In his journals, Puget reported that "the channel could not be termed Navigable therefore we had no Business to pursue [it]." Thus Vancouver missed the Skeena, which would soon become an important fur trading route. During his three seasons on the coast, he also missed the Fraser, Stikine and Taku, other important rivers in the Inside Passage. But he was only following orders: his instructions from the British admiralty stated he should not waste time in channels or rivers not navigable by ocean-going vessels. And the few large rivers that enter the Inside Passage all have extensive shallows at their mouths that can make them appear small.

The first white settlement on the Skeena occurred thirty years after Vancouver's survey, when traders for the Hudson's Bay Company established a fort near present-day New Hazelton, 180 miles inland. By the 1830s, as the Oregon Trail opened nearly 1,000 miles to the south and brought white settlers to the Inside Passage at Puget Sound, the Hudson's Bay Company had established several forts along the lower Skeena. Traders used canoes to bring beaver pelts to Telegraph Passage. In the 1850s, Canadian surveyors traveled the Skeena to determine the practicality of bringing the transcontinental railroad to its mouth. In the year 1859 a gold rush brought thousands of prospectors up the Skeena. In 1871 an entrepreneur built a store near the mouth of the river and soon developed a town site called Port Essington, which became a port of entry to the Skeena.

After the gold rushes, dozens of canneries opened along the lower Skeena, joining hundreds of others between Monterey, California, and southeast Alaska. By the late 1880s, Port Essington was a growing port city of a few thousand that shipped canned salmon to North American and Asian markets. A sawmill opened and inland logging operations floated timber down the river while handloggers on the coast delivered wood from the Inside Passage. Missionaries also used Port Essington as a base for their travels to remote Native villages. At the same time, as had already happened along the coast to the south, whites brought smallpox, measles and alcohol; by the turn of the century nearly three-quarters of the region's original inhabitants were dead.

■ ■ ■

We reached the northern end of Kennedy Island by midmorning and stopped for a snack before making a three-mile crossing to Smith Island. Seven miles to our northeast, the Skeena branched inland from Telegraph Passage. Several islands blocked our full view of the river, which looked like another arm of the sea. Big cumuli bloomed on the blue horizon beyond its mouth, like the river was literally water from the clouds. After a short rest, we began paddling for Smith Island, a four-square-mile island with low rolling hills covered in green forest. Blue water sparkled in the sun, and closely spaced swells a foot high drifted southward from Chatham Sound. Making strong paddle strokes, I knew we could reach Prince Rupert by dinner and have plenty of time to find a room and a place to store our boats. I had no idea how quickly things would change.

Like other crossings, my mind wandered as we paddled away from the forest and rocky shores. In pleasant sunshine, I looked forward to phone calls with friends and family, the first I would enjoy since Klemtu. But after forty-five minutes, I realized that Smith Island was still too far away. The crossing should have taken an hour at most, but the island remained more than a mile off. And something did not look right about our angle of approach. I looked over my shoulder to Kennedy Island, which should have been directly behind me, and was shocked to see it far to my left. While daydreaming a powerful current had carried us considerably eastward, insidiously sweeping us toward the mainland. When I stopped paddling, Smith Island glided sideways across my bow. To reach it, we would now need to fight the tide.

"Slow going, huh?" Bill called from 100 feet away.

"Yeah, I think we're being carried more toward the mainland than the island," I called.

"I know. I've been staring at Smith Island for ten minutes and it hasn't changed a bit."

I started paddling hard, using a point on the mainland to gauge my speed, and quickly determined I was moving more eastward than northward. Bill maneuvered closer to me, the veins on his arms bulging with each stroke.

"I could see bottom over there," he said, nodding backward while maintaining his paddle strokes.

I looked over the edge of my boat and noticed that the water had turned from blue to brown. We had reached the edge of the Skeena's mudflat, where millions of tons of sediment settled in the calm water of Telegraph Passage. As the tide continued ebbing, large parts of the mudflat could become exposed, stranding us for hours. While inconvenient, it was also potentially dangerous as some mudflats are as saturated as quicksand. With one hand, I stuck my paddle vertically through the murky water and was only partly relieved when I did not hit bottom. I knew that currents cut narrow channels through mudflats so that the water can be twenty feet deep in one spot but much shallower only a few feet away.

"We better paddle hard for Smith Island," I told Bill a little nervously. As the water grew more shallow, the current's speed would increase, carrying us farther from the island.

We pointed our bows at the island and paddled hard, leaning forward with each stroke and muscling our paddle blades toward us. At first, the island continued drifting west, requiring frequent course adjustments, but after twenty minutes, with my shoulders aching and my back muscles cramping sharply, I felt progress. The island's trees slowly gained detail, and finally, less than half a mile away, we entered the island's lee and began moving quickly toward shore. Ten minutes later, we ran our bows onto a small sand beach on the south side of the island, then climbed stiffly from our cockpits.

"Wow," said Bill, flopping down onto the beach, "instant peanut butter out there!"

"Almost an hour and a half to go three miles," I said. "We should reach Juneau by Halloween at that rate."

The tide flowed quickly past our beach toward the mainland. It piled three inches against a rocky point, like the side of a river, and created a small wake behind a partially submerged rock ten feet from shore. At a glance, the rock appeared to swim past the island.

8.1: USING THE MOON TO PREDICT THE TIDE

Tides result from the gravitational influence of the moon and sun, which varies as the earth's position changes. Because the moon is almost 93 million miles closer to the earth, its gravitational influence is more than twice that of the sun, and tides are more closely linked to its position.

As the moon circles the earth, its gravitational force creates a broad ocean swell, mirrored on the other side of the planet by centrifugal force. The swells, only twelve to eighteen inches high in the open ocean, follow the moon's position relative to the earth. However, friction with the ocean floor and local geography create a lag of roughly two hours. The swells rise considerably when they encounter the shallow depths of a continental shelf, then slowly flood its shoreline. In the Inside Passage, where narrow waterways form constrictions, they can raise the water level by more than twenty feet.

Peak tides occur within the time frame of the lunar day, which is roughly twenty-four

Obviously, there was no sense in paddling again until the tide changed.

"Low tide's not for another two hours," said Bill, lying on his back and holding the tide book open with both hands. "So much for beer and television," and he let his arms fall to his sides, the tide book landing facedown in the sand.

But I was not ready to accept defeat.

"Well, no…maybe when the tide reverses we'll catch a good ride toward Prince Rupert. At this speed," I said, looking at the water piling against the rocks, "we could still reach town by dinner."

He just nodded at me.

We ate lunch, then Bill leaned against a rock in the sun to write in his journal. I lay on my stomach to read. Periodically, I looked up to check the current, which after more than an hour still piled against the rocks. Irrationally, I still hoped we could reach the city by dinner. I wanted badly to take a break from being outside.

After almost two hours the current weakened, then disappeared. I woke Bill from a nap, and we packed our lunches and books into the kayaks. It was almost two in the afternoon when we entered the water. Fearing exposed mudflats to the east, we paddled west along the island's south side toward Chatham Sound. After slightly more than a mile, we would turn north to paddle three miles along the island's west side, then begin another crossing. Prince Rupert was twenty miles away.

"Right around the corner," Bill said, pointing his paddle westward across his deck, "we're going to hit an expressway for Prince Rupert. We'll be drinking Molsons and watching the Simpsons by seven."

"Hope you like hot showers!" I said, my spirits lifting as the trees along Smith Island slid past with satisfying speed.

Our first mistake, of course, was failing to recognize the influence of the Skeena. Its mudflats were illustrated in gray on our nautical charts, which should have been a warning to us. Any place with shallow water, especially the mouth of a river 360 miles long, will have strong currents often too complicated to predict without local knowledge. This would be particularly true during the big tides associated with a full moon. Our maps, tide books and the previous night's sky all held warnings we failed to recognize.

Our second mistake was paddling toward Chatham Sound on a sunny afternoon. Chatham Sound stretched fifty miles to our north and averaged fifteen miles wide, then joined Dixon Entrance, a mammoth opening in the Inside Passage that added to the sound's already significant fetch. In addition, northerly breezes consistently develop in the Inside Passage on sunny days, the result of high pres-

hours and fifty minutes, the amount of time it takes the earth to complete one revolution on its axis relative to the moon. In contrast, we live by the solar day, the amount of time it takes the earth to complete one turn on its axis relative to the sun, or twenty-four hours. Due to the difference, high and low tides occur approximately fifty minutes later each solar day. Local geography and the moon's phase create additional variations. Although some areas have only two peak tides per day, the Inside Passage follows a mixed semidiurnal pattern, with four peak tides (two lows, two highs) of varying heights occurring each day, roughly every six and one-quarter hours.

The size of tides varies throughout the lunar month, the amount of time it takes the moon to complete one revolution of the earth relative to the sun, or about twenty-nine and a half days. Two large tide cycles, called spring tides, and two small tide cycles, called neap tides, occur alternately within each lunar month. Spring tides occur during new and full phases of the moon, when the gravitational pull of the sun and moon are combined. Neap tides occur during quarter moons, when the sun and moon are at right angles relative to the earth, with their forces mitigating each other.

sure. The breezes are strongest in the afternoon, as cool sea air spills inland under rising air heated by the sun. Had we been more familiar with these processes, we would have known that paddling north into Chatham Sound was simply asking for trouble.

Fifteen minutes after leaving our beach, we rounded a rocky point, steered northward and were immediately blasted by a strong headwind. Chatham Sound came into view as we struggled past the point; the wind increased, eventually roaring in our ears. It pushed steadily at ten to fifteen knots without gusts or lulls as we struggled northward close to the island's steep shore. Soon our boats bounced on tightly spaced waves three feet high that broke loudly against the rocks. Heading directly into the wind, our heavy bows pierced the top of each wave and water washed over our decks all the way to our cockpits. The wind blew spray from each broken wave against our chests and faces, cooling us quickly.

None of the small islands to our north provided protection from the wind, the shore was too steep for landing, and we realized the wind would continue unabated for a few hours. We could have returned to our last beach, but that prospect was too discouraging. Although we obviously would not reach Prince Rupert that afternoon, at least we could shorten the following day's work. Paddling hard, reviving our earlier cramps, we set the north end of Smith Island, three miles away, as our next goal.

What dumb damn luck, I thought, knowing I would spend another night in the cramped tent, filthy from salt and sweat. It was frustrating that after three weeks of rain the first stretch of good weather actually worked against us. The accumulated frustration of the previous three weeks mounted inside me. The fact that the latest challenges came so unexpected, right as we looked forward to a break, seemed a cruel joke. Suddenly I wanted away from the "not nice coast."

My anger only wore me out. My paddle strokes became sloppy, and occasionally I reached down into a trough and missed the water entirely. Other times, big waves lifted my boat surprisingly high, and I responded with panicked braces. Finally, after ninety minutes we landed on a small island north of Smith Island. After almost ten hours of work, we were only twelve miles from our last camp.

Although white caps dotted the water the breeze was calm on our beach, and the sun was warm. We changed into dry clothes, then cooked another pasta dinner. Our island was small and showed signs of use, with a plywood table in a dirt clearing in the woods and a five-gallon bucket, some tent stakes and a few beer cans scattered near the sedges. It was obviously a popular camping spot only a day from Prince Rupert by skiff, pleasure boat or kayak, and after many nights on pristine beaches it felt like a busy state park. With so much wild land awaiting us in Alaska, camping on the city's margin seemed a waste of our valuable time. We went to sleep early, hoping for the first time that the next day would bring clouds or rain to mitigate the wind.

We awoke at seven the next morning to continued clear skies and quickly broke camp, hoping to make significant progress before the breeze developed. Prince Rupert was nearly twenty miles to the north, on Kaien Island. We would need to make several small crossings between islands, then paddle north along Kaien for six miles to reach the city. With more than twelve hours of daylight ahead and many twenty-mile days behind us, we knew it was an attainable goal.

We began paddling at eight-thirty, but already a steady breeze blew from the north. Our muscles were stiff from the previous day and progress was slow from the beginning. By ten we had covered only four miles with the wind building. After another hour, it reached more than ten knots; we began another long struggle against waves and spray. We pushed hard all morning and most of the afternoon, but when we eventually found relief from the wind close to Kaien Island, we began struggling against an ebbing tide channeled through a narrow passage leading toward the city. It felt like paddling up a river. The wilderness that had diverted our attention during earlier struggles was gone as we wound carefully through busy shipping lanes full of skiffs, pleasure boats, ferries and even a large tanker headed for the open Pacific.

Paddling along Ridley Island, less than ten miles from the city, we passed the Prince Rupert Grain Terminal, where wheat and grain from the Prairies was loaded from railroad cars onto container ships bound for Asia. Several enormous aluminum-sided buildings blocked the surrounding hills—a plume of white smoke poured from smokestacks. Train cars clanged loudly, men shouted to each other and forklifts and trucks moved in and out of big bay doors. Paddling past for fifteen minutes, I lamented our finite schedule,

185

knowing the struggle to Prince Rupert would cost us time in wilder places to our north.

At five, after another long day, we were still six miles from Prince Rupert. Exhausted and with nowhere in town to store our boats, we conceded a second defeat and set camp on a littered beach with Rupert in sight. We quietly consumed another bland meal, looking forlornly toward the city, and camped without hanging our food. Boats motored past, easily moving between Prince Rupert and Chatham Sound, traveling in mere minutes what had taken us more than two days to cover.

■ ■ ■

Kaien Island is less than a mile from the British Columbia mainland and roughly twenty miles north of Port Essington, across the mouth of the Skeena River. In the early 1900s, after thousands of years of use by Tsimsians, speculators associated with the Grand Trunk Pacific Railroad bought land on the northern part of the island and began a settlement which in 1907 they named after Prince Rupert of the Rhine, cousin of Charles II and first governor of the Hudson's Bay Company in the seventeenth century.

The speculators had convinced the railroad to put its transcontinental terminus at Prince Rupert, citing the area's large natural harbor,, one of the deepest north of Seattle, and the fact that it was two days closer to Asia than Vancouver. In the ensuing hype, Prince Rupert's population eventually exceeded that of Port Essington, and it became the primary port in the north. Port Essington continued as a cannery and fishing town for several decades, but was increasingly shadowed by Prince Rupert. Its population dwindled in the late thirties and forties; after two catastrophic fires in the early 1960s it ceased to exist.

Construction on the railroad began simultaneously in Prince Rupert and Winnipeg in 1907, and the last spike was driven in 1914. But by that time the railroad company was in trouble. In 1912, after a trip to Europe to attract investors, Charles Hays, the company's president, drowned in the North Atlantic with 1,100 other passengers aboard the *Titanic*. Hays was a driving force in Prince Rupert's development, and confusion and doubt followed his death. Overzealous speculation and the financial burden of World War I added further stress, and in 1914 the company declared bankruptcy. The Canadian National Railway took control of the company, but Vancouver, with its proximity to existing roads, rails and cities, became the focus of Canada's transcontinental rail system.

In the following decades commercial fishing grew as a major industry in Prince Rupert, and during World War II the U.S. used its harbor to transport troops to the Pacific and to build warships. Also during the war, the Canadian and U.S. armies built a road connecting Prince Rupert with the rest of the continent.

Today, with a population of about 16,000, Prince Rupert is the largest city on the British Columbia coast north of Vancouver Island. It is the northern terminus for BC Ferries, with service south to Port Hardy and west to Haida Gwai. It is also served by Alaska Marine Highway ferries. Logging, mining and commercial fishing are still major economic forces, but tourism is its fastest growing industry. The city already sees 350,000 annual visitors; with the completion of new cruise ship docks slated for 2004, that number could rise significantly.

■ ■ ■

We reached an abandoned wooden dock below Prince Rupert late the next morning after winding across a busy shipping lane. A young boy in jeans and a T-shirt fished from the dock, and behind him rickety stairs led up a short hill to town. The sun shone through broken clouds, and the boards felt warm as we hoisted ourselves from our boats.

"Hey," said Brendan Smith, the boy on the dock.

"Mind if I fish with you?" asked Bill after we tied our boats to a piling.

"Sure."

"What're we fishing for?"

"Spring salmon, cod…anything that'll bite," Brendan said.

"What kind of lure should I use?"

Brendan lay his pole down and dragged a small tackle box toward him. He was Native, with thick black hair that hung to his eyebrows and covered his ears. He told us he lived with his mother in the apartments above the dock. As he helped Bill put his fishing pole together, I walked up the stairs to price hotel rooms and find a place to store our boats.

After twenty-five creaking steps, I arrived suddenly at the edge of a busy street, with more cars passing me in ten seconds than I had seen since leaving my truck in Port Hardy. Powerful smells of diesel and a nearby McDonalds mixed with noise from an idling delivery truck and passing cars. Concrete and asphalt extended in three directions. Several ten-story buildings stood above lower shops and offices. A backfiring muffler startled me. I felt jumpy surrounded by all the noise, but excited to hear music and talk with people. I self-consciously ran my hand through my shaggy beard.

I waited for a traffic light to turn red, then cautiously crossed the street and walked into an outdoor clothing store. I asked an attractive girl behind the counter where I could store our boats. As she gave me directions to a harbor a mile away, I lamely tried to think of ways to prolong the conversation. I imagined she would find our adventures fascinating and would invite Bill and me to stay with her, storing our boats safely in her garage and taking us for wild adventures in the city. Maybe she would quit her job to join us for the rest of the trip, and we would eventually get married and live in a cottage by the sea. Bill could live next door. But her phone rang as we were talking, and she began making plans with a friend, waving goodbye to me with a pretty smile.

I walked south along clean sidewalks busy with people shopping or going to lunch, greeting almost everyone with a smile. I stopped in a few more shops to ask about a place to keep our boats or to find another attractive woman, one without friends always calling her at work. When I reached the harbor, which turned out to be a yacht club, a receptionist told me she didn't think they provided kayak storage and directed me to another dock about half mile away. There, a gruff man said he would store the boats for fifteen dollars per night, per boat, but was noncommittal about their safety. I visited another dock with much the same results and walked back to Bill after about an hour. On the way, I stopped in a few hotels and bought a couple sodas.

Brendan was still fishing, but Bill was asleep beside his pole, which had a new lure but was tangled in line. He awoke as I sat beside him and handed him a cold soda.

"What'd you find out?" he asked.

"Not much, really. There's two docks about a mile from here

188

that said we could leave our boats, but they didn't guarantee their safety. They were kind of ritzy places, like yacht clubs. When I started talking about kayaks they looked at me like I had two heads."

"You do," he said. "I've been meaning to say something."

"Yeah, well maybe I can I do something about that at the hotel. I found one for forty dollars a night."

Since I had only walked the area to our north, Bill walked to the south in search of a better place for our boats while I lay on the warm dock. I was surprised when he returned after only thirty minutes.

"We're all set," he said, handing me an ice cream cone. Such simple pleasures were luxurious after all the pasta.

"I stopped by the tire shop, eh, and this guy said a friend of a friend was a big sea kayaker that would probably help us out. He called the guy up—his name's Howard—and let me talk to him. He got all excited about our trip, eh, and said he would pick us up at the tire shop when he gets off work, which is at six."

"Wow, that's great, eh."

The hotel was only a few blocks away, so we shuttled our gear and kayaks to the street, then took turns walking to the hotel with the rifle, radio, tent and food. We then closed the kayaks and leaned them against low shrubs in front of a fast food place where the manager agreed to keep an eye on them. We took showers at the hotel and at six walked back to the tire shop, where we learned that Howard really was a big sea kayaker. Standing six feet tall and weighing at least 225, Howard had big eyebrows and a thick mustache on a jowly face. A few strands of brown hair stuck to his forehead below his ball cap; his eyes were big and black. He arrived at the tire shop in a big green pickup at five minutes past six and shook our hands warmly.

"Welcome to Prince Rupert," he said with a booming voice, "You guys can stay at my house just a few kilometers from here. I have a dinner date tonight but tomorrow after work we can talk. I have lots of questions for you."

He was disappointed when we told him we already paid for a hotel room.

"Okay, well let's get your boats in my truck. I have to leave soon for dinner, so you guys stay here and tomorrow we'll have dinner together, okay?"

After Howard left, we went to the hotel restaurant and ordered steaks, baked potatoes and two big salads, a delicious dinner after almost a month with little meat or fresh vegetables. Afterward, we lay in our beds eating potato chips, drinking beer and watching television. It felt odd to relax at night without first setting up the tent or tying the boats to something. Bill suggested the balcony as a good place to hang our food.

The next day, our room was a mess. The tent hung from the curtain rod in front of the window, and our dry bags, which we had washed in the bathtub, hung inside-out from hooks, racks, door knobs and a couple of lamps. The water filter, stoves and cookware, all cleaned in the sink, were drying on the bathroom counter. The food was organized into four piles beside one of the beds. The rifle, gun-cleaning kit, marine radio and a pile of batteries littered the dresser beside the television; six rounds of ammunition, headlamps and a fuel bottle lay with our books and maps on the nightstand between our beds. We hung the Do Not Disturb sign to discourage the maid.

After spending the day apart to make phone calls, write letters and walk around the city, we met in the hotel room late in the afternoon. Howard was not due to pick us up for a couple hours, so we spread our Alaska maps on the beds to plan the second half of the trip.

"I talked to my dad today," Bill said as we placed the maps next to each other. "He's doing real well, walking around and talking about going back to work soon. My mother sounds a lot more relaxed, too."

"Good," I said, "That must have been a pretty big scare for everybody."

"Yeah, but like I said, things sound a lot better now. And I feel a lot better about continuing the trip. I mean, as long as things keep going well there, I'm committed to paddling to Juneau."

We had never reached closure regarding our heated words during the storm near Work Island, which created underlying tension. During the following week, I struggled quietly to think how to ask about Bill's intentions while recognizing the seriousness of his father's heart attack. That he broached the subject before me was a relief.

"Before we start," Bill said, "let's talk about when we're going to get to Juneau. Let's set a date for it, then figure out where we can go."

190

"I thought we already had a date," I said, "Second week of June, right?"

"Okay, yeah, well I just want to make sure," he said, but I thought there might be more to it.

We ran through the agenda we had set before the trip started, adjusting the dates for places we hoped to visit: Misty Fiords, LeConte Glacier, Admiralty, Taku. Since we were seven days behind our original itinerary, we had to shave a few days from some of the excursions and eliminate most of the buffer time incorporated for bad weather.

"I don't know," Bill said looking down at the maps. "It seems like we're setting ourselves up for a lot of paddling."

"What do you mean?"

"Well," he said looking at me, "I think this plan is too much for the amount of time we have. What if we get into a situation like Chatham Sound again, where it takes three days to cover thirty miles?"

I have since learned that I can be unrealistic and even manipulative when planning backcountry excursions. I become wide-eyed about hiking, skiing or kayaking to remote locations; back-country bowls or far-off bays on a map lure me into planning trips for which I might not have adequate time. When friends express doubt, I point to contour lines or sandy beaches and explain excitedly how quickly we can ski this or paddle that. Sometimes my ambitious plans have created stress or hardship that a shorter itinerary might have prevented. But in our Prince Rupert hotel room, I had not yet learned that lesson. As Bill talked about fetch in Dixon Entrance, currents in Rudyerd Bay or some of the marathon days my plan required, I pointed to places on the maps where I thought we could duck from winds and cover long distances, regardless of the weather.

But after more than three weeks of setbacks and delays, and too many long days of paddling, Bill rejected my reasoning. He, at first gently then more adamantly, informed me that in order to avoid increasing tension we would have to omit certain destinations. He told me we needed more buffer days for bad weather, but I stubbornly held to each point on the map.

"Think of this as an exploratory mission," he reasoned. "We can come back some other year and hit the places we miss this time."

"Some other year?" I exclaimed, "This is once-in-a-lifetime, Bill."

The conversation was becoming heated, but it was almost time to meet Howard.

"Look," said Bill, standing up and walking to the small refrigerator laden with dry bags and toiletries, "I agree that we should see as much as possible, but let's just make a contingency plan for skipping some spots if time gets short. It'll just make us ready if the weather gets real shitty again."

He took two beers from the fridge and twisted off their caps, throwing them onto the floor. Then he clinked the bottles together, insinuating we had agreed on his statement, and handed me one while taking a long sip from the other and looking at me. I grudgingly sipped my beer. I was accustomed to leading the trip and was caught off guard by his assertiveness. I resented it, but remained quiet. I knew he was right.

We met up with Howard and piled into his truck. Howard played Def Leppard on his truck stereo. The music was too loud for normal conversation, but he asked questions about our trip anyway. From my seat near the window, I had to lean over Bill and talk loudly to participate in the conversation. After ten minutes, we pulled into a gravel driveway next to his prefabricated house, with our kayaks and six others leaning beside the door.

"How do you like your boats," he asked as we walked to the kayaks. For twenty minutes we talked about different brands and styles, how plastic compares to fiberglass and what equipment we preferred on long trips. Although he asked questions about our trip, the conversation revolved mostly around his collection of boats. He was knowledgeable about styles and models and enjoyed examining the features of each boat.

Inside, Howard handed us beers as we sat in his den. He had plastic flowers above the television and a wood-framed image of a sunset on black and orange velvet above a pellet stove. There were pictures of him with friends in kayaks and a small bookshelf with magazines, photo albums and books. A stack of cardboard boxes lined the wall by the door.

"My girlfriend moved out a couple months ago," he said gesturing toward the boxes, "and that's the rest of her stuff." He was about to say more, then changed his mind and shook his head.

We drank a couple beers and talked about where we were from, but by the end of the second beer, Howard dominated the conversation and I got the impression guests were not common in his home.

"Well, how about pizza?" he asked after an hour.

We agreed on toppings, and Bill and I insisted we would pay for the food. He had helped us enormously by picking up and storing the boats.

"How can it take an hour to get a pizza out here," he exclaimed after hanging up the phone. "I could walk there and get it in less time."

Howard talked about his job, his life in Prince Rupert and his ex-girlfriend as we waited for the pizza. When talking about his ex-girlfriend, anger crept into his voice and I began thinking he had drank a few beers before picking us up. He only asked us about our lives or our trip during lulls in the conversation, as if briefly self-conscious about talking too much.

I was relieved when the pizzas arrived. The three of us gathered around the door, and I handed money to the delivery girl, a teenager with Native features who thanked us with a friendly smile. But Howard snatched the money back, startling the girl, and pushed it toward me, crumpling the bills in his big hands. He then paid for the pizza himself and carried the boxes to a flimsy table in his small kitchen. He handed us plates and two more beers, even though we had only half finished the ones in our hands. As we dug into the pizzas, two oily larges with sausage and pepperoni, Bill asked what sounded like a harmless question about health care in Canada.

"Hey," he said, after taking a huge bite from his slice, "the regular guy is working his ass off to make ends meet!" He paused for a moment to swallow, then wiped about half the cheese from his mustache with the back of his hand. "The government taxes us to death up here, and all everyone says is 'well, we have state health insurance.' Well, *bullshit!* I'd still pay out the nose if I got sick!"

Howard's face turned red and his neck was sweating. He knit his big eyebrows angrily over his black eyes as he washed down big bites of pizza with loud gulps of beer.

"I'm sorry," he said, calming down and laughing a little. "I just get so damn angry when I think about how much we pay in taxes up here—oh, and don't even get me started on the Native thing!"

I quickly tried to think of a way to change the subject, knowing he was about to get started on the Native thing, but I was too slow.

"You're from the east, right?" he asked us, leaning conspiratorially across the table and setting his pizza down. "Well you did the right thing back there, you see.... You killed all the friggin' Indians! Out here, we didn't kill *enough* of them!"

He chuckled, seeming not to notice that Bill and I were not laughing. Instead, we were thinking of Patrick in Klemtu, Belle and her family, Brendan, the nice girl that had delivered our pizza.

"Now we have all these goddamn treaty negotiations with every friggin' First Nations from here to Vancouver," he continued before we could change the subject. "They want all the land, the trees, the gold, the fish. They want *everything*, but they're already getting free friggin' money from us, the taxpayers. We send their kids to school; we fix their houses." He pounded his fist on the table, knocking over a beer bottle and rattling the silverware. "We pay for their goddamn welfare when they don't work for a whole year!"

What could we do? Howard had stored our boats safely, picked us up at our hotel and bought us pizza. He had even offered us a place to stay. I suddenly felt cheap accepting his help, as though betraying friends made earlier in the trip. All I could think to do was keep changing the subject and start yawning. I yawned repeatedly, made my eyes look tired and stretched my arms in the air. Eventually, Howard grew tired, too, and drove us back to our hotel. Exhausted, we walked to our room and went to bed without even turning on the television.

PART II

ALASKA

To the lover of pure wildness Alaska is one of the most won-
derful countries in the world.

John Muir

CHAPTER NINE

Back to the Grind

I leaned over the back railing of the MV *Matanuska*, one of the nine Alaska Marine Highway ferries, and watched the wake churning forty feet below. It left a foamy trail across the sparkling blue water of Dixon Entrance. Ten miles to the east, the mainland hills were green and blue with occasional snowy mountains behind them. To the west, beyond a small island, the open ocean met the horizon of a hazy blue sky.

I had eventually relented to Bill's reasoning and agreed to omit some destinations from our itinerary. First, we decided to ride the ferry from Prince Rupert to Ketchikan, Alaska. This eighty-mile trip took us across Dixon Entrance, which forms a gap in the Inside Passage almost as large as the one along Queen Charlotte Sound. Under the best conditions, paddling to Ketchikan would have taken us a minimum of four days, but recalling our experience in Queen Charlotte Sound, we knew significant delays were possible. We also eliminated an eight-day excursion to Misty Fiords National Monument. This 2-million-acre designated wilderness near Ketchikan, known for its steep-walled fiords, high mountains and expansive forests, was high on my list of places to visit. I had to repeatedly remind myself of the glaciers and mountains to our north as the ferry passed by the narrow channels reaching deep into Misty Fiords.

At the *Matanuska*'s railing I was joined by Tina Post, her long brown hair blowing across her face. She had wispy eyebrows above dark brown eyes and was short with a muscular build. She was twenty-five and after a winter with her parents in Michigan was on her way to Ketchikan for a second summer as a wilderness ranger for the U.S. Forest Service. We had met in the boat's forward lounge, looking at an easel full of maps.

"When does work start?" I asked her.

"Two days. There's a couple weeks of training and office work, then I'm in the field for most of the summer, until sometime in September."

As with hundreds of other seasonal employees, the Forest Service provided low-cost housing for Tina and food and gear while she was in the field. Her fieldtrips were ten days long and entailed educating backcountry travelers about low-impact camping and hiking deep into the rain forest to survey vegetation and wildlife populations.

"It's amazing," she said, sweeping hair from her face, "we spend a few days in popular areas talking to boaters and kayakers, then head to remote areas to do surveys. We bushwhack for days with these big packs and don't see a single person or hear any motors."

"How was the weather last year?" I asked.

"Pretty terrible," she laughed, "It rained most days. And even when it wasn't raining we'd get soaked pushing through all the vegetation. I'd come back from those trips totally beat up. I'd have cuts on my hands and these big bruises and I'd be itching all over from the bug bites. I'd just sleep for the first couple days back in town—but I was in the best shape I've ever been in. How's the weather been for your trip?"

"Rainy until about five days ago, but it's been mostly clear since then, which has me dreading the next rain cycle. I'm sure we'll pay for all this sun."

"Yeah," she laughed, "I remember that feeling. But that's life on the Tongass, right?"

■ ■ ■

The Tongass National Forest encompasses a little less than 80 percent of southeast Alaska. At approximately 17 million acres, more than twice the size of Vancouver Island, it is by far the nation's biggest national forest. And with the largest remaining old-growth temperate rain forest in the world, it is also one of the most contentious national forests. In many ways, the Tongass is southeast Alaska. It borders each of the region's fifteen major communities and nearly all of its private land, stretching from beaches to mountaintops and providing recreational and economic opportunity for all of the region's 73,000 residents. As a result, the Forest Service is an integral part of life in southeast Alaska.

Ideally, the U.S. Forest Service represents the meeting of democracy and land management, where specialized knowledge combined with public input determines policy. Unlike the National Park Service, which manages federal lands primarily for preservation, the Forest Service manages its lands for multiple uses. This challenging mandate requires dividing the 191 million acres of national forest between diverse interests, including recreational, municipal and commercial needs as well as preservation. Using forest plans written every ten to fifteen years, land managers map each forest, allocating lands for varying uses such as grazing, logging, mining and developments such as power lines, reservoirs, campgrounds and ski areas. They plan construction and maintenance of thousands of miles of trails, which they divide between snowmobilers, cross-country skiers, mountain bikers and hikers. They also designate parcels for wildlife habitat, research, clean water and wilderness. Federal law, agency policy and often intense political pressure complicate each designation; lawsuits commonly stall management plans as interest groups jockey for a bigger piece of the federal pie. Like any democratic institution, the Forest Service is not immune to manipulation and bias. And of the 155 national forests in the United States, this is perhaps nowhere better evidenced than in the Tongass.

In response to increasing deforestation in the "Lower 48," Teddy Roosevelt set aside part of southeast Alaska as the Alexander Archipelago Forest Reserve in 1902 and six years later combined the reserve with the Tongass National Forest. From the beginning, the Forest Service tried to bring stable economic development to southeast Alaska by offering cheap timber to companies willing to build local mills. But rugged terrain, distance from ports and competition with mills in Canada, Washington and Oregon kept big companies away. The only regular customers were handloggers, who used steam donkeys mounted on barges to feed Tongass timber to small sawmills.

Logging on the Tongass increased during World War II, when the Forest Service signed a contract with the Canadian de Havilland Company to supply timber for British warplanes. Sitka spruce was the preferred tree, and, as stated earlier, by the end of the war most of the big spruces beside the water were gone. After the war a shortage of newspaper continued deforestation in the rest of the U.S., and the postwar housing boom further increased logging on the Tongass. In 1947, Congress passed the Tongass Timber Act, which enabled the Forest Service to offer generous incentives to timber companies while guaranteeing enough annual funding to cover the losses of subsidized sales. Finally large-scale logging became economically viable in southeast Alaska.

In the early 1950s, the Forest Service promised more than 8 billion board feet of timber over fifty years to a Bellingham, Washington, company that agreed to build a pulp mill in Ketchikan. Several years later, the agency signed a similar contract promising 5 billion board feet over fifty years to a Japanese consortium that would build a pulp mill in Sitka. To make the latter contract legal, the consortium, Alaska Pulp Company (APC), formed an American corporation based in Juneau. This politically popular idea fostered economic development in southeast Alaska while providing forest resources to Japan, whose forests were decimated during the war. To promote competition in this environment, the Forest Service provided roughly one-third its annual allowable cut to independent loggers and small mills.

By 1960, both mills were dissolving Tongass timber into pulp, the basis for cellophane, rayon, diapers and other household products. The longterm contracts had replaced inconsistent, low-wage jobs at independent mills with year-round, high-paying work at the pulp mills. Ketchikan and Sitka became busy logging towns with improved roads, schools, services and revenue that benefited the entire region. And in the eyes of the Forest Service and timber companies, the Tongass became a crop. Managers used terms like "overmature" to describe old-growth forests, which they claimed clearcutting would replace with healthier, more productive second-growth stands.

But as vast stump fields appeared in the region in the mid-1960s, some residents, including fishermen, hikers and both recreation and subsistence hunters questioned the emphasis on logging. Wildlife biologists, some within the Forest Service, issued early warnings that continued large-scale logging could damage the Tongass permanently. The controversy grew at the end of the decade; several conservation groups formed in southeast Alaska to push for wilderness protection under the recently passed Wilderness

Act. They gained support from national organizations in the early 1970s, when the Sierra Club sued the Forest Service over its plan to sign a third longterm contract. The contract included building a pulp mill in Juneau and logging Admiralty Island, southeast Alaska's third-largest island and home to one of the world's densest populations of brown bears. At about the same time, hunters sued to stop a timber sale on Prince of Wales Island near Ketchikan. Admiralty Island ultimately won protection, but Congressional legislation overturned an injunction on the Prince of Wales sale. Environmentalists learned that timber had powerful allies in Washington, D.C.

As opposition to cutting on the Tongass grew, legislation in the early 1970s led to increased logging. For years, Alaska Natives had argued that it was illegal and unethical for the federal government to do anything with Alaska lands—cut, mine or protect them—without first providing lands and economic opportunity to the region's original inhabitants. But the disorganized groups lacked political power and support built slowly.

In the late 1960s oil discoveries on Alaska's north slope forced the issue of Native land claims as oil companies realized a pipeline across Native land was the only way to get oil to port in south-central Alaska. In 1971, just three years after the discoveries, Richard Nixon signed the Alaska Native Claims Settlement Act (ANCSA). The law awarded Natives more than 960 million dollars and the right to select 44 million acres from federal lands in Alaska for development of their resources. It also created twelve regional Native corporations and allowed smaller communities to form their own corporations, which would manage the ANCSA assets to ensure all Alaska Natives received dividends.

In response to increasing calls for conservation, ANCSA also instructed land managers to designate wilderness and national parks in Alaska. This set the stage for a heated Alaskan lands debate that would last almost ten years and attract national attention, with increasing numbers of Americans calling for federal protection of Alaskan lands. It culminated in the election year of 1980 and resulted in the Alaska National Interest Lands Conservation Act (ANILCA), signed into law as one of Jimmy Carter's last acts as president.

ANILCA is a sweeping document of nearly 100 pages that addresses most lands issues in Alaska, including Native subsistence,

201

commercial fishing and preservation. In southeast Alaska, it set aside 5.4 million acres of wilderness, the first after passage of the 1964 Wilderness Act, and turned the 2-million-acre Glacier Bay National Monument into a national park. But ANILCA also included major breaks for the pulp mills, brokered by Alaska's republican delegation. It established an annual timber supply fund of $40 million to support timber sales and set a logging target of 4.5 billion board feet per decade. Incidentally, ANILCA also allowed the possibility for oil and gas development in the Arctic National Wildlife Refuge (ANWR), a hotly contested issue today.

At the same time that ANILCA allowed timber companies to increase their logging of the Tongass, Native corporations completed their land selections in southeast Alaska. They chose roughly half a million acres of the region's most productive forest and began a decade of almost lawless clearcutting in an attempt to make their corporations profitable. Within ten years, they razed nearly as much land as the pulp mills had since the 1950s.

Throughout the 1980s, conservation efforts intensified as biologists increasingly demonstrated the harmful effects of clearcuts on wildlife. They also discovered that the inventories used to establish the longterm contracts in the 1950s were grossly flawed. At the time, foresters estimated timber volume on the Tongass by analyzing aerial photographs with the same formulas used to gauge timber volume in Washington and Oregon. But at higher latitudes, the trees on the Tongass grow shorter than those in Washington, and the estimates provided the pulp mills with an unsustainable timber supply that would eventually cost the Tongass all of its most productive stands, leaving none for protection.

In 1981, a successful lawsuit brought against the pulp mills by an independent logger also demonstrated that the longterm contracts hurt business in southeast Alaska. The case showed that by the 1970s the two companies had created a monopoly by purchasing or forcing from business every major mill in the region. The companies used the mills as fronts to consistently outbid competition on federal timber sales and artificially depress the pulp market in southeast Alaska. Combined with a system of unfair lending practices, this made it almost impossible for independent loggers to survive and eventually forced many from business. Simultaneously, it ensured enormous profits for the two companies.

Embarrassed by the discoveries, the Forest Service launched an investigation that revealed the two companies had fraudulently hidden their profits in order to keep Tongass timber cheap. The Ketchikan mill, now owned by Louisiana Pacific, had concealed its huge profits by distributing them to parent businesses, making the mill appear barely profitable. The Sitka mill, still owned by APC, did the same by shuffling its profits through a convoluted network of Japanese businesses.

In the mid-1980s, after fraud and antitrust activities were proven in a district court and upheld by a federal appeals court, the Forest Service requested involvement from the justice department. But under Ronald Reagan, who had appointed a former Louisiana Pacific executive to oversee the Forest Service, the justice department refused to investigate.

Amazingly, as the pulp mills were still fighting in court, a pulp market recession in the early 1980s enabled them to renegotiate timber prices with the Forest Service. They eventually settled on an average of less than $3 per 1,000 board feet of Tongass timber, roughly one-fiftieth the price of timber in Washington and Oregon. They also received generous tax breaks from the federal government, increasing their already enormous profits.

Direction from ANILCA and support from the Reagan administration and Alaska's congressional delegation kept Tongass logging

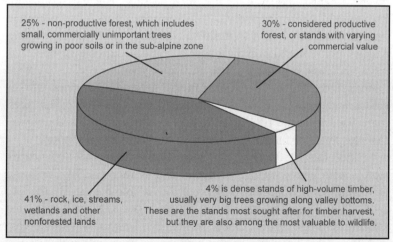

25% - non-productive forest, which includes small, commercially unimportant trees growing in poor soils or in the sub-alpine zone

30% - considered productive forest, or stands with varying commercial value

41% - rock, ice, streams, wetlands and other nonforested lands

4% is dense stands of high-volume timber, usually very big trees growing along valley bottoms. These are the stands most sought after for timber harvest, but they are also among the most valuable to wildlife.

Chart 9.1: Percentages of Tongass that are productive forest, ice, rock, muskeg. Tongass National Forest lands are roughly 17 million acres.

in high gear throughout the 1980s. In addition, the Native corporations responded to the deepening pulp recession by increasing logging on their lands. It was a desperate but generally failed attempt to escape debt—by the end of the decade nearly a million acres of southeast Alaskan rain forest had been clearcut since 1950. Although that may seem a small amount of the Tongass' 17 million acres, it is important to realize that almost half of the Tongass is rock, ice, muskeg and other nonforested lands, and that another quarter is considered nonproductive, or with low commercial value. Only about 4 percent of the forest produces high-volume old-growth forest.

Opposition to the longterm contracts grew in the late 1980s. As more people learned that the Forest Service was losing millions of dollars on the Tongass timber program, taxpayers joined salmon, deer, wolves, bears, fishermen, hunters and small businesses in the growing list of victims of the longterm contracts. In 1990, Congress responded with the Tongass Timber Reform Act (TTRA), which served environmentalists a major victory. It did not cancel the contracts, but it designated almost a million acres as either wilderness or roadless areas, increased buffers around salmon streams, abolished the $40 million timber fund and decreased the target cut.

Alaska's republican governor, Wally Hickel, and its republican delegation fought the TTRA and even managed to increase logging on the Tongass shortly after the bill's passage. But they could not help the pulp mills themselves, which by the 1990s were in trouble on a growing number of fronts. The continued recession in the pulp market took a big toll on their profits, increased global competition made their aging mills obsolete and, after years of neglecting basic maintenance, the mills required major upgrades to meet worker safety and environmental standards. In addition, the mills faced huge fines from the EPA and Alaska Department of Environmental Conservation for their long history of air and water pollution.

Since the 1950s, the companies had heavily polluted nearby waters with heavy metals, methanol and sulfuric and hydrochloric acids and emitted large quantities of dioxin into the air. By the late 1980s, a marine dead zone existed outside the Ketchikan mill, and sulfuric acid releases poisoned workers and neighbors with increasing frequency. Historically, the companies dealt with pollution by either paying the fines and continuing to pollute or by appealing violations. But by the early 1990s, both companies owed millions of dollars in fines. They also faced lawsuits from former employees and area residents, and finally, in 1993, APC closed its Sitka mill. The following year it closed its Wrangell mill and left southeast Alaska. In 1997, Louisiana Pacific followed suit by first closing its Ketchikan pulp mill, then its smaller mills.

Although Alaska's congressional delegation and others had warned for years that ending the longterm contracts would have dire economic consequences, southeast Alaska's economy survived the mill closures. In the 1990s, cruise ship visits to the area grew exponentially, charter boat licenses nearly doubled and tourism became the region's top-grossing private-sector industry. In Ketchikan, unemployment rose only slightly after the closures, softened by booming construction and tourism industries. In Sitka, unemployment also rose, but tourism and a growing health care industry provided new jobs.

However, many of the new jobs paid less than the pulp mill positions; in smaller communities dependent on logging, the effects were greater. In Wrangell, for instance, unemployment soared and many left the area. The 2000 census showed that several smaller communities were simply disappearing. To help affected residents, Bill Clinton signed legislation appropriating $110 million for retraining, relocation and economic development.

Meanwhile, logging on the Tongass remained a hotly contested issue. In 1997, a new Tongass Land Management Plan offered protection for wild and scenic rivers, bigger buffers for salmon streams, additional roadless acreage and a significantly reduced annual cut. After thirty-three appeals from industry and Native and environmental groups, it was finalized in 1999 with even stronger protections, including logging moratoriums in sensitive areas and longer logging rotations in critical wildlife habitat. In addition, it reduced the annual allowable cut to less than a third of 1980s levels.

In 2001, after two years of study, 600 public meetings across the country and over a million largely favorable public comments, the Forest Service instituted its Roadless Initiative, which further decreased logging on the Tongass. But shortly after, when George W. Bush took office, the Forest Service suspended the rule and asked for more public comment. In addition, the Forest Service suspended the logging moratoriums of its 1999 management plan.

Today, the Forest Service, Alaska's pro-development delegation, the Bush administration and Native, timber and conservation groups are still struggling to find the right balance for timber management on the Tongass.

■ ■ ■

It took three trips to carry our kayaks and gear from the ferry. We walked alongside a metal car ramp, which clanged loudly under cars, trucks and RVs driving single-file from the ferry to the parking lot. After piling our gear beside a window in view of the ferry terminal cashiers, we took a short walk along the road to Ketchikan.

After centuries of Tlingit occupation, whites settled in Ketchikan in the 1880s to build a fish saltery. At the turn of the century, the town boomed as mines opened on Prince of Wales Island and thousands headed north for the Klondike. Afterward, canneries, fishermen and handloggers kept the town alive before the arrival of big timber in the 1950s. Today, Ketchikan is the second largest town in southeast Alaska, with 15,000 residents. It is on the southwest edge of Revillagigedo Island, occupying a narrow strip of relatively flat land sandwiched between mountains and the sea. Tongass Narrows, a channel averaging less than a mile wide, borders one side, while steep mountains border the other.

At roughly 1,100 square miles, Revillagigedo is the fifth largest of the more than 1,000 islands in southeast Alaska. It has thirty miles of paved road extending from Ketchikan and several hundred miles of logging roads winding through clearcuts and second-growth forests north of town. But each road terminates in forest. And like all but three southeast Alaskan towns, Ketchikan is accessible only boat or plane.

We walked along a narrow sidewalk past faded aluminum buildings, weathered storefronts and wooden houses, as busy traffic consisting largely of pickup trucks whirred alongside us. Tongass Narrows was 100 yards to our right. As the primary way in or out of town, it was even busier than the street—float planes buzzed loudly as they landed and took off, pleasure boats and skiffs passed each other slowly with small wakes, another ferry moved toward the terminal and men worked on fishing boats and barges beside wooden docks. Across the channel, a 737 thundered along Ketchikan

International Airport's single runway, which provides daily service to Seattle, Juneau and Anchorage.

In another week, the first cruise ship of the season would arrive, adding to the activity in Tongass Narrows. Sometimes five ships dock in Ketchikan in a single day, swelling the population by as much as 10,000. Buses bring tourists to a small city center area, where they buy souvenirs from gift shops. Some take flightseeing or taxi tours, but most never see more than downtown.

We stopped at a grocery store for meat and fresh vegetables, then ate sandwiches beside our boats before joining the traffic in Tongass Narrows. Two hours later, we set our camp at the head of a log-strewn beach not far from the pulp mill. To the south, the ocean turned gray, and gray-brown tendrils of rain dragged along blue mountaintops. Light rain began as we sat on driftwood eating burritos with fresh vegetables.

I awoke at five the next morning to hard rain battering our tent. With my head inches from the wall, I could hear water washing down the rain fly and splashing against a nearby rock. With the tent still dry inside and my sleeping bag warm, I lay comfortably drifting in and out of sleep for two hours. Near seven I could no longer ignore my bladder and unzipped the tent door. Outside, a gray ceiling only 300 feet above the water made southeast Alaska look much like what we had seen of British Columbia; dark green conifers covered the lower portions of hillsides that rose steeply into thick clouds.

I rubbed against the rain fly as I exited the tent, and cold water streamed down my lower back. As I stood, rain drops quickly moistened my hair. I hurried to my kayak, fished out my rain gear and then walked into the woods to eat breakfast. Afterward, we packed quickly and began paddling northwest in Tongass Narrows. We reached the channel's end less than an hour later and began bobbing on two-foot waves at the edge of Clarence Strait. The strait extended thirty miles to our south, where it opened into Dixon Entrance. Ahead, it veered northwestward, disappearing into a gray abyss. With cold rain hammering our decks and dripping from our hoods, we rafted together near Point Higgins to consult our maps.

In order to continue along the mainland, we needed to travel west-northwest across the mouth of Behm Canal, which opened to our north. This seven-mile crossing would bring us to Caamano

207

Point at the southern end of Cleveland Peninsula. From there, we would follow the west side of the peninsula northwest into central southeast Alaska.

With waves to two feet at its edge, we expected rough water in the middle of the crossing. To our north, gray clouds blended with the surface of the sea in Behm Canal and completely concealed Betton Island, only three miles away. Visibility was only slightly better to the south, where small clouds blew along the sea, fading in and out of larger clouds hovering above the water. The rain hissed all around us. It was weather George Vancouver commonly called "thick and rainy."

■ ■ ■

Vancouver entered southeast Alaska in late July, 1793, after spending several weeks surveying Dixon Entrance. Midway through his second season, he was tired of the poor weather and referred to it often in his journal as gloomy, inhospitable, unfavorable and irksome.

On July 24, with the *Chatham* and *Discovery* anchored in the protection of Salmon Cove near Dixon Entrance, Vancouver led a survey party in two small boats to investigate southern southeast Alaska. After a week in Portland Canal, he traveled north to explore what is now the west side of Misty Fiords National Monument. On August 7, he entered Behm Canal, which forms a 120-mile horseshoe around the east, north and west sides of Revillagigedo Island, leaving the south open to Tongass Narrows and Revillagigedo Channel.

Entering the eastern mouth of the fiord, Vancouver expected yet another dead-end extension of the sea, but three days later, after traveling sixty miles, the channel remained wide. In addition, he found three mainland channels requiring his exploration, which slowed his progress. More than 120 miles from Salmon Cove and running low on food, he feared he would have to turn back before surveying the extent of Behm Canal. He loathed the thought of a second survey of the channel, which would only extend his stay on the coast.

The channel finally narrowed and veered sharply westward on the afternoon of August 11. Watching the direction of the ebbing tide, Vancouver correctly surmised that he was circumnavigating a large island. The following day, as the channel widened again and veered southward, he knew he was heading back toward Dixon Entrance and his ships. That afternoon, a large group of Natives approached the party in several canoes and made signs they wanted to trade. They were likely Tlingits, whose historical territory included almost all of southeast Alaska.

While Joseph Whidbey remained on the water in one boat, Vancouver and Peter Puget rowed to shore in the other, accompanied by some Natives. Vancouver went ashore, but soon noticed Puget arguing with the Natives, who had stolen a musket. Tension rose quickly, and the Natives caught the group unarmed when they raised their spears in anger. Vancouver quickly negotiated with the chief, and for a few minutes it seemed violence had been averted.

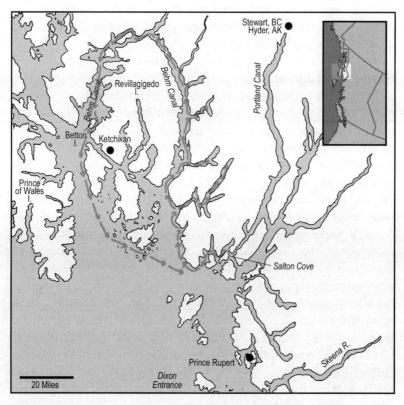

Map 9.1: Vancouver's route through Dixon Entrance and southern southeast Alaska.

But as Vancouver and Puget tried to leave the beach, fifty Tlingits surrounded their boat, preventing their departure. Again they raised their spears before Vancouver's men could arm their weapons.

By this time, Whidbey was quickly moving toward shore, accompanied by several canoes. With violence seeming inevitable, Vancouver ordered Whidbey's men to fire; several Natives fell dead in the water and on the beach. Others capsized their canoes in shallow water and waded ashore using them as shields. As Vancouver's men reloaded their weapons, the Natives scrambled into the forest. Moments later, they reappeared on a bluff thirty yards away, where they threw stones and fired one shot from the musket.

Two of Vancouver's men lay injured in the boats, struck with spears, and somewhere between six and a dozen Natives lay dead or injured on the beach. Vancouver ordered his men to row from shore, having lost three muskets, ammunition and some books. With screams emanating from the forest, the men passed a point Vancouver named Escape Point and rowed south in the widening channel. That night, with Caamano Point in view to their west, they camped at Point Higgins. Vancouver named nearby Betton Island for one of his injured men.

With little remaining food, the party traveled southward for the next three days, determining the extent of Revillagigedo Island and observing Prince of Wales Island to their west. On August 15, they recognized Portland Canal and knew they were within a day of Salmon Cove. That night they dined on a half pint of peas each, then rowed and sailed through the night across Dixon Entrance. At seven the next morning they arrived at Salmon Cove, much to the relief of their waiting crew.

The party had been gone twenty-three days and had traveled more than 700 miles. But because these miles included the circumnavigation of Revillagigedo Island, Vancouver had not "advanced our primary object of tracing the continental boundary, more than twenty leagues from…the vessels. Such were the perplexing, tedious, and laborious means by which alone we were enabled by degrees to trace the north-western limits of the American continent." Reflecting on the events in Behm Canal, Vancouver admitted that his comfort with Natives, after two seasons of peaceful contacts, had put his crew in danger. However, the incident would be the only instance of bloodshed during Vancouver's three seasons on the coast.

■ ■ ■

With waves pushing us toward Point Higgins, we took a compass bearing toward Caamano Point and began paddling across Behm Canal. Betton Island was still not visible, and the point looked ghostlike through the rain. Since the crossing would take at least two hours, we risked becoming lost in fog far from shore if the weather deteriorated. The situation could become dangerous if we drifted south into Clarence Strait, which quickly widened to nearly twenty miles between Revillagigedo and Prince of Wales Islands. But it was a calculated risk. The compass would help us navigate in fog, and the northward-trending waves combined with the flooding tide would eventually push us against Cleveland Peninsula if we became disoriented. The likelihood of becoming lost in the larger body of water to our south was remote.

The rain fell steadily, but in light wind the waves remained below three feet. Less than a mile to our north, the gray water of Behm Canal quickly blended with the low sky. Caamano Point remained visible throughout the crossing, and after two and a half hours we pulled our boats onto its rocky headland. The point faced south toward Clarence Strait and the brunt of each winter's strong winds; big gray logs lay stacked against a forest tangled with downed trees and thick brush. Ducking through soaked vegetation, we retreated to the edge of a mossy hillside where a leaning cedar filtered the pouring rain. We sat on spongy moss eating moistened sandwiches as the rain ran down our hands. We quickly grew cold and returned to the water after only forty minutes.

We continued northwest along Cleveland Peninsula with the rain hissing at the sea, dripping from our hoods and drumming against our kayaks. Visibility steadily decreased to less than a mile, with the ceiling sinking to between 200 and 500 feet. The heavy clouds seemed stuck against the steep coast, as though the sun would never return, and the pleasant weather of Grenville Channel seemed a dream.

Near three, we went ashore to set camp on a short gravel beach facing southeast into an increasingly cold breeze. As Bill piled our food and kitchen gear at one end of the beach, I set the tent at the

9.1: Navigation by Compass in a Kayak

With charts or maps, kayakers can use compasses to determine their location by taking bearings on two or three distinct landmarks such as mountains or points. Their location is the place where lines drawn along the bearings intersect. They can use the information to set a course to a bay or island too distant to be distinguished, then follow the course by monitoring the bow's position relative to a landmark near the destination. This is more reliable than following the compass needle because wind and current will create drift, so that a kayaker trying to paddle due west may move significantly north or south, which also increases the length of the crossing. Calculating the rate of drift requires additional bearings throughout the crossing, which will result in more accurate estimates of the crossing's duration. But as long as conditions remain clear, paddlers will reach their destination by keeping the chosen landmark at a consistent position on their bows.

However, poor weather is common in the Inside Passage, and decreased visibility makes calculating drift much more difficult. If leaving a beach in fog that conceals the destination, kayakers need some visible reference points to determine their course. In addition, they must have

other on a small gravel platform beneath the sprawling branches of a Sitka alder. Although the tent was soaked inside and out, I set it close to a rotting bluff, hoping to shelter it from the rain. By the time I finished, my pruned hands ached with cold and I felt chilly in my wet clothes.

It was too early to crawl into our sleeping bags and changing would only soak our remaining dry clothes, so we retreated to the kitchen tarp to drink hot chocolate and listen to the weather forecast. A monotone female voice, like some stern bureaucrat, read a bleak weather synopsis: Tuesday, rain; Wednesday, chance of showers; Thursday, showers; Friday, rain likely; Saturday, rain likely. The chance for precipitation each day ranged between 60 and 90 percent.

At five we cooked dehydrated black beans and rice and by six-thirty had cleaned the dishes and hung the food. Soaked and cold and with nothing left to do, Bill climbed inside the tent, but I decided six-thirty was too early to lay in my sleeping bag. In steady rain, I stood outside watching water stream down the craggy bluff and disappear into gravel. Above the tent, young alder leaves shook with each rain drop, their brown branches wet and glistening. Behind the tent, bright green skunk cabbage grew in mud beside a pond only ten feet across. Big drops from hemlock branches popped against its black surface. In every direction, rain and mist filled the dim air.

I walked along the edge of the water, then along a bear path in the woods. With bluffs on either side of the beach and thickly vegetated hills rising quickly behind camp, I could not go far. After standing at the bases of a few big spruces, I finally retreated to the tent, hung my wet rain gear beneath its vestibule and climbed into my sleeping bag at seven-thirty.

I tried to read but fell asleep inside of an hour, then awoke at eleven-thirty having to urinate. Outside, the night was black and rainy with a chilly breeze. I could hear small waves breaking only ten yards away, but the sea was invisible. The rain quickly moistened my hair and bare chest, and I was cold when I climbed back inside. I tried to sleep, but the rain crackled loudly at the tent and the end of my sleeping bag was wet from resting against the door. For the next three hours, I read and wrote in my journal, each breath visible in my headlamp's beam. Listening to the steady rain, I finally fell asleep near three.

Rain still crackled against the tent when I awoke feeling tired at seven. After reading and napping until after nine, we crammed our sleeping bags into dry bags, packed away our books and unzipped the tent door to another gloomy day. We had agreed that paddling for at least a few hours would be better than spending a rainy day on

knowledge about their average paddling speed and the direction and speed of waves, wind and current. If passing islands more than a half mile from shore paddlers can pause to note the speed and direction of drift, then use well-practiced formulas to determine the rate of drift over the course of a mile. If fog moves in during a crossing, paddlers may be forced to paddle according to the compass needle, which again requires good knowledge of the speed of waves, wind and current. Of course, before setting out on a crossing, especially one that could lead to open water, strong currents or channels susceptible to strong winds, paddlers should listen to the weather, pay attention to weather developments and be familiar with how wind and current create drift so that they can make educated guesses in a bad situation.

The following are some tips on compass use that can help with safe crossings:

When taking bearings, landmarks should be between forty-five and ninety degrees from the bow and within a few miles. Landmarks too far away or at too small of an angle from each other can turn small inaccuracies into large ones.

A hiking compass will work while kayaking, but it must be aligned with the boat's centerline and either wedged into the map case or securely fastened to the bow with duct tape or shock cord. A marine compass seated in a compass well is much more accurate and easy to use.

Waves and the action of paddling will move the bow from side to side, making it difficult to follow a compass needle or point at a landmark. Often kayakers must aim for an average direction.

Paddlers should learn formulas for determining speed and drift and practice them often. If they are well-rehearsed, they will be easier to use and more accurate in rough or otherwise challenging conditions.

Paddlers should be familiar with their average paddling speed in order to accurately estimate drift without a nearby landmark and to estimate the duration of a crossing.

Because wind and current drag near shore and often create eddies, estimates of drift should be done more than a half mile from shore.

If darkness or fog conceal landmarks, kayakers can navigate using wave direction. If a paddler knows the waves are traveling due north, then hitting them at a forty-five-degree angle would be traveling in a northwesterly direction.

A GPS unit is effective for determining direction and location, but it does not replace the need for good map and compass skills.

Fundamentals of Kayak Navigation has great information on kayak navigation.

the small beach. After a big breakfast of bagels, cereal and apples, we pushed our boats into the water.

By noon, the moisture from my rain gear had soaked through my undershirt, and every paddle stroke brought cold clothes against my skin, sending chills through my body. The rain increased to a downpour and ran from the front of my hood in narrow streams. A steady breeze from the south urged our boats northward but kept us struggling to stay warm. The ceiling remained low, with visibility varying between three and eight miles. Half a mile away, along Cleveland Peninsula, bands of mist steamed upward from between trees and disappeared into a dishwater sky. Our maps showed peaks approaching 3,000 feet, but all we saw were dark, forested hillsides rising quickly into clouds.

The storm blurred the boundaries between land and water. While paddling, its misty clouds fragmented our views, washing together narrow channels, snowy summits and rolling forests. On land, it dropped from the trees, hissed on rocky beaches and ran down our rain gear on its way back to the sea. Several times we paddled through clouds too heavy to rise, where light mist danced in the air between bigger raindrops.

Late in the afternoon a pleasure boat passed within 100 yards, and a man in short sleeves opened his cabin door to wave at us. We waved back, but while cold and wet, neither of us really wished to be aboard the boat. Although drinking hot cups of coffee while wearing T-shirts inside a warm wheelhouse would have been nice, it would have removed us from too much. Beyond windows, the flat sea and green forests of the Inside Passage can become tame scenery. But in kayaks it was impossible to forget the sea's coldness, strong currents and unsettled waves or the soaked and dynamic nature of the forest. For us, the coast had become textures we felt daily—soft moss, wet leaves, cold rockweed, smooth drift logs—that we never would have known from beyond the windows of a boat. Its soundtrack surrounded us. Ravens, gulls, wings on water, twigs snapping in the night, barnacles crunching under rubber boots—things we could not have heard beyond the drone of an engine. Each day, as the rain washed over us, our senses became more intimately attuned to the coast.

"That's forty-eight straight hours of rain," Bill said that night, looking at his watch. We were beneath the kitchen tarp, eating pre-made Indian food and rice. "I think I have moss growing behind one of my ears."

Tired and wet, we retreated to the tent by seven. I fell asleep by nine-thirty but woke up several times throughout the night to rain battering our soaked tent. The rain finally turned to showers late the next morning as we turned east from Chatham Strait and entered Ernest Sound, a ten-mile opening between Cleveland Peninsula and Etolin Island. Misty sunlight hit distant water as the thick clouds slowly disintegrated. The main layer of clouds rose to 3,000 feet and revealed small patches of blue sky, but lower clouds made a mess of the surrounding land. It looked like the aftermath of a big party, with puffy clouds strewn against everything. Narrow streaks of mist were horizontal brush strokes across mountainsides. Misty clouds rose like smoke from narrow valleys, rolling above the forest and dissipating quickly. A few narrow columns of flat-bottomed cloud hovered 300 feet above the water and billowed upward more than 2,000 feet, where they bloomed outward below the main ceiling.

Late in the afternoon, a cluster of snowy mountains appeared on the south end of Etolin Island, with the largest close to 4,000 feet high only a few miles from tidewater. Thick white clouds stuffed their alpine valleys, wrapped around their forested sides and overflowed their peaks like gobs of molten marshmallow. Fragments of

9.2: PROTECTING BEARS FROM OUR FOOD.

Camping in bear habitat requires knowledge of bear behavior and a sense of responsibility about keeping bears away from human food and garbage, which is equally important to bears and campers.

Because bears in the Inside Passage hibernate for up to five months each year, they have to consume in as little as seven months enough food to get them through the entire year. They are voracious omnivores, either replenishing fat lost during winter or adding enough fat to prepare for hibernation, and will always remember an easy meal. If kayaks, dry bags, tents or other camping equipment provide food, bears become conditioned, forever associating humans and their gear with easy food. Conditioned bears eventually get too close to camps or act aggressively toward humans, and although in rare instances they attack humans, it is far more common that they are shot. Such bears are often called "problem bears," but in reality their behavior is a result of problem campers.

mountain tops heaped with snow appeared briefly, mixing with the clouds in a combination of blue and white.

We went ashore in a large bay and laid all of our gear against boulders, then finally changed into dry clothes. After dinner we spotted a black bear, the first of the trip. It slowly approached our camp while feeding in the long band of sedges between the intertidal and the forest. As we watched with binoculars it came within fifty yards of our kitchen, occasionally looking at us or waving its nose in our direction. After twenty minutes it ambled into the forest, where leafy alder branches quickly concealed it. Fifteen minutes later, we inspected the mowed sedges where it had been feeding and found a mound of fresh, grassy scat.

Contrary to the recent weather report, the next morning was only partly cloudy. We decided to take the day off from paddling and laid all our gear and clothes on the beach, then spent the morning reading and napping in variable sunshine. No boats visited our bay as we enjoyed a soundtrack of scoters, gulls and eagles. Seals occasionally surfaced with wet breaths; ravens inside the forest sounded like screaming monkeys.

Across Ernest Sound a cluster of immense mountains on Etolin Island shone brightly against large areas of blue sky. Deep snows covered the peaks, and sharp cornices that must have been fifty feet high extended from the ridges like visors. Long fracture lines ran across the tops of big bowls as rumpled piles of avalanche debris filled alpine basins. Rocky summits and sheer cliffs interrupted the thick snow. The size and complexity of the peaks surpassed anything we had seen in British Columbia.

Prince of Wales Island filled the distance to our southwest. Vancouver named POW in late September, 1793, honoring the eldest son of King George III. Several weeks after his adventures in Behm Canal, Vancouver had surveyed the mainland east of the island in worsening autumn weather. On September 20, after rounding its northern end, he decided to return south, concluding his second season on the coast. Much to his frustration, he had only covered about 315 miles of latitude in almost five months.

Prince of Wales is the largest island in southeast Alaska and the second largest island in the state, after Kodiak. It is 132 miles long and 45 miles wide with a land mass of over 2,200 square miles. It has extensive areas of porous limestone substrate, or karst, which is unique in southeast Alaska, where much of the substrate consists of poorly drained glacial till or nonporous bedrock. The well-drained karst combined with abundant rain formed extensive caves on POW that the Forest Service and independent scientists have only recently

Here are some rules for camping in bear habitat:

Cooking closer than 100 feet from the tent can leave food scents that may attract a bear to the camping area. In the Inside Passage the intertidal provides the perfect kitchen, where incoming tides quickly erase food scents.

Keep a clean camp. Before hanging food, campers should carefully check the kitchen area for garbage and food scraps.

Always hang food at night or while away from camp. Food should be hung at least twelve feet from the ground and ten feet from the trunk of a tree. Black bears are nimble climbers and can easily access food hung twenty feet from the ground but only a few feet from the tree's trunk.

Keeping food in a kayak is a bad idea. A bear's sense of smell is extremely strong, and even well-wrapped food in a closed compartment can be an attractant. In addition to conditioning a bear, keeping food in a kayak puts the kayak at risk to damage from a curious bear. Kayaks should be cleaned regularly and checked nightly for wrappers and spilled food.

Cookware, dishes and silverware should be cleaned thoroughly and either hung with the food or placed somewhere distant from the tent.

Hikers should avoid carcasses and make noise near streams or in thick brush, where bears may not hear or see well.

begun to study. Already, human bones close to 10,000 years old and much older bear bones found there have contributed to the understanding of early life in the Inside Passage.

Since karst drains well, carrying surplus water from the soil, it provides ideal conditions for tree growth, especially for Sitka spruces in low-lying river valleys. Naturalists have found spruces on Prince of Wales more than six feet across and almost 200 feet tall. They are remnants of a forest that once held the highest concentration of big trees in the northern Inside Passage. But its size, big trees and proximity to growing ports in the southern Inside Passage, made POW an early target for loggers. By the 1950s, when Ketchikan Pulp Company began cutting the island's interior, hand-loggers had removed all of the big trees from its shoreline. In the 1980s, as Native corporations liquidated their land claims assets on the island, local environmentalists dubbed it Prisoner of War Island. The timber reforms of the 1990s were too late for much of Prince of Wales. Today it is an enormous monument to poor logging practices. Over 1,500 miles of brown logging roads course its once-rich valleys and hillsides, surrounded by thousands of acres of clearcuts and tight second-growth forests. Erosion from logging roads and clearcuts is widespread, dumping tons of sediment into salmon streams. Much of the devastation is concealed from boaters by a thin margin of forest surrounding the island's shores, but air travelers can clearly see that large parts of the island's forest are gone.

■ ■ ■

The temperature rose to near 60°F around noon, and we took separate walks from our camp. While Bill explored more than a mile of gravel beach and rocky bluffs, I struggled inland through thick vegetation along a swift creek. Its clear water rushed down a steep grade and through narrow notches of basalt and granite. Three hundred feet above our beach, I napped beside a calm pond surrounded by forest.

Returning to camp, I took a thorough bath in a cold stream running down our beach, then watched the clouds change the lighting on Etolin Island's mountains. Later, with the dishes clean and the food hung, we watched the sun set over the peaks. They formed a jagged line of blue and white against a golden sky.

We made leisurely progress northward during the next three days, eventually traveling along western Wrangell Island. The weather continued improving, with clear skies and warm temperatures by the third day. The views also improved, with the mountains on Etolin Island growing higher and closer with each turn. Paddling along Wrangell Island, we fixed our eyes on the chutes, peaks, and heavy snows immediately to our west.

We also caught our first glimpses of the mountains along southeast Alaska's border with British Columbia. The highest peaks, close to 9,000 feet, jabbed at the pale blue sky with daggers and spires too steep for snow; a jumbled wall of snowy mountains surrounded their bases. They rose from the Stikine Ice Field, a pool of glacial ice occupying more than 1,000 square miles between the Stikine and Whiting Rivers. At one point, I thought I could see where the LeConte Glacier, North America's southern-most tidewater glacier, began its downward slide from the mountains. I hoped we would paddle to the face of the glacier in three days, but as usual, unforeseen challenges delayed our arrival.

CHAPTER TEN

High and Dry on the Stikine—
Big Rivers in the Inside
Passage

We continued north for another day along the west side of Wrangell Island, with clear skies and temperatures in the sixties. Bill was about a quarter mile ahead of me for most of the morning, and as I rounded a forested point I found him standing on a beach talking with a couple by an aluminum skiff.

Once ashore, he introduced me to Susan and Mark Woodling, a Native couple in their fifties. They both wore flannel shirts with old jeans tucked inside rubber boots. Susan chatted with us as Mark plopped the skiff's anchor in the intertidal, then tied its line to a rusty post above the high tide line. She pointed to their single-level home, which was half concealed in thick forest 100 yards away. On the wall beside its front door was a red and black wooden carving of a bear in the northwest coast native art style.

"We're ten miles south of the road," she said as her husband carried a box of groceries along a trail to the house, "so we take the skiff to town for supplies."

After chatting for a few minutes, Susan asked if we had read any John Muir.

"Well this is where he almost got himself killed," she said. "By Tlingits. The missionaries from Wrangell stole a totem from the village that used to be here. They chopped it down with an ax so they could take it to some museum down south. The Tlingits captured them and would have killed them all, but Muir talked them into letting them go. They liked Muir."

John Muir first arrived in southeast Alaska in July, 1879, aboard a steamship delivering mail to Wrangell and Sitka. An avid naturalist, he had traveled from his home in California's Sierra Nevada "to gain some knowledge of the regions to the northward." For eleven years he had explored the Sierra Nevada, particularly the Yosemite Valley, studying its plants and developing new ideas about its geology. Whereas most contemporary geologists attributed the steep-walled valleys of the Sierras to cataclysmic floods, Muir suggested glaciers had created their unique shapes. By visiting southeast Alaska, he hoped to confirm his theories while witnessing first-hand the erosional force of glacial ice.

From the beginning, Muir's "grand object" of learning about the region's natural history raised curiosity, even controversy. He was unlike other white visitors to southeast Alaska, who for more than a century had come in waves to take the area's furs, salmon, gold and trees. But Muir seemed only obsessed with the area's nature, studying plants and glaciers with the same fervor his contemporaries applied to seeking gold. His odd pursuits were sometimes unsettling to both whites and Tlingits.

On one of his first nights in Wrangell, Muir inadvertently caused a stir while watching a storm from atop a nearby mountain. He had quietly departed Wrangell at dusk and climbed the mountain in a driving rainstorm to "see how the Alaska trees behave in storms and hear the songs they sing." Well after nightfall, he arrived atop the mountain, where "the glad rejoicing storm in glorious voice was singing through the woods, noble compensation for mere body discomfort." Using punk, twig shavings, then sticks and eventually logs, he built an enormous bonfire that illuminated the trees around him and reached forty feet into the low clouds.

Muir's fire could not be seen from town, but its glare lit the clouds blowing across the mountaintop. Near midnight, some Tlingits noticed the glare and hurried to a missionary's home, begging him to pray for protection from the evil spirits in the sky. Soon a group of whites and Tlingits gathered outside to see the strange lights. Concealing their alarm, the whites speculated that spontaneous combustion or perhaps a volcano was causing the glow. The following morning, when they learned of Muir's bonfire, few could understand why he would camp atop a mountain during a harsh storm. It was only the first of many times John Muir would attract such attention.

Muir's first visit to southeast Alaska lasted nearly six months.

Basing himself largely from Wrangell, he took extensive trips by steamship and canoe throughout the northern Inside Passage and became the first white person to explore Glacier Bay, where the Muir Glacier still bears his name. Whenever he could, he set off for days without much more than some bread, dried salmon and a bundle containing his sleeping roll and tent. A skilled mountaineer, he climbed high peaks and made daring treks across glaciers, more than once risking his life to discover the source of glaciers or gain views of their surrounding mountains. His treks lasted well into the night and often occurred during nasty autumn storms.

Muir returned to southeast Alaska four times during the following twenty years, and his writings were published as *Travels in Alaska* in 1915, less than a year after his death. The book chronicles his bold adventures and celebrates southeast Alaska's nature with relentless exuberance. His passion for the region's plants, mountains, glaciers and even weather sharply contrasts the dour writing of George Vancouver, who complained often about the weather, dead-end channels and disordered forests of the northwest coast. While Muir seemed barely able to contain his enthusiasm, even in miserable conditions, Vancouver expressed almost no affection for the region during three seasons of surveys, as illustrated in the following passages.

From *The Voyage of George Vancouver, 1791–1795* June, 1793: "Neither the sea nor the shores afforded us the smallest refreshment, nor the least relaxation; and the weather being extremely unpleasant, without any prospect of a change, necessarily increased the labor, and retarded the progress of our boats in the examination of this inhospitable region; whose solitary and desolate appearance, though daily more familiarized to our view, did not become less irksome to our feelings."

From *Travels in Alaska*, Muir in July, 1879: "New scenes are brought to view with magical rapidity. Rounding some bossy camp, the eye is called away into far-reaching vistas, bounded on either hand by headlands in charming array, one dipping gracefully beyond another and growing fainter and more ethereal in the distance. The tranquil channel stretching river-like between…while mellow, tempered sunshine is streaming over all, blending sky, land and water in pale, misty blue."

222

■ ■ ■

"Want to go see a totem?" asked Susan.

Using a walking stick for support, she led us along a faint trail in the woods. Fractured sunlight spilled through the canopy and rested like puddles over shaded logs and underbrush. Two varied thrushes high in the trees sounded like referee whistles in the distance. After a quarter mile we stopped by a crooked spruce attached to what at first appeared to be a dead tree.

"That's the totem," Susan said. "It won't be here much longer, but it's the oldest one near Wrangell. Probably one of the oldest in all of southeast."

The spruce had grown from a crack in the bottom of the totem, eventually splitting it open and tilting it to a sharp angle. Its split center embraced the spruce, as though trying to remain upright for as long as possible. Soon it would fall to the mossy ground and sink slowly into the duff, where it would nurse spruce and hemlock seeds lying dormant under our feet.

We walked around the old totem and ran our fingers through barely distinguishable carvings filled with small mosses. Susan explained that the top piece had fallen off years earlier and that the remaining carvings represented a bear and a beaver. I wondered how many totems and other artifacts I had unknowingly passed while walking in the rain forest, where plant succession quickly conceals them.

We walked slowly back to the beach, chatted for a few minutes, then Bill and I climbed inside our kayaks. We paddled north for the afternoon, then set our camp at the edge of a grassy meadow beside a calm stream. As we cooked dinner, gulls chattered in the intertidal and two herons stood motionless, knee-deep in the stream. While we ate on intertidal rocks, a big eagle outstretched its wings to land gracefully atop an old root wad lying in grass thirty yards away. High clouds gradually moved from the south, turning the sky a hazy white.

After dinner, we took a long walk through meadows and muskegs as light rain began falling. In the muskegs, which are saturated peat bogs, our boots squished through red, orange and yellow mosses, sometimes sinking as much as two feet in the wet ground. Muskegs are too acidic for spruce, cedar and western hemlock, but they support a widely spaced forest of shore pine and mountain hemlock. The shore pines were only four feet tall; their gnarled branches struck freakish poses, while the hemlocks grew forty feet tall with ashen trunks ten inches in diameter. Stringy lichens, pale green and up to eighteen inches long, hung from their branches like tangled hair.

Susan had mentioned that brown bears and wolves lived on the island, and we looked for their tracks in muddy areas near the stream. We never found any, but late that night, during a break in the rain, I heard a lone wolf howling from somewhere in the mountains behind camp.

The following morning was cold with steady rain. Thick, white clouds hovered between 500 and 1,000 feet; the dark trees behind camp sagged in the rain. Big bands of white mist rolled across the meadow, forming ghostly dogs and horses that slowly dissolved and spun upward like spirits. On the flat water, a misty shark fin fifty feet high glided past our camp, then twisted upward and eventually passed overhead with spindly fingers. The mountains we had seen in previous days were invisible.

We entered our boats by nine and within an hour began paddling beside the road to Wrangell, with pickup trucks hissing alongside us on wet pavement. Early in the afternoon we hauled our kayaks onto a stony beach near the center of town and walked to a nearby diner for coffee and phone calls.

Outside the diner's stained windows, the rain became torrential, splattering in muddy puddles. A few teenagers in leather coats, with wet black hair and glum faces, kicked a beer can down the street, abandoning it in a muddy gutter. I had been to Wrangell before and knew it had a friendly, small town atmosphere and spectacular views of the jagged peaks above the Stikine Ice Field. But that day people seemed quiet, and the gray ceiling hid everything but the lowest portion of the surrounding hillsides.

■ ■ ■

Like so many places in southeast Alaska, Wrangell was an ideal location for early inhabitants. The island provided abundant deer and berries, and all five Pacific salmon species, as well as steelhead, gathered each summer at the mouth of the nearby Stikine River. The river likely provided early people with one of the first routes to the coast from the continent's ice-free interior, and beginning about 3,000 years ago its delta became the central territory of the Stikine Tlingits.

Of all the northwest coast Native groups, the Tlingits occupied the largest territory, stretching more than 600 miles from Dixon Entrance to the Copper River. Throughout the region, dozens of subgroups, or kwans, claimed subsistence territories often centered around rivers. Kwans included the Tongass, Sumdum, Taku, Chilkat and others still represented by place names throughout southeast Alaska. Trade, marriage, potlatches and war were common between Kwans.

Vancouver passed Wrangell in September, 1793, before concluding his second season on the coast, but Russian fur traders were probably the first whites to settle the area. They built a fort there in 1834, called Redoubt Saint Dionysius, to protect their interests from increasing trappers. But six years later, with Russia losing its grasp on Alaska, they leased the fort along with the rest of southeast Alaska to the Hudson's Bay Company, who renamed it Fort Stikine. The settlement remained small until the early 1860s when the first gold rush up the Stikine River brought thousands of miners. Soon, steamers and sternwheelers regularly traveled the 160 miles between Wrangell and Telegraph Creek, British Columbia, the end of the Stikine's navigable waters.

When the U.S. purchased Alaska in 1867 for $7.2 million, or roughly two cents an acre, Fort Stikine became Fort Wrangell, a small community of Tlingits, miners, handloggers and missionaries. The community remained quiet until its second boom in the mid-1870s, when the Cassiar gold rushes attracted another wave of miners. In 1879, as the rush faded, John Muir reported that over 1,800 miners passed through in one season on their way up the Stikine, and that most of the forest surrounding town had been cleared.

In the 1880s, Wrangell built its first canneries and sawmills, which provided steady seasonal work for the small community. A decade later it experienced a third boom when Klondike miners used the Stikine to reach the Yukon before pioneering the famous route through Skagway. When the boom ended, Wrangell returned to a small community of cannery workers, fishermen and handloggers. It remained that way until longterm timber contracts with the

Forest Service provided steady employment and boosted the population. Wrangell suffered when the APC mill closed in 1996, but today roughly 2,300 people live there. Local government, manufacturing from a small mill, tourism and fishing provide the majority of jobs. Unemployment reaches 16 percent in winter, but in summer it drops to 4 percent.

■ ■ ■

We sat in the diner for two hours watching rain smack the dirt parking lot and misty clouds blow across nearby hills. As I read newspapers and magazines, Bill made several calls to his friend Judith Brink in New York. At fifty-two, Judith had long dreamed of kayaking in southeast Alaska and had made tentative plans to accompany us during the last week of our trip. But in a series of phone calls between Bill, Judith, the airlines and a charter boat in Juneau, they agreed instead to meet in nine days at a remote bay on Admiralty Island.

The rain only increased throughout the afternoon, and three o'clock looked like dusk outside the diner. With no excuses left for staying inside we finally returned to our kayaks and paddled seven miles in hard rain to a tiny island north of town. The rain turned to showers and cold mist as we landed on a sand beach only ten feet wide between steep bluffs. We climbed over a giant log half covered in moss and set our camp on lumpy ground below big trees, then cooked a quick dinner of macaroni and cheese before climbing into the tent. Once warm and dry, we looked over our maps and planned our route to the LeConte Glacier, which we hoped to reach in two days.

The rain stopped overnight, and we awoke to a cold northerly blowing tattered clouds below a dense ceiling at 2,000 feet. From our camp we needed to paddle a few miles north to an island at the edge of the Stikine Flats, a series of mudflats reaching northward twenty miles across the mouth of the Stikine River. The aptly named Dry Strait, which is almost all mud at low tide, provides the only route across the flats. It runs between Mitkof Island on the west and several islands at the mouth of the Stikine on the east and separates Sumner Strait, on the south, from Frederick Sound on the north (see Map 10.1). We hoped to cross the flats in one day, camp by the

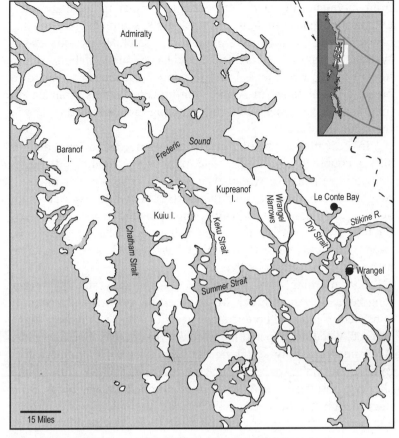

Map 10.1: Wrangell, Sumner Strait, Stikine Flats, Frederick Sound

mouth of LeConte Bay, then paddle the next day to the face of the glacier, where we would spend two days.

Crossing the flats would not be a simple task, as they are only entirely submerged during a couple hours near high tide. As the tide recedes, the mud eventually connects islands and the mainland. When the tide drops to mean sea level, which is the average of the lowest low tides, a muddy plain twenty miles from north to south and up to ten miles from east to west forms a gray plume at the mouth of the Stikine.

Alaskan mudflats usually form where big rivers deposit glacial silt in protected marine waters, and they are notoriously dangerous. The silt is finely ground particles of rock that glaciers have eroded

227

from mountainsides and light enough to float in moving water. Often called glacial flour, it settles as muddy sediment at the mouths of rivers, with the unsettled top layer often saturated like quicksand. Walking across the mud is difficult and hazardous, with boots sometimes sinking a couple feet and forming a vacuum that is hard to break. Several times in Alaska, unfortunate boaters stranded on mudflats have become stuck while walking to shore and drowned in the incoming tide.

In order to cross the flats in one day, we needed to arrive at their edge a couple hours after low tide, right as the flooding tide began inundating them. We would then need to cover twenty miles in roughly seven hours before the next ebbing tide exposed them again. Complicating the equation, an impending new moon created big tides, with lows four feet below mean sea level and highs almost twenty feet above it. Strong tidal currents would assist us in some areas but work against us in others.

That morning's low tide revealed a bouldery slot fifty yards long below the small beach we had used the previous afternoon. It consisted of jumbled boulders covered in barnacles, mussels, algae and rockweed that tapered into a rocky fissure only five feet wide. After unsuccessfully searching the steep shores for an alternative route to the water, we began carrying our boats and gear through the slippery obstacle course. Anemones drooped in wet blobs from intertidal bluffs, slimy sea cucumbers lay motionless between rocks and buried clams shot streams of water three feet into the air. The tide rose steadily as we worked, and it was two hours before we made our first paddle strokes. An hour later, we reached the edge of the mudflats, already covered by the tide. Although behind schedule, a strong northward current gave us optimism about reaching LeConte Bay that afternoon.

Paddling at the edge of the Stikine's delta, we passed expansive meadows teeming with gulls and thousands of shore birds. Each spring and fall, over 500,000 shorebirds and 120 species of migratory birds, including Canada geese, sandhill cranes and tundra swans, rest and feed at the mouth of the Stikine. Each May, the world's second-largest congregation of bald eagles, numbering between 1,500 and 2,000, uses the delta to feed on spawning eulachon. At one point, I counted eighteen eagles perched on driftwood and feeding in the intertidal across less than half a mile of meadow. Seals, sea lions, otters, bears, wolves and moose also use the delta.

The clouds lifted and broke apart as we passed a small island and gained our first views up the Stikine. It cut a broad, flat valley between steep walls rising thousands of feet, forming one of few routes inland from the Inside Passage. Big piles of black driftwood covered dozens of sandbars; short trees clumped together on low islands periodically flooded by the big river. Above either side, an endless jumble of snowy peaks defined the border between the U.S. and Canada, which was only thirty miles away. Some of the peaks reached more than 7,000 feet only a few miles inland.

The Stikine is nearly 400 miles long and begins in the Skeena Mountains only fifteen miles from the headwaters of the Skeena and Nass Rivers. It drains 20,000 square miles, more than New Hampshire and Vermont combined, and flows generally southwestward through northern British Columbia. Beginning at 6,000 feet under an unnamed glacier, it flows through high alpine, dry montane forests and sandstone cliffs before turning to fierce whitewater in the Grand Canyon of the Stikine. This chasm 1,000 feet deep and sixty miles long drops an average of forty feet per mile. In one spot, the enormous river is pinched to just six feet wide.

Twelve miles downstream from the canyon, near Telegraph Creek, the Stikine slows considerably and is navigable for 160 miles to the Inside Passage, even as it cuts through the Coast Mountains at the international border. In autumn of 2001, I spent nine days with two friends sea kayaking the river from Telegraph Creek to Wrangell, enjoying five days of sunny weather east of the Coast Mountains before suffering through several days of sideways rain and cold wind near the coast. In the arid interior, bright yellow aspen and cottonwood leaves clacked in light breezes as we hiked among lodgepole pines, juniper and sagebrush. As we entered the Coast Mountains, with thick clouds washing over their peaks from the west, the forest changed to lush cedar, hemlock and spruce with blue-white glaciers drooping from rounded peaks. On either side of the range, wolf, moose, deer, otter and black and brown bear tracks crowded each silty beach—evidence of the corridor's biological wealth.

■ ■ ■

229

After covering twelve miles in three hours we pulled our boats onto a meadowy beach on Farm Island. With a large plain nourished by silt from the Stikine, the island supported several farms beginning in the late 1800s and lasting until the 1950s. They provided produce and meat for Wrangell until regular barge service brought more reliable supplies.

With sunshine pouring through big holes in the clouds, we ate peanut butter and jelly sandwiches and trail mix while sitting at the edge of a big meadow. The tide had begun to recede, but we estimated it would not expose the mud until more than three hours later. We spent twenty minutes watching a black bear eating sedges about fifty yards away, but hurried back to our boats when we noticed the water had receded thirty yards, revealing a long, muddy beach.

From Farm Island we paddled past Dry Island, then began a series of short crossings between small islands. We covered five miles in less than two hours, but as we veered north between two islands, we began fighting a strong ebb coming from LeConte Bay and the Stikine's North Arm. Since the largest volume of water moves during the third and fourth hours of each tide cycle, we knew the ebb would only increase. In addition, the water had become murky, and expansive mudflats surrounded the islands behind us. We were still three miles from our intended camp.

"I just hit bottom!" I yelled to Bill, who was a short distance ahead of me. More than a mile from land, my hull had rubbed against mud in just six inches of water.

"I think we're still okay," he called, sinking his paddle perpendicularly into the water. "I can't feel bottom over here."

I dug my paddle into the soft mud and pushed myself into deeper water. Then I paddled quickly toward Bill, and we rafted together.

"I don't think we'll make it to LeConte," I told him, "I think the mud's going to appear pretty quickly now."

"Yeah, I agree. Want to head back toward those islands?"

"Either that or make a straight shot for the mainland. I think it's less than a mile, and the map shows a Forest Service cabin there."

"Yeah, let's try that. It'll get us closer to LeConte, too."

We turned east and paddled hard for the closest point on the mainland, leaning forward into each stroke. For ten minutes we made progress without feeling the bottom, and the trees on the mainland gained detail. But then my paddle struck mud one foot under my boat. Seconds later my bow rose from the water atop mud under just three inches of water. I used my paddle to back off the mud, then paddled to the right of it. Bill had somehow missed the shallow spot and paddled ahead of me.

"Pretty shallow," he called back. "About two feet. I think it might be deeper to the right, though." He veered to the right and then steered again for the mainland.

We could tell that channels of varying depth meandered through the mud below us, but the murky water prevented us from seeing them. Pointing our bows toward the mainland and paddling hard, we left it to luck to paddle over the channels.

"Stuck!" called Bill from 100 feet ahead.

A moment later my hull struck bottom again. Then suddenly, as though someone had pulled a plug, the water around me disappeared. It seemed to evaporate quickly, leaving my boat surrounded in gray mud with a silvery sheen. I looked toward Bill and could see the mud connected our boats. Then I looked north and my heart sank: All of the water was gone. We were on a brownish gray plain that appeared to reach the mainland and all the mountainous islands within twenty miles. I looked over my shoulder and found mud connecting the islands we had paddled between less than an hour earlier. My beached boat rocked from side to side as I looked around.

I released my spray skirt, sat up on my rear deck, then swung my legs over my beam to test the mud. It felt surprisingly firm, and I rose slowly, then took tentative steps toward Bill. My feet slid across the greasy mud, revealing an oily layer of black silt below its surface, but they sank only a few inches. I had pictured sinking to my knees.

Bill and I stood by his boat, still wearing our life jackets and spray skirts even though we were now miles from the water.

"Well, four hours until the water returns, right?" Bill asked.

"I think so. Of course, I'm also the one who said we had seven hours to cross the flats."

"Yeah, good point. Let me see that tide book."

We examined the tide book and maps, trying to estimate when the water would return.

"Do you think the boats would be alright if we walked ashore?" Bill asked.

"I suppose. We just better get back out here in time," I said. "In

10.1: Rule of Twelves for Predicting Tidal Activity

The rule of twelves is an easily remembered method of predicting the rate of flooding and ebbing tides and can help prevent situations like we encountered on the Stikine Flats. It requires determining the tidal exchange, the difference in feet between high and low tides and dividing it by twelve, then applying the following formula:

In the first hour of a tide cycle one-twelfth of the exchange will move into or out of the area. In the second hour two-twelfths (one-sixth) will move. Three-twelfths, or one-quarter, of the tidal exchange will occur in each of the third and fourth hours. In the fifth hour the rate returns to two-twelfths, and in

fact, we should be out here a little early to make sure. I mean, we could start walking back here and have the tide fill in around us before we reached the boats. Then the boats would float away…and we'd drown."

"No, I think the hypothermia would get us first."

"Damn, that would be an embarrassing way to go."

"Think we could drag them ashore?"

We removed our life jackets and spray skirts, threw them into Bill's cockpit, then pulled together on his boat's bow line. The boat moved forward slightly, but the friction of the mud and the weight of the loaded boat dug the rope deep into our hands.

"Well, shit," said Bill, "We know the water can't come back for two hours because low tide's not until after six, right? So let's just walk to shore, cook dinner in the cabin, then come back out here an hour after low tide. We'll paddle to LeConte after dinner."

We grabbed dinner food and a stove and started for shore. For much of the walk our feet sank only two or three inches into the mud but slid frequently on its oily surface. However, we crossed several areas where our feet sank four and five inches and stuck in the mud. Each time we freed one boot, it slid across the slippery surface before sinking again. The mud squished and gurgled under our feet and smelled like sewage.

After a quarter mile we reached a steep-sided trench six feet deep and twenty feet across where a channel of the Stikine flowed through the mud. The channel was roughly sixteen inches deep, and we tip-toed across it to prevent the water from flooding our boots. On the other side, we clawed up the steep mud embankment and continued toward shore.

We had to cross two more river channels and finally reached the grassy shore twenty-five minutes after leaving our boats. Our hands, arms, pants and boots were covered in mud from climbing in and out of the channels. Behind us, more than half a mile away, the boats were tiny red spots in the middle of a muddy moonscape. Beyond them, blue mountains created an uneven horizon below thickening clouds.

A Forest Service recreation cabin stood twenty yards from the high tide line, one of roughly 150 that the agency maintains throughout southeast Alaska. Like many of the cabins, it was accessible only by boat or plane and required reservations and a fee of twenty-five dollars per group, per night. With no sign of people, we let ourselves inside. Four bunks lined the walls, a wood stove sat beneath one of the stained windows and a ladder led upward to a small loft. Random cans of soup and beans filled a cabinet above a plywood counter covered in mouse turds.

After resting for half an hour, I

the sixth hour it diminishes to one-twelfth. In other words, on an incoming tide with a twelve-foot tidal exchange, the water will rise one foot in the first hour, two feet in the second, three feet in both the third and fourth hours, then two feet in the fifth, and one foot in the sixth. The figures grow more complicated with an exchange of nineteen feet, which is more common in the region.

The rule is not exact, and some local variations will make it seem inaccurate, but it is a good tool for understanding tidal movement and can help determine when tidal currents will be strongest or weakest. It can also help predict how much beach an incoming tide will cover or how much an outgoing tide will reveal.

wandered outside for a short hike. The clouds had lowered again, lopping off the mountains above 2,000 feet, and light rain was falling. I followed a well-worn bear trail south through tall sedges, with mature forest on one side and mudflats on the other. Varied thrushes whistled and red squirrels chattered from inside the forest, while Canada geese honked from grassy islands in the mud.

After a quarter mile I followed a set of big moose tracks onto the mudflat. They were deep and defined, as though the moose had ambled at a relaxed pace. But after a short distance they became widely spaced skid marks where the moose had suddenly started running. At first I assumed Bill and I had unknowingly spooked the moose while walking across the mud, but 100 feet further I noticed huge brown bear tracks intersecting the moose tracks. The bear's prints were larger than my head, with deep claw marks three inches ahead of each front paw print. It appeared the bear had not chased the moose, but that its presence on the flats had scared the moose into a gallop. Both tracks were distinct, obviously made in the few hours since the last high tide.

Before returning to the cabin I looked south into Dry Strait, where mud connected the mainland to the surrounding islands, including the mountainous Mitkof Island to the west. Boating to Wrangell at any tide looked impossible. To the north, where our maps said Frederick Sound was supposed to be, brown mud appeared to meet the blue mountains in the distance.

James Johnstone also thought Dry Strait was impassable when he viewed it in August, 1793, from a few miles north of Wrangell. After several failed attempts to cross the mud, he reported to Vancouver that the Stikine Flats and Mitkof Island were both part of the continental shore. It was a mistake that added many days of surveying in dangerous weather to Vancouver's crew and that would not be fully understood until more than a year later.

After rejoining the *Chatham* and *Discovery* in Salmon Bay following the attack in Behm Canal, Vancouver took five days to sail across Dixon Entrance and up Clarence Strait to Caamano Point. The following day, on August 22, he sailed back into Behm Canal and anchored the *Chatham* and *Discovery* in Port Stewart, only eight miles from where the Tlingit attack had occurred ten days earlier. The crew readied the cutters and launches for more surveys that afternoon; the following day Joseph Whidbey led a survey along

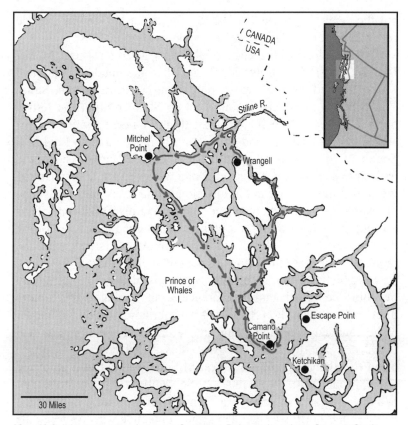

Map 10.2 Johnstone route between Caamano Point and northern Sumner Strait.

Behm Canal's west shore while Johnstone began a survey south out of Behm, then north in Clarence Strait.

In persistently poor weather, Johnstone surveyed the mainland shore along Cleveland Peninsula and east of Etolin and Wrangell Islands. On August 26, he passed the present-day Wrangell airport, entered Sumner Strait and continued north toward the Stikine River, which he mistook for another arm of the sea. On August 28, seven miles south of the river, he reached shallow water at the edge of the Stikine Flats and veered west, expecting to find a channel northward. Traveling west along the edge of the flats in six to nine feet of murky water, he made several attempts to sail north toward the Stikine and Dry Strait. As Vancouver later reported, "many unsuccessful attempts were made at this time to pass [the Stikine Flats],

235

but the depth decreased too fast to venture further, and as the tide fell, patches of dry sand became visible in all directions."

After following the edge of the flats to southeastern Mitkof Island, Johnstone falsely concluded that the muddy plain and Mitkof formed the continental shore along northern Sumner Strait. The following day, continuing west in Sumner Strait, he turned north to survey Wrangell Narrows, a thin channel separating Mitkof and Kupreanof Islands and connecting Sumner Strait to Frederick Sound. If Johnstone had persisted in Wrangell Narrows he would have drawn the continental shore along western Mitkof Island, making only a minor error, but in low clouds, the rocks and shoals nine miles into the narrows convinced him he had reached its end. Thus mistaking the narrows for a long bay, he returned to Sumner Strait, then traveled west along southern Kupreanof Island with the impression he was still following the continental shore.

At Mitchell Point, nine days and approximately 100 miles from the ships, he turned south in Clarence Strait, hoping to find a more direct route back to Port Stewart. After four days, late on September 3, he rounded Caamano Point and returned to the *Chatham* and *Discovery*. Shortly after, the two ships sailed north in Clarence Strait to Mitchell Point, then west in Sumner Strait to a protected cove. From there, beginning on September 10, Johnstone and Whidbey began two surveys in windy, wet weather. Thinking the land to their north was mainland, their objective was to survey the extent of Sumner Strait. Of course, if Johnstone had found Dry Strait or Wrangell Narrows, the continuing surveys of Sumner Strait would have been unnecessary.

Johnstone returned to Mitchell Point, then traveled west to investigate the craggy shores and numerous bays of southern Kupreanof Island. The next day, he entered present-day Keku Strait, which divides Kupreanof and Kuiu Islands and, like Wrangell Narrows and Dry Strait, links Sumner Strait to Frederick Sound. But at present-day Rocky Pass, a narrow channel clustered with shoals and rocks, Johnstone made a third miscalculation. Without reaching Frederick Sound, he concluded he had reached the navigable extent of Keku Strait and reported to Vancouver that what is now Kuiu Island was also part of the mainland. Meanwhile, Whidbey surveyed southern Kuiu Island west of Keku Strait in strong winds and heavy rain. He lost his rudder and sternpost on a rock and spent several days pinned ashore by weather before reaching big swells and violent surf where Sumner Strait meets the open ocean, a point Vancouver would soon name Cape Decision. On September 20, after ten days of risky and difficult surveys, Whidbey returned to the *Chatham* and *Discovery*.

Based on Johnstone's surveys, Vancouver believed Mitkof, Kupreanof and Kuiu Islands were all part of the mainland, which appeared to turn sharply west at present-day Dry Strait and extend roughly ninety miles to the Pacific. Based on Whidbey's observations at Cape Decision, which occurred in low clouds and showers, he believed the continental shore continued indefinitely northward, indicating further surveys would require sailing in the open ocean. "By no means satisfied with the progress...during the summer," which had covered a little more than 300 miles of latitude in four months, Vancouver decided to head south from the nasty weather. On September 22, he passed Cape Decision and sailed south to survey the west side of the Queen Charlotte Islands and the California coast south of Monterey.

When Vancouver departed the northwest coast in 1793, he believed he had reached the extent of an archipelago stretching from the Strait of Juan de Fuca to Sumner Strait. He believed the remaining surveys, from Sumner Strait to Cook Inlet, would be along solid shores and therefore much easier. He would not learn of Dry Strait until after completing his surveys more than a year later, when the captain of a trading vessel at Nootka corrected his charts. And he never learned of the Stikine, which like the Fraser and Skeena does not appear on his charts. However, also like the Fraser and Skeena, the Stikine's mudflats would have made the river unnavigable by ocean-going vessels.

■ ■ ■

Back at the cabin, we chopped wood, lit the stove and cooked an enormous pasta dinner with pesto, bottled artichokes, olives and feta cheese. It was our favorite dinner, and we cooked too much of it. After gorging ourselves, we struggled to stay awake in the warm cabin as light rain tapped hypnotically on the roof.

"We better go," said Bill, "Low tide was a half hour ago."

We quickly packed our food and cookware into a backpack,

then walked out to a cold evening of light rain. As we slogged across the mud, I grew increasingly paranoid that we had waited too long in the cabin. If the tide reached our boats before we did, the water could easily wrap around us and strand us on a shrinking island of mud as our boats floated away.

We crossed the three channels and after twenty-five minutes reached our boats wet from rain and sweat and covered in mud. The water still seemed far away, but it was hard to tell in the rain. We had intended to resume paddling three miles to the north, but neither of us wanted to wait for the tide to return. The cabin was a warm alternative, especially after nine consecutive nights of sleeping in the tent.

"Should we try to drag them again?" I asked Bill.

"Yeah, maybe gloves will help."

We dug our neoprene gloves from our deck bags and pulled together on one of the bowlines. The boat moved forward slowly, but the rope still dug into our skin, forcing us to switch hands frequently.

"What about carrying it?" Bill asked after one hundred feet.

"We can carry them one at a time in short intervals. Maybe we can get to one of those channels and paddle closer to the cabin."

We walked 150 feet across the mud to my boat and hoisted it onto our shoulders, then began carrying it toward Bill's boat. But after fifty feet of slipping in the mud, with the heavy boat's hull digging painfully into our shoulders, we had to rest.

"Alright," I said, rubbing mud from my aching shoulder. "I have an idea."

I put my life jacket on, then used spare rope from inside my cockpit to fashion a harness around my shoulders and across my chest. Fifteen feet of rope trailed behind me, which I tied to the front grab-loop of my kayak. Then I began walking forward, my life jacket preventing the rope from digging into my shoulders and chest.

"Mush!" cried Bill as I bent forward, my chest almost parallel to the mud.

I moved slowly, but with much better progress than our earlier attempts. My back and shoulder muscles strained under the weight, but as I crossed shallow depressions covered in half an inch of water, the boat glided forward, providing a break from the hard work. A minute later I passed Bill's boat.

238

Steady rain struck the smooth mud, smacking it loudly and creating small craters as we dragged our boats forward. Before long the tide caught up with us, covering the mud in watery fingers only an inch deep. They stretched slowly ahead; soon we were sloshing through two and three inches of water. Although the water lifted the boats, relieving us of their weight, it was too shallow for us to paddle and made the mud more slippery. As we continued toward the cabin we slid frequently, almost falling.

We outpaced the tide after 100 yards, and the full weight returned to our backs and shoulders. Leaning forward, we continued toward the cabin and soon reached the first channel of the Stikine. The tide had filled it to three feet, leaving slick walls of mud too steep for us to use for climbing into our boats. Already wet and muddy, we lowered the kayaks into the water, removed our boots and socks, then slid into the channel while holding onto our bow lines.

The boats slowly drifted upstream with the tide as we cautiously waded across the channel. It was a waist-deep combination of 45°F sea water and recent snowmelt from the Stikine, which quickly made our feet ache with cold. Once across, we awkwardly climbed a muddy bluff with our knees and elbows, then hauled the boats back onto the mudflat. With the next channel only fifty feet away, we left our boots in the boats and pulled the soaked ropes back over our life jackets. As we continued forward, cold mud squeezed between our toes, which we curled downward for traction. At the next channel, also three feet deep, we again waded through cold water.

Close to ninety minutes after leaving, we climbed barefoot into the grass outside our cabin. We were soaked, with mud all over our hands, arms, faces and rain bibs. Behind us, the tide had covered the mud to within a quarter mile. We carried the muddy kayaks onto the porch of the cabin, changed into dry fleece, then chopped firewood. Later, we fell asleep with our muddy clothes hanging above the stove.

It was mid-May, and we were close to 57° N latitude. Although sunset was a little after nine and sunrise around four-thirty, it stayed light from about three in the morning until eleven at night. The four hours in between were dark in cloudy weather, but seemed lit by a full moon in clear weather, with snowy mountains glowing and forested hills visible as black silhouettes. The sky was darkest to the south, where only a few stars were bright enough to shine, but in the north it was always light blue and green. We had not seen stars to the north since early April. Each morning, the songbirds in the forest woke us a few minutes earlier.

I awoke at three-fifteen to a cacophony of robins, thrushes, warblers and dozens of other songbirds. Pale light filled the cabin. Through the window I could see a large area of clear sky changing from purple to light blue. I rose quietly from my bunk, stepped outside and looked north into Frederick Sound. The water was gray and flat as glass under partly cloudy skies. On its mainland side, about ten miles away, a long series of cliffs rose between 1,000 and 2,000 feet straight out of the water. They were dark blue in the predawn light, with a thin band of white mist stretching half a mile along their bottom. Beyond the cliffs, a jumble of snowy mountains, some up to 6,000 feet, formed the horizon.

I stood near the water for a few minutes, watching the light strengthen and the colors change. The pale blue in the northern sky gradually spread southward; big clouds high above the mountains turned from gray and brown to purple, blue and white. The snowy peaks on the horizon turned creamy, and slowly a big cornice and the wrinkled surface of a snow-covered glacier gained detail.

The high-pitched chattering of songbirds in the forest grew louder and more diverse. Soon a group of crows joined with raspy caws as gulls near the edge of the grass whined loudly. A loon gave a mournful call from somewhere on the water.

Bill stepped onto the porch and stretched.

"What are you doing up?" I asked.

"Who can sleep with all the racket," he joked, pointing his thumb toward the songbirds in the woods and walking toward the water.

"Those boats?" he asked, frowning toward LeConte Bay.

It looked like four white boats were at the mouth of the bay, about six miles away. Each had a hint of blue on the bottom but didn't seem to be moving.

"I think they're icebergs," I said. "They must be. They're probably grounded on shallows at the mouth of the bay."

"Let's go see them," he said after a moment. "The tide's going out, but we probably have about two hours before it exposes the mud, right?"

"You want to leave now?"

"Yeah. We could probably reach the glacier by early afternoon, set up camp, and relax for a couple days."

"Alright, but if we go, we better go now, before the tide goes out much further."

We pulled our dried clothes from hooks above the stove and forty-five minutes later had our boats ready at the edge of the muddy embankment in front of the cabin. With the first rays of sun turning the snowy peaks to the north soft pink and searing a hint of orange into the distant cliffs, we ate a quick breakfast, then slid our boats into glassy water and began paddling for LeConte.

We paddled north for half a mile as progressively lower mountains turned pink in the rising sun. The cliffs shed their blue veil and turned orange, then blood red. The flat water turned slowly from gray to slate blue and scoters, harlequins and gulls flew low overhead. As Bill continued paddling, I paused to take pictures of his kayak against the dawn's slowly changing colors. But after a few minutes he called back to me.

"Better hurry," he yelled, "the water's only two feet deep here."

I put my camera away and paddled quickly toward Bill, but after fifty yards my bow rose out of the water and stopped in mud. The water was deeper only twenty feet ahead, so I quickly got out of my boat and dragged it through shallow water. As I hopped back inside and began paddling, I looked up to see Bill get out of his boat. The mud ahead blended perfectly with the flat water and he appeared to walk on the surface of the sea, pulling his boat behind him. After fifty feet he climbed back inside and resumed paddling.

Bill paddled ahead, but I got stuck a second time. This time the water was deeper only a few feet away, so I quickly got out of my boat and dragged it to the left, then got back in and started paddling hard. Behind me, mud extended more than half a mile to the cabin. We were at the edge of the ebbing tide, racing it across the flats.

I got stuck and had to drag my boat one more time, but after fifteen minutes we rafted together in deep water with the mud flats behind us and LeConte ahead of us. Four miles away, several blue-white icebergs floated in Frederick Sound. They were my first icebergs in nearly three years and the first of Bill's life.

CHAPTER ELEVEN

The Land that Ice Built— Dodging Icebergs in LeConte Bay

The last great ice age of the Pleistocene reached its maximum extent 20,000 years ago, when continental ice sheets covered much of Canada and the northern United States. By 12,000 years ago the ice sheets had melted, but considerable glaciation still covered the Sierras, Cascades, Rockies and Coast Mountains. It was not until roughly 10,000 years ago that the channels of the Inside Passage became largely free of ice, although large ice fields remained in the high elevations of the Coast Mountains. About 7,000 years ago temperate rain forest occupied the region below an average of 2,000 feet.

Since the end of the Pleistocene, periodic climatic cooling trends have initiated glacial advances in the Inside Passage, the most recent called the Little Ice Age, which occurred between roughly 3,000 years ago and the year 1750. The advances occurred when heavy snows in the Coast Mountains led to increased glaciation in the ice fields. As the ice fields overflowed, many valley glaciers advanced to tidewater and already existing tidewater glaciers surged forward in their fiords. However, the increased glaciation reached only a fraction of Pleistocene levels; most glaciers in the Inside Passage have been steadily receding for about 300 years.

Like the majority of glaciers in southeast Alaska, the LeConte has surged and retreated several times since the end of the Pleistocene. During each advance, it bulldozed ahead an enormous pile of underwater debris consisting of everything from silt to giant boulders. During each retreat it left the huge pile, called a terminal moraine, at the point of its farthest advance. By studying these moraines scientists can read local glacial history, but parts of the story remain unknown since some glacial advances obliterated earlier terminal moraines.

At some point at least 1,500 years ago, the LeConte filled all of LeConte Bay and calved icebergs directly into Frederick Sound, which is twelve miles from the glacier's current location. When it retreated, it left a moraine that is visible today as a low spit and a small island linked by a shallow bar across the mouth of the bay. The bar accelerates tidal currents and at low tide strands dozens of icebergs.

■ ■ ■

Bill and I arrived at the mouth of LeConte Bay shortly before six on the morning of our narrow escape from the Stikine Flats. Dozens of blue-white icebergs ranging in size from VW Beetles to semi-trucks crowded the mouth of the bay, stranded by the ebbing tide. The receding water had exposed parts of the bar and left some bergs completely out of the water, providing a rare view of their entire mass. Their tops were level platforms a foot or two thick that overhung jagged bases twenty feet tall. The thin tops steadily dripped melt water and represented the small percentage of each berg's mass that was visible when floating. They were broader than their bases because ice melts fastest under water.

Beyond the stranded bergs, LeConte Bay narrowed into an arm one mile wide between cliffs several thousand feet tall. Thick ice choked its dark gray water, which curved between mountains and disappeared. Twelve miles away the bay ended at the face of the LeConte Glacier, which we hoped to see by early afternoon.

Six A.M. was broad daylight, but thickening clouds had concealed earlier patches of blue sky and lowered to kiss the tops of the mountains. A cool breeze urged us forward as we searched the line of bergs for an opening into the bay. When we found it, we battled a strong ebb across the bar, with small icebergs racing past us toward Frederick Sound. With low tide only an hour away, we hoped the impending flood would boost us toward the glacier.

Once across the bar, we paddled through scattered icebergs for an hour, then encountered a wall of thick ice stretching the width of the fiord. Many locomotive- and cottage-sized bergs, all blue and white, stood high above a mass of smaller, crushed ice packed tightly together. Knowing icebergs can roll, split or collapse without warning, we approached the ice near the smallest bergs and plotted a route that avoided the largest ones.

We slowly nosed our bows into chunks of ice varying in size between ice cubes and beach balls, then forced our paddles between them to bring the full length of our kayaks into the ice. We separated the ice by rocking our bows from side to side with our hips. The smallest chunks crackled against each other, but from softball-size and up, they thudded percussively against our bows as though we had struck rocks. Their jagged edges made a ripping sound against our plastic boats.

We aimed diagonally across the fiord, trying to stay among small bergs, but quickly realized that the breeze and currents were shifting the ice. Soon we encountered larger bergs—ottomans, love seats, sleeper sofas—amid the crushed ice, which was so thick we had to clear it from our way just to get our paddles into the water. Twice we arrived at dead-ends where we had to move bergs larger than our kayaks by firmly planting our paddles into their fissures and leaning toward them. They bobbed heavily as they slowly moved from our path.

The bergs varied in size and shape but were mostly nondescript chunks with jagged edges. Their outer layers were often white, where exposure to air had loosened their crystals, but their interiors and recently broken edges revealed the blue of densely compacted glacial ice. Without direct sunlight to create bright reflections, they glowed against the gray water, varying from pale and almost turquoise to a dark purple bordering on black. Their surfaces were cold, smooth and wet; some had hundreds of tiny fractures, like shattered windshields. While resting in the mass of ice with no open water in sight, we broke off bits of bergs that tasted slightly of salt. They were the compacted snowflakes from eighty or more winters earlier.

As we slowly advanced, our paddles scraped powerlessly against dense ice, while the bergs thudded and ground against each other. With the temperature around fifty they were constantly melting, releasing pockets of pressurized air created decades earlier when layers of snow condensed into ice. The pockets snapped, crackled and popped around us, like a giant bowl of cereal. The eerie sounds, dark cliffs and thick clouds made the fiord seem lifeless and frozen.

After forty minutes of slow progress we reached gaps of open water and paddled ashore at a small talus. We lugged our bows onto cobbles, stripped from our PFDs and skirts, then found some flat boulders where we could snack. Afterward, I reclined and closed my eyes as Bill investigated a nearby stream, but minutes later I heard a sharp crack, then the unmistakable knocking of huge boulders.

"Avalanche!" Bill called, pointing across the fiord and hurrying toward me.

The rumble was loud, even from a mile away, as a thick teardrop of snow unfolded quickly through a narrow notch in the fiord wall. The fracture had occurred out of sight but released an enormous load that dropped toward the sea from 2,000 feet. The wet snow quickly buried willows, alders and a cascading stream but did not create a big powder cloud. As I sat up and focused I saw enormous chunks of snow, ice and rock falling over cliffs and shattering onto ledges at the head of the slide. In thirty seconds the leading snout fell more than a thousand feet, followed by an increasingly brown slurry of snow, rock and dirt. Then it slowed significantly and advanced in jumps and starts to 500 feet above the sea. For the following five minutes a seemingly endless stream of snow continued flowing above the snout, showering from cliffs and exploding against ledges, gushing like water in some spots and creeping like cement in others. Ten minutes later, with most of the action over, occasional rocks continued knocking against the mountain.

"I don't see many avalanches in New York City," said Bill, still looking up at the mountain.

A steady headwind developed as we continued toward the glacier, still nine miles away. It robbed the benefit of the incoming tide and created waves to one foot that splashed against our bows and the surrounding icebergs. Thick, white clouds crept over mountaintops like ghostly fingers, while blowing mist mixed with rocky crags in steep valleys as the ceiling dropped to between 1,000 and 2,000 feet. Intermittent ice forced us to change course frequently, and periodic showers of hard rain blew from the direction of the glacier.

LeConte Bay is a crooked finger extending northeastward into the mainland. Each paddle stroke brought us deeper into the heart of

245

the Coast Mountains. Whereas in Canada the higher peaks that we saw were usually well inland, now the fiord walls reached 3,000 feet a mile from shore and rose quickly to more than 4,000 feet. Several peaks near the British Columbia border, only fifteen miles away, were above 7,000 feet. With cliffs too steep for much mature forest, only small clusters of ragged spruce filled gullies or clung to moderate inclines, which were rare. More commonly, narrow patches of willow and alder grew on ledges or in steep ravines where they suffered the ravages of frequent avalanches. Steep streams with high waterfalls coursed almost straight lines down the dark walls.

We made slow progress against the wind and passed increasingly large icebergs, with one giant angling to a point five stories high above a base 200 feet across. It was dark blue and parked against a brown cliff with many smaller bergs scattered around it. In the coming weeks it would calve large bergs that would splash into the water and send waves rolling across the fiord. As the ice under water melted, offsetting its balance, it would roll or send chunks shooting suddenly to the surface. Knowing such "shooters" could sink a large boat and easily prove fatal to kayakers, we gave the berg wide berth.

At midmorning we passed Thunder Point and encountered a cold breeze blowing from the surface of the glacier, still seven miles away. The point was named decades earlier, when the LeConte was still close enough that its thunderous calvings seemed to shake the ground. In the mid-1990s carbon dating of the sea bed near Thunder Point revealed a terminal moraine from 200 years ago, at the end of the Little Ice Age. Continuing toward the glacier the surrounding land would increasingly show the effects of recent glaciation, including young soil and loose rock, so that paddling forward was like traveling back toward the Pleistocene. Our time travel would climax at the face of the glacier, where recently uncovered land would resemble how the Inside Passage looked 10,000 years ago as receding glaciers gave birth to fiords.

A mile past Thunder Point we reached another line of thick ice extending the width of the fiord. Sharp points and precarious ledges jutted haphazardly into the air, like wrecked train cars, with many more large bergs than we had encountered earlier. As we looked for a safe spot to enter the ice, a thick squall swallowed the cliffs ahead and turned the air over the ice gray. With mist blowing into our faces we entered the pack near the smallest bergs and zigzagged north-eastward trying to avoid the bigger ones. The ice ground and crack-led around us as we forced our paddles between bergs, moving forward more by prying and rocking than by paddling. Within a few minutes we pulled our hoods over our heads as the mist turned to steady rain.

Some of the surrounding bergs were dark blue blocks three sto-ries high with deep fractures that looked ready to collapse at any moment. Others supported large chunks of ice or carried silt, gravel and boulders that would soon become part of the ocean floor. One had several azure tubes up to ten feet in diameter reaching deep into its center. They were former moulins, icy pipes that carry surface melt water into the glacier's complex plumbing. On a glacier's sur-face, these cylindrical holes can reach dozens or even hundreds of vertical feet to rivers raging inside or below the glacier.

After thirty minutes, with gusty winds blowing chilly rain into our faces, we reached an opening fifty yards across. Fast raindrops shattered the water's complexion. And enormous bergs—houses and tire shops—reached upward in every direction. Although small bergs filled the gaps, we couldn't see a path wide enough to keep us safely distant from the big bergs. A quarter mile to our south, verti-cal cliffs rose from the water, leaving nowhere in sight flat enough to land.

Just as I began thinking we might be in danger, we heard a sharp report and a rush of water behind us. I looked back quickly and saw an SUV-sized chunk of ice bobbing next to a large berg less than a quarter mile away. Waves radiated from the fallen block of ice, knocking smaller bergs against each other. The larger berg rocked back and forth heavily and then began to roll, with one of its sides rising ten, then twenty feet as the other side sank slowly. Salt water rushed from holes in its side and splashed onto nearby bergs. Within thirty seconds the berg rolled onto its side, changing shape com-pletely and revealing a royal blue that had been under water moments earlier.

I tried to relax, knowing that most of the surrounding ice was stable, but with no clearings in sight and the wind gusting to twen-ty knots I felt trapped and vulnerable. The sound of moving ice sur-rounded us. I suddenly realized our clearing was shrinking, with ice-bergs approaching us like city buses. We made a quick decision to paddle north toward the other shore, which was close to a mile away but appeared horizontal enough for us to land. Within minutes our clearing had decreased to ten yards.

We paddled into the smallest bergs and tried to angle north toward shore, but the moving ice gathered against our boats and carried us back toward Thunder Point. The quick maneuvers necessary to avoid big bergs were impossible in the tight ice, and I was uncomfortably close to jagged bergs many times my size. As they creaked and groaned I tried not to think of the consequences of their rolling or splitting. Falling ice was only one threat; a capsize in the freezing water would cause almost immediate hypothermia. Already, the cold water radiated through the hull of my boat and chilled my feet and calves.

"There's another opening up here," Bill shouted to me. He was thirty feet away and making better progress. "Well," he called a minute later, "I guess it's closing pretty fast."

Only as a matter of chance, the shifting bergs opened enough that I could make progress through an area of crushed ice. I dug my paddle hurriedly between bergs and moved as fast as I could toward Bill, my bow slamming against ice boulders. In a few minutes I was paddling in the clearing behind his boat, headed for the north shore.

The wind and rain continued strong, dropping the wind chill into the high thirties, as we squinted under our hoods navigating through the ice. Eventually we approached a tall berg 100 feet long that blocked our view of the other shore. We tried to hurry past its east side, leaving a berth of fifty yards, but became mired in thick ice moving toward it. Then a big block that had appeared safely distant a moment earlier approached us quickly from the east, with smaller bergs rising along its leading edge like surf against a ship's bow. It would soon crush us against the big berg to our left.

"Can we back up?" Bill asked, still directly ahead of me.

I looked back and saw our path filled with crushed ice.

"Yeah, we can. It's pretty thick, but they're mostly small bergs right now."

We back-paddled twenty feet, knocking ice away with our sterns, then found a path of small bergs leading diagonally to our right between the two big bergs. Frantically moving ice with our paddles, we plowed through the path and slipped between the two big bergs with less than 100 feet separating them.

We struggled nervously through another half mile of thick ice, our wet hair matted to our foreheads and our hands aching in the cold wind. After fifteen minutes we forced our boats through a small bay choked with crushed ice and went ashore at a marshy beach. It was only two in the afternoon but already nine hours since we had made our first paddle strokes. During that time we had narrowly escaped the Stikine Flats, battled strong headwinds, fought through two areas of dense ice and almost got crushed between icebergs the size of small houses. Agreeing that was enough for one day we set up camp and napped.

■ ■ ■

Glaciers are slow-moving rivers of ice that behave much the same as flowing water, with eddies, falls, pools and varying currents. In southeast Alaska their headwaters are the immense ice fields of the Coast Mountains, where more than 100 feet of snow falls annually at about 5,000 feet and higher. Not much snow melts in the short, cool summers at that elevation, so each winter's accumulation compacts the previous winter's snow. After as little as five years, the pressure of continued, wet snow squeezes air from between snow crystals and condenses them into solid glacial ice, which is almost ten times denser than newly fallen snow. Because of the density, glacial ice absorbs light at the red end of the color spectrum, making it appear blue to the human eye. Glacial ice appears white when melting or the presence of air bubbles reflects sunlight.

Some ice fields in southeast Alaska are more than 4,000 feet deep. Each year's heavy snow adds pressure to them that squeezes glacial ice through mountain gaps, where it flows into pre-existing valleys as glaciers. The ice flows downhill until it reaches an elevation where melting exceeds supply from the ice field. That elevation depends largely upon the amount of ice field a glacier drains, just like a river's volume depends upon the extent of its headwaters.

The smallest glaciers, called alpine glaciers, are small tongues confined to areas above treeline, while the larger valley glaciers flow past treeline, often terminating with tumultuous rivers or big lakes. Tidewater glaciers are typically the largest and flow from high in the mountains to sea level, like the LeConte. Regardless of size, almost all glaciers constantly move forward. Acting like conveyor belts, they carry new ice from the ice field to the glacier's terminus, where it melts or breaks away. They also transport rocky debris from higher to lower elevations, slowly changing the faces of their mountains.

Glaciers advance, or grow longer, when ice supplied from the mountains exceeds melting at the terminus, which can result from increased precipitation in the ice field or cooler temperatures near the terminus. They recede, or shrink, when melting at the terminus exceeds the flow of ice from the mountains, which can result from decreased precipitation or warmer temperatures. In either case, the glacier continues flowing forward, grinding away at its mountain, and the ice at its terminus continues melting and calving.

Most glaciers flow less than a few feet per day but advance or recede between fifty and one hundred feet per year. A typical example is the Mendenhall Glacier, a valley glacier in Juneau with an average daily flow of a couple feet that has receded about a mile since 1962. However, some glaciers surge or retreat catastrophically for short periods, moving at many times their averages. For example, the 300-foot-tall face of Black Rapids Glacier in interior Alaska surged forward as much as 250 feet per day for a few months in 1936, threatening to dam a nearby river and destroy a road before its flow returned to normal. In contrast, the LeConte provided an example of catastrophic recession in the mid-1990s.

The LeConte receded 2.5 miles between 1887 and 1962, a steady rate comparable to other glaciers in southeast Alaska outside of Glacier Bay National Park. From 1962 to the early nineties it remained generally stable, but in late 1994 it began a rapid recession, losing nearly a mile in one year. It stabilized again for more than a year, with normal oscillations of up to a quarter mile occurring seasonally, then lost another almost half mile by the fall of 1998. Today it is relatively stable, with seasonal variations of nearly 500 feet.

Scientists are still studying the cause of the rapid retreat, but most agree that during the normal course of recession the glacier's face reached a deep trough in LeConte Bay that partially floated the glacier. The resulting instability led to increased calving until the glacier reached more shallow water. It is possible that the glacier is now close to pulling up onto land, revealing the end of LeConte Bay and becoming a valley glacier.

Although the LeConte now recedes at a normal rate, it still produces an enormous amount of icebergs. While visiting the area in the summer of 2001, I spent time with a charter boat operator who had dropped five kayakers in LeConte for a weeklong trip the previous summer. Like Bill and I, they encountered thick ice with many fast-moving bergs and eventually became pinned between large bergs. With ice grinding and cracking around them, they evacuated their boats and climbed onto the floating ice. They hauled their boats from the water as best they could and scrambled on slick, unstable ice as the grinding bergs threatened to roll them into icy water. They spent twenty minutes in that terrifying situation before a change in wind direction created an escape route.

"They thought they were done for," the charter boat captain told me.

■ ■ ■

We awoke shortly before seven to a leaden ceiling at 3,500 feet. Ice still choked our bay, but the steady stream of bergs flowing past appeared lighter than the previous day. In the distance, the LeConte thundered deeply every minute or two as columns of ice up to twenty stories tall collapsed into the sea. We agreed to leave camp set up and make another attempt to reach the glacier, which was only four miles away. After breakfast we packed lunches and pushed our boats into the water, hoping to reach the glacier well before midday. If the ice proved too thick, we would look for a place to hike or simply return to camp to relax.

We pushed through thick ice in our bay, then turned left into moderate ice in the main arm. Rounded domes of largely bare rock rose abruptly from either side of the fiord and reached 3,500 feet, where the heavy sky dragged across their summits. Bright snow covered their top 500 feet, contrasting their broad foundations of dark rock. Dirt-stained snow from a winter's worth of avalanches filled alpine basins and long gullies that ran to sea level; ragged spruce forests clung to the less-severe aspects and filled narrow valleys between the mountains. The bergs glowed blue against the dark cliffs, and the flat water between them provided vivid reflections of ice, snow and mountains.

Ahead, the mountains around the glacier slowly pulled apart as we paddled forward, revealing the glacier's powder blue horizon at

1,000 feet below hulking mountains covered in deep snow. Moraine on the glacier's surface formed thick, black lines, like tire tracks running up the glacier, that curved around the mountains and illustrated the fluid movement of the ice. Where the ice flowed down a steep slope, deep crevasses shone royal blue under the thick clouds. Although we still could not see the face, which was 200 feet tall, the glacier's thunder grew louder and more frequent, with some calvings lasting half a minute and echoing against the mountains.

We snaked through moderately thick ice and covered one mile in a little less than thirty minutes, then entered an increasingly dense pack. Steering close to sheer cliffs on the north shore, we covered another quarter mile through small eddies of open water before thick ice forced us back toward the middle of the channel. We advanced slowly for another ten minutes but eventually got stuck between a couple piano-sized bergs drifting steadily toward a blue monolith fifteen feet high. The ice crackled around us as a lone gull flew overhead, virtually the only sign of life we'd seen since entering the area more than a day earlier.

Through prying and rocking we freed ourselves from the jam, then forced our way through thick ice toward the north shore where a big stream emptied over a bouldery talus. Above it, a carpet of spruce filled the lower quarter of a thin valley between bare walls 2,000 feet high. About four miles beyond, a steep glacier plunged 700 feet down the side of a gray mountain outlined by a big patch of blue sky.

The ice was thick until 100 feet from the stream, where the rushing water held the bergs at bay. We left our boats in the water with their bowlines tied to boulders, then climbed thirty feet up the talus and looked toward the glacier. A jumble of broken ice covered the water for as far as we could see, with no apparent routes to the glacier. It could take hours to get through the ice, and getting back to camp would be difficult and dangerous.

"I think it'd be easier to reach the glacier beyond these woods than the LeConte," Bill said.

"Yeah, I don't want to mess with that ice anymore. Let's try a hike."

We carried our boats above the high tide line, evident as a line of bleached rocks, then carried them thirty feet higher, knowing big waves are possible near tidewater glaciers. As I tied the boats to a sturdy spruce Bill packed lunch, maps and a first aid kit into a back-pack. Thick clouds still covered most of the sky, but broken clouds in the direction of our hike revealed patches of blue.

With water gushing loudly around us, we hopped between boulders and splashed through shallow pools to the top of the talus, then struggled through a nest of wiry alders overhanging the stream. Once inside the dim forest, we continued walking in the stream, assuming the woods on either side were thickly vegetated. We knew following the water would eventually bring us to the glacier.

Big boulders, some of them twenty feet high with moss and small trees growing from their tops, divided the stream into several channels that alternated between gushing torrents and shallow riffles. Two hundred years earlier, our destination glacier had deposited the boulders as it receded from LeConte Bay. In earlier centuries, it had filled the valley and joined the LeConte Glacier, delivering ice and rock as far as the moraine at the edge of Frederick Sound. Today, its terminus is three miles up-valley, shrinking steadily into an alpine glacier.

After a quarter mile, steep valley walls pinched the stream into a narrow notch filled with turbulent water, forcing us to seek higher ground. From beside the noisy water Bill threw our backpack twenty feet up the hillside, then clambered over mossy boulders and a steep bluff to the forest edge. From firm ground fifteen feet above me, he reached down for the rifle, then I began my ascent using alder branches and clumps of moss for handholds. But ten feet above the stream one of my flimsy handholds failed and I slipped backward over the rocks, breaking my fall with my elbow, shoulder and face before sliding calf-deep into rushing water. As I hurried from the stream, cold water filled my boots and the taste of blood filled my mouth.

My arms were scraped and muddy, and I could feel a large bump forming on my forehead. Sitting by the stream I poured water from my boots, which would remain uncomfortably wet for days, and dabbed a sleeve at my bloody lip. After a minute, I made a slower but more successful ascent into the forest. From there, we climbed higher over mossy boulders and downed spruces to comparatively level ground where we could take a break.

The forest was a parklike stand of even-aged spruce on a lumpy surface of moss-covered boulders. The trees were all about fourteen inches in diameter and sixty feet tall and grew evenly spaced, roughly ten feet apart. Typical of even-aged stands, they formed a thick canopy that blocked most sunlight. As a result, few live branches grew in the dim light below twenty feet; only short, dead stubs covered in thick moss extended from the lower trunks. The dim light also prevented thick understory, leaving only a carpet of soft moss and low herbs that uniformly covered the boulders, as though manicured. It was up to two feet thick and extended as far as we could see, like a shag carpet experiment from the 1970s gone wild.

"This makes me homesick for my Chia Pet," said Bill, patting the soft forest floor. "I sure hope my roommate's remembering to feed it."

As a glacier recedes, it exposes smoothly sculpted bedrock that has not seen sunlight in centuries and is devoid of vegetation. In the first years following the ice's retreat, rain and moving snow bring silt and debris together in small pockets where the first lichens and mosses eventually form the foundation for future soil. Seeds collect in these small pockets, perhaps brought there by wind or birds, and pioneer plants such as fireweed and lupine soon colonize the primitive soil. Lupine is particularly important because it excretes nitrogen as a waste product of photosynthesis, which along with dead material from the plants enriches the soil. After twenty-five years enough soil exists to support shrub willows and alders, which create dense thickets that shade out lupine and fireweed. These plants continue to colonize barren areas while the willows and alders add dead leaves and branches to further build the soil. Like lupine, alders fix nitrogen into the new soil, and after a couple decades of thickening brush, the first spruce and cottonwood seedlings take hold. The resulting forest is thick as jungle but provides new habitat for mountain goats, porcupines, squirrels, voles and many songbirds, enriching its diversity and attracting eagles and even bears.

Roughly fifty years after deglaciation the first spruce and cottonwoods reach above the thicket of willow and alder, beginning a transition to coniferous forest that will take decades to complete. As the spruce increase, their thickening canopy shades out the deciduous trees and after about 200 years forms an even-aged stand with little understory. In our stand by LeConte we found many rotting alder stumps buried in the thick moss that were remnants of the deciduous forest that had preceded the spruces.

As the spruces grow bigger in coming decades, some will topple from wind or disease, creating holes in the canopy that will permit sunlight to hit the forest floor. A diverse understory will quickly crowd the opening, with berries, devil's club and small trees all competing for light. Hemlock seedlings will be among the competition, representing the next transition in the forest. Given enough soil and sunlight they will reach the canopy after about 150 to 200 years. At that point, 350 to 400 years after the glacier's recession, the forest will be an uneven-aged mix of spruce and hemlock with a mosaic of understory growth and much dead and downed wood crisscrossing its floor. This is the slow process that created the vast old-growth forests of the Inside Passage after the Pleistocene ice retreated. If we were to make it to the glacier at the head of our valley, we would enter earlier stages of forest succession in more recently deglaciated areas.

■ ■ ■

We made easy progress through the forest, eventually finding a faint trail with deer and goat prints. Infrequently, we caught glimpses through the thick forest of the surrounding mountains and the glacier ahead. The only sounds were the rushing stream 100 feet below and our muffled steps on the mossy floor.

The slope gradually grew steeper; after thirty minutes we reached the first of several slide paths choked with alders. For a quarter mile, avalanches had either swept away the spruce forest or never given it a chance to develop. We struggled through the tangled alders, which angled down-slope from the weight of recently melted snow and still had dirt and moss wedged between their branches from avalanches. The first two thickets required battling through knotted brush, but the third forced us to our hands and knees, where we climbed through alders and willows so thick we often were a few feet from the ground. The only relief came when we reached a patch of granular snow, similar to big clumps of sugar, that still held the vegetation to the ground. Dirt and branches littered the snow, which had small holes melted through that revealed a small stream trickling below.

The spruce forests between slide paths grew shorter, and after the third path we found more alder growing amid the spruce, repre-

11.1: Advantages of Topos / Nautical Charts

Sea kayaking is a daily combination of travel by land and sea, making both nautical charts and topographic maps essential pieces of safety equipment for any kayak expedition. Each has advantages that complement the other.

Nautical charts are maps for mariners provided by NOAA and Canada's Hydographic Service, Department of Fisheries and Oceans. Except for exact renditions of the coastline and major rivers, peaks and other features useful to marine navigation, they reveal little about the shape of the land. However, they provide details about the water not given by topographic maps, including the location of navigational aids, kelp beds and eddies and information about current speed and direction. Whereas some topographic maps indicate shoals and rocks near shore, nautical

senting a slightly earlier stage of forest succession that would make progress more difficult. One hundred feet below, the stream crashed through a narrow bedrock gorge bridged by a downed tree. We backtracked a short distance to a mossy area between spruces and had lunch above a sheer-walled gorge that pinched the stream into a raging current. Speeding water fanned over flat boulders and crashed against a rock wall with powerful hydraulics. Bright green moss glistened through mist above the water. Below the gorge, a water ouzel did deep knee bends on a wet rock surrounded by thundering water.

After lunch we climbed a couple hundred feet above the stream, trying to find a good view. We climbed over jumbled boulders and wound our way around steep benches with sheer walls until we finally reached a rock platform where we could see the surrounding mountains through the tops of spruce trees. A big wall on the other side of the valley hid the LeConte, but above it jagged fingers of impossibly steep rock pierced the clouds. Many were too steep for snow, but deep snow and ice surrounded their bases. Looking up our valley, jagged ridges with snowy couloirs stood above a glacier clinging to a steep mountainside. Although fractured, it was the best view we could find from the thick forest.

We made one more attempt to

reach the glacier, but after crossing another slide path encountered thick alders that slowed our progress to a crawl. Realizing it could take hours to travel the remaining two miles, we backtracked through two slide paths, then climbed to a ledge for another fractured view. Less than an hour later we returned to our boats and paddled back to camp through moderately thick ice.

We arrived back at camp at three in the afternoon. Bill spent the next hour fixing his rudder cable, which was frayed and close to splitting, and I reorganized our remaining food and burned trash in the intertidal. Afterward, we sautéed garlic and onions and fried quesadillas beside our small bay as a rain shower obscured the other side of the fiord. To the south, big mountains close to 6,000 feet glowed through a hole in the clouds above barren cliffs rising abruptly from the water. To the west a vibrant rainbow arched over a big, blue berg. To the east, the LeConte Glacier was a confederate blue triangle between intersecting ridges. An endless parade of oddly shaped icebergs drifted quickly past our camp like bumper-to-bumper traffic, some smaller ones detouring into the packed ice of our bay.

The tide receded quickly as we ate, stranding a dozen bergs on our beach. They had appeared small when we paddled through them a few hours earlier, but when the water receded charts show both their exact location and the tide level where they become hazardous. In addition, they display continuous depth readings, which kayakers can use to predict current anomalies and rough surf. Nautical charts are also updated more frequently than topographic maps.

While topographic maps do not offer nearly as much about the ocean, they provide far greater information about the land. With detailed contour lines they reveal the shape and size of small knolls as well as large peaks, and depict manmade objects like roads, cabins and towns as well as streams, glaciers, muskegs and variations in treeline. They show whether a shoreline consists of rock, sand, mud or cliffs, which helps kayakers determine good places for camping and drinking water. They are helpful for planning hikes inland, but the contour lines are also useful while on the water, showing kayakers steep hills that may provide protection from wind or deep valleys which can funnel strong winds onto the water.

some of them stood fifteen feet tall. Rain showers returned after dinner, and we retreated to the tent by nine to organize our maps and plot our course for the next few days. We would travel north in Frederick Sound to Petersburg, where our next food delivery awaited us, then continue fifty miles to Admiralty Island to meet Bill's friend Judith.

I soon fell asleep but awoke in the middle of the night to a loud crack and a rush of water as an iceberg somewhere nearby calved. Before I could fall back to sleep I realized water was lapping very near our tent. Shining my headlamp into a twilit night I looked straight across the surface of the water at scores of icebergs floating quietly as little as fifteen feet away. Patting the grass outside I felt cold water only one foot from the door. Although our tent was above the sedges, which almost always meant we were safe from the tide, the new moon had created the highest tides of the month.

Thirty minutes later, at high tide, water lapped against the door and crept twelve inches below our tent. Bill was awake, and we bent our knees to pull our sleeping bags away from the door. After another thirty minutes the water had receded more than a foot, but I lay awake for a little while longer hoping no breaking icebergs would send waves into our tent. When I awoke at seven the next morning, five icebergs—four scattered suitcases and an ice—sculpted swan—lay on the marshy ground within twenty feet of our tent.

Both John Muir and George Vancouver were also flooded by tides while camping in southeast Alaska. For Vancouver, it happened around two in the morning on July 26, 1793, shortly before his adventures in Behm Canal. Although he had set his tents "at least twenty feet above the surface of the water at our landing," it flooded his tents and forced his men to spend an uncomfortable night sleeping in their small boats. For Muir it happened in August, 1880, while he camped near a tidewater glacier not far from Juneau. He awoke in the middle of the night to cold waves battering his tent after the glacier had calved. His Native guides, who had slept in a canoe anchored off shore, fared much better.

CHAPTER TWELVE

Humpbacks, Eagles and Bears—Wildlife on Admiralty Island

After a third winter visit to Hawaii, George Vancouver sailed north in March, 1794, to perform his last season of surveys on the northwest coast. Rather than working from south to north as he had in previous years, he sailed directly to Cook Inlet at 60°N latitude. From there he traveled east to Prince William Sound, then southeast roughly 500 miles to Cape Decision, where he had concluded the 1793 season.

Vancouver began in Cook Inlet because he believed it was among the most important and time-consuming areas left to survey. He was an officer on the 1778 expedition when James Cook concluded the inlet was the mouth of a large river and was eager to disprove the theory that it connected to a Northwest Passage. He did not want to risk leaving this task to the end of the season, when poor weather might drive him from the region. In addition, reports from traders and his own observations from Cape Decision convinced him most of the remaining coastline southeast of Cook Inlet was unbroken and therefore easier to survey.

Vancouver arrived in Cook Inlet on April 12, but a combination of tides, shoals and ice from the thawing Susitna River prevented immediate surveys. Cook Inlet has the world's second-largest tides, with a possible exchange of more than forty feet in roughly six hours, and their powerful currents slammed large chunks of ice against the *Discovery* and complicated its passage between shoals. It was almost a month before Vancouver determined no navigable river entered the inlet. Visiting Russian trading posts and exploring Prince William Sound took additional time; unfavorable winds east of the sound also further delayed his progress. The two ships did not reach Cross Sound, 200 miles north of Cape Decision, until July 8.

Cross Sound is the northern-most point where the Inside Passage meets the open Pacific. On July 10, with the *Chatham* and *Discovery* anchored in a calm cove near the mouth of the sound, Vancouver dispatched Joseph Whidbey with three boats and fourteen days of food to survey the region. On July 12, the men struggled through shifting icebergs in Icy Strait and passed a large glacier at the mouth of what is now Glacier Bay. Today, a little more than 200 years later, the glacier has retreated an impressive sixty miles from Icy Strait. The next day, the party entered Lynn Canal, North America's deepest fiord, and followed it north for several days to its end at present-day Haines, Alaska. Following its eastern

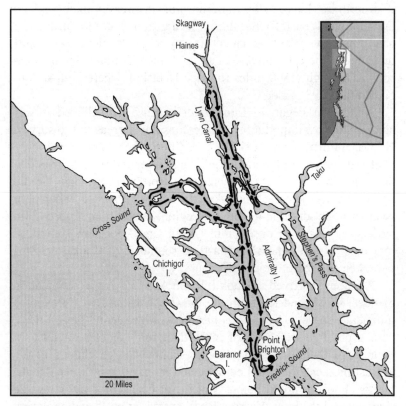

Map 12.1: Whidbey's route through northern part of Inside Passage, including Admiralty Island, Cross Sound, Icy Strait, Glacier Bay, and Lynn Canal.

shore southward on July 18, they entered Stephens Passage, which runs between the mainland and Admiralty Island.

That afternoon near Auke Bay, part of present-day Juneau, Whidbey encountered an unfriendly group of Tlingits, who despite several warning shots followed his boats well into the evening. In poor weather and fading light, he reached a narrow passage with many shoals and rocks that he mistook for the end of Stephens Passage. He intended to camp on a nearby beach to confirm this the next day, but when the Natives "got possession of the beach. . .[and] drew up in battle array" he returned northward and paddled through the night. He passed the northern tip of Admiralty Island, which Vancouver later named Point Retreat, and finally went ashore the following morning on the island's west side, which he believed was mainland. Unnecessarily, he spent the next five days surveying Admiralty's west coast southward for over 100 miles. He passed the southern tip of the island and reached Point Brightman before returning to Cross Sound on July 26, sixteen days after his departure. He did not realize Admiralty was an island until several weeks later, during the last days of the survey.

Vancouver left his Cross Sound anchorage on July 28 and two days later reached the southern tip of Baranof Island, only thirty miles northwest of Cape Decision on Kuiu Island and fifty miles south of Point Brightman. According to his charts, which showed Kuiu and Admiralty Islands as mainland, only one body of water remained unexplored on the northwest coast: the large gap south of Point Brightman recently visited by Joseph Whidbey. That gap, which Vancouver would soon name Frederick Sound, separates Admiralty Island on the north from Kuiu and Kupreanof Islands on the south.

Vancouver anchored on eastern Baranof Island and sent Whidbey with two boats north to Point Brightman, instructing him to survey eastward along Frederick Sound's north shore. Simultaneously, he sent Johnstone with two boats south to Cape Decision, instructing him to survey northward along the west side of Kuiu Island, then eastward along Frederick Sound's south shore. Ideally, the two would meet somewhere in Frederick Sound, thus concluding their exhaustive survey of the northwest coast. Vancouver wrote in his journal that "this appeared to be no difficult task" since both Cape Decision and Point Brightman were visible from his anchorage; he estimated the mission should take only a week. However, with previous experience along the coast in mind, he supplied both groups with provisions for fourteen days.

Frederick Sound is the largest opening in the Inside Passage north of Dixon Entrance. It is shaped a little like a boomerang, with one side angling southeastward fifty miles to Dry Strait and the other angling southwestward forty miles to Chatham Strait. It is the northern limit for western red cedars, and north of the sound the temperate rain forest consists primarily of Sitka spruce and western

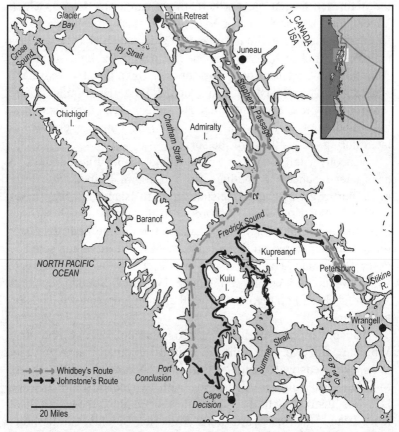

Map 12.2: Whidbey (gray) and Johnstone (black) routes through central southeast Alaska, at the conclusion of Vancouver's surveys. While Whidbey was realizing the insularity of Admiralty Island, Johnstone realized he had previously missed Keku Strait between Kupreanof and Kuiu Islands. Neither found Wrangell Narrows or Dry Strait, other passages between Sumner Strait and Frederick Sound.

hemlock, although small amounts of yellow cedar grow in poor soils. Each summer, Frederick Sound also hosts one of the largest congregations of humpback whales in southeast Alaska.

■ ■ ■

We awoke early in LeConte Bay to partly cloudy skies and almost constant rumblings from the LeConte Glacier. We ate our breakfast on a marshy spit standing over small bergs deposited by the overnight high tide, then broke camp and packed our boats. Entering the water at eight, we pushed through thick ice in our small bay, then caught a strong ebb through relatively light ice toward Frederick Sound. Traveling west in the bay, out of the Coast Mountains, the severity of the cliffs gradually decreased and thick rain forest returned to either shore. At the mouth of the bay an ebb whisked our boats, along with several icebergs, into Frederick Sound.

The sound was nearly ten miles across and flat as glass under clear skies. After a short break we began a diagonal crossing of twelve miles to Mitkof Island. Leaving the mainland, the barren spires of the Stikine Ice Field rose slowly over lower mountains covered in forest and alpine meadows. Thirty minutes into the crossing, three humpbacks surfaced a quarter mile ahead and kept pace with us for fifteen minutes, as though escorting us across the sound. To our south, the Stikine Flats were a brown plain between the mainland and Mitkof, with sinuous channels shining silver in the sun. Except for light green clearcuts in the distance on Mitkof Island, it was the same view Joseph Whidbey had in August, 1794.

■ ■ ■

Whidbey departed Baranof Island on August 2nd and reached southern Admiralty Island the following day. For the next six days, he surveyed northward along the island's east shore in nearly constant rain and reached the vicinity of present-day Juneau on August 8. That afternoon he passed the same village where Tlingits had pursued his boats earlier in the trip. With Tlingits again paddling toward him, he recognized his surroundings and finally realized the insularity of Admiralty Island, after circumnavigating its nearly 600 miles of coastline. For the sake of thoroughness, he continued northward to Point Retreat before beginning the long trip southward along the mainland side of Stephens Passage. As before, Tlingit warriors pursued his boats near Juneau and only retreated after he fired at their canoes.

Rain fell for at least seven of the next eight days, often pouring heavily as Whidbey traveled south in Stephens Passage, investigating the many bays and inlets along its mainland side. Perhaps as a result of the poor weather, his surveys were not as thorough as earlier work. He correctly surveyed Stephens Passage, but inlets such as Tracy Arm, Port Houghton and Thomas Bay were either missed altogether or drawn much smaller than their actual size. It is not hard to imagine that Whidbey and his crew held no belief in a Northwest Passage at this point and after three seasons on the coast were both tired of investigating dead-end channels and eager to conclude the survey.

The weather finally turned fair on August 16. That morning Whidbey reached the southern end of Frederick Sound and, as Vancouver wrote, found it "entirely closed by a beach, extending all round the head of it." The beach was the Stikine Flats, and Whidbey could see Dry Strait leading south through the mud. However, remembering Johnstone's failed attempts to cross the flats from the south the previous August, he did not pursue the channel. Instead, he steered north to survey eastern Mitkof and Kupreanof Islands, which were still considered part of the mainland. Like Johnstone the year before, he missed the Stikine River. However, while the river would later prove important to the fur trade, the mud would have made navigation by Vancouver's ships impossible.

As for LeConte Bay in the southeast corner of the sound, Vancouver wrote "a large body of ice, formed in a gully between the mountains…entirely covered the surface of the water." The ice, grounded on LeConte's terminal moraine, probably formed a line that prevented Whidbey from seeing the bay. Whidbey surmised the ice had fallen from the surrounding mountains. LeConte Bay also did not appear on Vancouver's charts. Later, Archibald Menzies, the expedition's naturalist, wrote that the surveys of Frederick Sound and Stephens Passage "had been too hastily relinquished."

■ ■ ■

We reached the rocky shores of Mitkof Island early in the afternoon, ate lunch and then napped on black rocks in the sun with Frederick

Sound lapping nearby in one-inch waves. Across the sound, forested mountains with snowy peaks rose quickly from the water. Beyond them, several peaks along the Canadian border reached more than 7,000 feet with gray headwalls and sheer needles too steep for snow. Two large valley glaciers spilled from the ice field, cutting white gaps through blue-green forest and disappearing behind ridges.

We napped for more than an hour, then paddled only a half mile to a shallow bay where we set camp. I spent the afternoon lying on a big drift log, our boots and tent drying nearby on the beach, while Bill investigated the forest behind camp. At dinner and again while lying in the tent, three humpbacks sounded with deep breaths a mile from shore.

We were up early the next morning and made good speed toward Petersburg, the spruces and hemlocks of Mitkof Island almost whirring past under blue skies. Near the mouth of Wrangell Narrows, a narrow lane leading to Petersburg, we paddled through a loose group of a dozen boats ranging from skiffs to forty-foot cabin cruisers, all trolling for king salmon. After chatting briefly with one of the captains, we turned left into the narrows and caught a powerful flood toward town. Hardly paddling, we covered two miles in fifteen minutes, with the water on either side swelling in big boils and spinning in deep whirlpools. Houses with grassy lawns backed by thick forest swept past on our left as the low buildings of downtown Petersburg quickly gained detail.

The temperature was in the mid-sixties as we climbed onto a warm dock near downtown. The harbormaster, a jocular man in his sixties with a scraggly gray beard, promised to keep an eye on our boats, and we climbed a narrow ramp toward town. When we reached its top we found several hundred people, many in T-shirts, lining either side of Petersburg's main thoroughfare and a nine-piece jazz band playing "Let's Dance." A dozen vendors offered pizza, hot dogs, tacos, Chinese food and cookies from plywood counters near the bandstand, and a big banner over Main Street read "Welcome to Petersburg's Norway Days."

Petersburg is the only settlement on the 211-square-mile Mitkof Island and has a population of roughly 3,000. Peter Buschmann, a Norwegian businessman who built a sawmill and cannery along Wrangell Narrows and used ice from LeConte Bay to pack fish, founded the town in 1899. Buschmann attracted other Norwegians to southeast Alaska, and many settled in Petersburg; even today the town's phone book lists dozens of Nilsons, Petersburgs and Olsons, representatives of several generations of Scandinavians. Norway Days, a weekend-long celebration including concerts and a parade, celebrates the town's unique Scandinavian heritage.

Fishing has historically been Petersburg's main industry. Part of Buschmann's original cannery still stands attached to the Petersburg Fisheries Inc. Cannery, a salmon-processing plant that cans 300 tons of salmon each year. Six hundred fishing and crabbing vessels operate from Petersburg, and several large refrigerated warehouses line Wrangell Narrows near downtown. Logging, tourism and state and federal jobs also fuel the town's economy.

The fried food and live music railroaded our plans to find a hotel room and retrieve our food delivery from the post office. After visiting a few of the food stands, I found a lawn chair on a sunny deck overlooking Nordic Drive while Bill walked around downtown. With the sun high in the sky, I pulled off my dank boots and socks, removed the fleece pullover I'd worn for most the preceding forty days and felt hot for the first time in months. While using my knife to pick devil's club prickers from my salt-stained hands, my reflection in a nearby window caught my eye: two stained dry bags containing my clothes lay beside my lawn chair, along with my faded boots, fleece and torn socks. My green pants were stained nearly brown, I had a shaggy beard and I still had a fat lip and cut on my forehead from our hike in LeConte. My arms, usually tan by late May, were milk white.

I sat for hours listening to the band and watching hundreds of people mill around downtown, their arms and legs as white as mine. Food smells and music—trumpet, clarinet, piano, banjo, cow bells— filled the air. They drifted toward the shaggy forest that overhung the other side of Wrangell Narrows, where the only sounds were eagles, ravens and occasional whale breaths. They dissipated over Frederick Sound, long before reaching the snowy peaks and jagged spires of the ice field, where wind blew snow and whistled between rocks.

"It's kind of funny," said Bill when he returned, "There's no hotel rooms available this weekend. The hostel's full, too, and I heard there aren't any rooms at the bed and breakfasts, either."

266

"Really," I said. I had been looking forward to a hotel room and a hot shower.

"Yeah. We can look through the phone book and make some calls, but I think we'll be camping in Petersburg tonight."

We dialed a few numbers from the yellow pages and quickly confirmed no lodging was available. Late that afternoon we took showers at the community gym and eventually met a minister who let us sleep on the church floor that night. Before lugging our valuables to the church, Bill talked briefly with Judith, who was flying to Juneau in the morning. He confirmed we would meet her in three days.

We got our food when the post office opened the next morning. After carrying the two big boxes to the dock, we spent two hours reorganizing food and gear, then departed Petersburg early in the afternoon under continued clear skies. Across Frederick Sound, the mainland peaks rose sharply, with Kates Needle and Devils Thumb between 9,000 and 10,000 feet less than twenty miles inland. Big valley glaciers flowed between sharp mountains and spilled through forest into unseen valleys. Thomas and Farragut Bays branched inland on the east side of the sound, with glaciers, mountains and forests that could take weeks to explore. With 15,000 miles of coastline, southeast Alaska alone offers a lifetime of exploration.

That afternoon we passed the beach on Kupreanof Island where Johnstone and Whidbey met at the conclusion of the Frederick Sound surveys.

While Whidbey was busy in Stephens Passage and southern Frederick Sound, Johnstone spent nearly two weeks surveying the many inlets on western and northern Kuiu Island. Passing between Kuiu and Kupreanof Islands in Keku Strait, he realized he had mistakenly considered Kuiu as part of the mainland the year before.

On August 16, while sailing south along eastern Kupreanof Island, Johnstone met Whidbey escaping an attack by Tlingits. The two crews sailed a few miles north, then set camp to celebrate the end of three long seasons on the northwest coast. They flew the British flag, fired three volleys from their muskets and formally claimed to the surrounding trees and ravens that everything between Cross and Puget Sounds was the possession of England. Then each member of the crew was given two servings of grog to drink the health of the king of England. Two days later they arrived back at

267

the ships in pouring rain. On August 28, 1794, Vancouver sailed from the northwest coast for the last time. He named his anchorage on eastern Baranof Island Port Conclusion.

On separate occasions, Johnstone and Whidbey had missed both Dry Strait and Wrangell Narrows, with Johnstone approaching from the south in 1793 and Whidbey from the north in 1794. The passages separate Mitkof and Kupreanof Islands, which the men reported as part of the mainland. Wrangell Narrows never appeared on Vancouver's chart, but in September, 1794, the captain of a trading vessel in Nootka told Vancouver he had sailed through Dry Strait. Vancouver's final chart included this correction but combined Kupreanof and Mitkof as one island.

■ ■ ■

Late the next day we landed on a gravel beach near Cape Fanshaw, the western-most mainland point in Frederick Sound. The beach was 100 yards long with big piles of bleached driftwood and the first wildflowers of our trip; chocolate lilies, shooting stars, paintbrush and lupine crowded along the mossy border between beach and forest. Fifteen miles to our west across Frederick Sound snowy mountains on Admiralty Island formed a jagged horizon above dark forest. High clouds had turned the sky hazy white and, in cool temperatures, rain seemed imminent.

We set our tent on gravel fifty yards from a sheer cliff and cooked dinner on driftwood benches that faced Frederick Sound and Admiralty Island. After dinner we hung our food from the cliff, then took a walk into the dim woods behind camp. Within a quarter mile we reached a big blowdown with saplings growing haphazardly from root wads over thirty feet tall. We climbed along downed trees for a while, then returned to camp and found fresh moose tracks passing ten feet from our tent and leading through our kitchen before disappearing into the woods. At 9:30, we watched a fiery sunset through holes in the clouds.

We awoke early the next morning to drizzle and fog. Gray clouds blew low across the water, obscuring small islands less than two miles from shore and completely concealing Admiralty Island. With Judith meeting us on Admiralty the next morning and showers increasing during breakfast, we

268

realized we needed to navigate by compass across Frederick Sound.

From our beach we had to make an eight-mile crossing to two small islands four miles from Admiralty. Through the fog we could see the Storm Islands, a small chain roughly two miles from shore and two miles north of our course. Although we could not see it, our maps showed the Five Finger Light on some small islands five miles from shore and five miles north of our course. With visibility hovering around two miles, we knew we could use the Storm Islands as reference for the first few miles, but it was less likely we would see Five Finger Light. It was possible that up to five miles of the crossing would entail paddling blindly through fog.

With their details blurred through blowing clouds, we took compass bearings on the Storm Islands and a mainland point a little less than a mile to our south. We used the bearings to pinpoint our location on the map, then drew a course of roughly 280 degrees to the islands eight miles away, our map rustling in the breeze. After double-checking that our compasses were adjusted to Frederick Sound's twenty-seven degrees of magnetic declination—the difference between magnetic north shown by our compasses and the true north represented on our maps—we duct taped them to our decks.

Ideally, following the course would bring us to the islands in less than three hours. However, the southeast breeze was likely stronger a few miles from shore and could blow us well north of our destination over the course of eight miles. If we passed the islands on the north, we could paddle as much as five additional miles before hitting Admiralty. On the other hand, a strong ebb was simultaneously draining south through Frederick Sound, which at the least would mitigate the northward drift created by the breeze. If the ebb was stronger than the breeze, we could pass the islands on the south and become lost in the big body of water between Admiralty and Kuiu Islands. It would be eight or more additional miles before we reached land.

It was impossible to gauge the effects of wind and tide from shore, but if the Storm Islands remained visible for the first thirty or forty minutes of the crossing we could use them to estimate the rate of our drift. Then, as they disappeared in fog we could factor that rate into our course for the remaining distance. Unfortunately, this plan did not provide a formula for the fact that both winds and tides were likely stronger several miles from shore. While imperfect, it was our only available method, and we did not feel the risk of missing the islands warranted our waiting out the weather, which would have stranded Judith on Admiralty the following day.

The Storm Islands flickered through blowing clouds for thirty minutes as we paddled over northbound waves between one and two feet. As the islands disappeared into gray air behind us we agreed the wind was stronger than the outgoing tide and adjusted our course southward to avoid being carried too far northward. As the waves grew to two and three feet we turned further southward, cutting into them at a thirty-degree angle and hoping the Five Finger Light would appear soon to provide some reference.

The rain came in intermittent but heavy showers, with thick mist blowing across the water. Visibility decreased to one mile. Three miles from shore the seas rose to three and four feet, pushing northwestward toward Admiralty. For an hour we paddled with no land in sight, the gray waves with white tops rolling from one edge of the fog to the other. We tried to remain on a consistent course, cutting diagonally into the waves, but as time passed we felt our compasses grow useless.

After almost two hours we saw the Five Finger Light flashing pale white through a rift in the fog to our northeast. It was visible for only ten minutes, but with no other available reference we could not use our compasses to positively determine its distance. Consulting our maps and estimating the light was three miles away, we determined our course would carry us one mile north of our destination in roughly ninety minutes.

The wind drove rain against our backs while the waves continued at three and four feet, breaking noisily around us and jostling our bows northward. To compensate, we cut further southward, pointing toward the backs of the waves at forty-five degrees. After ninety minutes without any sign of land, we began peering into the thick air for the islands, which we hoped to see directly in front of us. After another thirty minutes, with our legs and backs cramping, we became concerned that we had missed them. Increasing rain added to our discomfort.

Finally, close to four hours after leaving Cape Fanshaw the islands materialized suddenly through a rift in the blowing mist. Their ragged canopies were gray through the clouds; white surf surrounded their rocky shores. About a mile south of them, we had overestimated the power of the waves and almost paddled past them. We turned north with the waves and within thirty minutes slipped between the islands and entered a calm bay on their north where we set camp. It was past two in the afternoon when we finished lunch. With visibility hovering around a mile, we decided to leave the remaining four-mile crossing for the following day.

In continued showers we rested in the tent, then I explored the forest behind our bay. Following narrow trails that wound between trees at the island's edge, I found piles of broken urchin shells left by otters. Their scat smelled strongly of fish, and their paths led into dark hollows beneath trees.

When I returned to camp a forty-foot pleasure boat had anchored in our bay. I could see Bill's kayak tied to its afterdeck. After fifteen minutes he paddled ashore. Gray fog blew across the water outside our bay and obscured everything beyond the boat.

"Got some halibut for dinner," he said as he dragged his boat onto the gravel. "The couple in the boat are teachers in Colorado, and they just caught a thirty-pound halibut at the edge of our bay."

Sitting on our PFDs under our tarp we dumped the two big steaks into oil and garlic and cooked a side dish of rice with broccoli. The wind rushed heavily through the canopy above, and the temperature dropped to the high forties.

"Should we hang the food tonight?" Bill asked.

"I think it'll be okay in the boats," I said, "Admiralty's four miles away."

Admiralty Island is roughly 1,700 square miles, making it southeast Alaska's third-largest island after Prince of Wales and Chichigof. With approximately 1,700 brown bears, or one per square mile, its brown bear population is one of the densest in North America. Angoon Tlingits, who still occupy a portion of Admiralty's west coast, called the island *Kootznoowoo*—Fortress of the Bears.

Brown bears are the coastal equivalent of grizzly bears. They are the same species, *Ursus arctos*, but the contrast between coastal and interior habitats has created differences in behavior and size. For instance, brown bears on the coast, where berries and fat-rich salmon are abundant, are more tolerant of each other and require much less territory per individual than their inland relatives. The population

271

density on Admiralty would never occur at Yellowstone, where a single adult male can require a territory of 500 square miles. Coastal bears also average greater size, with some giant males on Kodiak Island exceeding 1,400 pounds. Adult males on Admiralty average 500 pounds, although some are thought to reach more than 700 pounds; interior bears such as those in Yellowstone average less.

No black bears live on Admiralty. Blacks and browns share similar diets, roughly 80 percent vegetarian, but are different species and usually avoid the same territory. Black bears, *Ursus americanus*, are smaller than brown bears, with adult males weighing between 300 and 600 pounds, and are far more tolerant of other bears and humans. Whereas the U.S. brown bear population outside of Alaska is less than 1,000 and confined to undeveloped wilderness in five western states, black bears number in the tens of thousands and live in almost every state, often close to human settlements. Blacks have smaller claws than browns, which enable them to climb trees. They typically lack the large hump of muscle between the shoulders that distinguishes brown bears. Color is not a reliable way to tell the difference between the two species, as browns can be golden brown through black, and blacks can be cinnamon, black, blue or white.

Although they obviously prefer remaining on land, both black and brown bears are good swimmers and commonly move between islands in the Inside Passage. Young adults struggling to claim their own territory, especially during lean times, are most likely to swim to islands like those where we were camped in search of food. Although I felt safe leaving our food in our boats that night, I later learned that adult males have been seen on the islands.

■ ■ ■

The next morning was dry and calm but foggy, with mist sifting through the canopy and obscuring tree trunks only 100 feet from camp. Our bay was flat and blue and sharply reflected the white boat and its foggy veil. As we pulled our breakfast food from the kayaks, a loon called mournfully from the fog. During breakfast we tried to hail Judith's charter boat, the *Wilderness Swift*, on our marine radio. With Juneau only ninety miles north across Frederick Sound and Stephens Passage, we hoped to reach the boat soon after it left town to establish a rendezvous. Standing on a big rock near the water's

272

edge, Bill held the antennae high as he repeatedly tried to reach the boat.

"*Wilderness Swift... Wilderness Swift...* This is kayakers on sixteen."

With no response, we packed camp and moved our boats to the water's edge, then plotted a northwest course four miles to a rocky point on Admiralty Island. The fog was thicker than the previous day, but navigating by compass was not nearly as daunting; as long as we paddled somewhere between west and north we would hit Admiralty in a little more than an hour. With no wind, the tides would create only minimal drift over the short distance. As we stood over our maps, the couple aboard the boat pulled their anchor, its heavy metal chain clanging against the bow and echoing in the fog.

We paddled into fog at the end of our bay, and our islands quickly disappeared behind us. In all directions, flat water extended into white mist. When I paddled more than 100 feet from Bill, he faded into the fog. The only sounds were the slosh of our paddles and a ship's foghorn blowing regularly somewhere to the south. After thirty minutes the fog turned bright white overhead, as though the sun might soon appear.

We failed to notice that the monotonous foghorn gradually got closer until it suddenly sounded very loud, and we both stopped paddling. In the ensuing silence we heard the dull rumble of a large ship's engine. Then the horn blew again, a low tone sounding very close.

"Where's that marine radio?" I asked, but Bill was already trying to find it, fumbling through the dry bag on his deck.

I watched the water for a wake and peered into the fog to the southwest, where it sounded like a barge or ferry was moving between Admiralty and the islands behind us. Perhaps its captain had detected us on radar and was trying to warn us. If our radio had been on, we might have heard the captain issue a securitae to vessels in the area, a warning that captains of large ships provide when they pass through fog or narrow lanes, where smaller vessels need to move from their path.

"There it is," I said as Bill switched on the radio. "Pretty close."

A fragment of a Princess cruise ship suddenly appeared a half mile away through a hole in the fog four stories above the water. It was only large enough to reveal a few letters at a time, which like a

12.1: Basic Marine Radio Protocol for Kayakers

A marine radio is among the most important pieces of kayaking equipment and can mean the difference between life and death, especially where cold water emergencies require quick response. Because most captains use marine radios, creating the potential for crowded airways, kayakers should be aware of marine radio protocol and regulations established by the FCC and U.S. and Canadian Coast Guards.

In the U.S., operators of private vessels are not required to carry marine radios, but if they do the Coast Guard requires they monitor channel sixteen. All commercial vessels are required to monitor marine radios and to respond to emergencies in their area. To maximize efficiency in emergencies and prevent congestion, the FCC and Coast Guard have set certain channels aside for specific purposes. Here are the most important examples:

Channel sixteen is a calling and distress channel only, which means it can be used to establish communication with other vessels or to make a distress call. Once parties establish communication in a non-emergency, they must move to another channel. The Coast Guard uses sixteen to broadcast special messages or weather bulletins and to

streaming message slowly spelled *Princess Dawn* above a row of black windows. We never saw the ship's deck, bow or stern; just a section of its white side before the fog drifted closed again. The ship's motors rumbled in the dense fog as, less than a minute later, we bobbed on its three-foot wake.

"*Wilderness Swift...Wilderness Swift...*This is kayakers on sixteen."

Ten seconds later the radio crackled to life.

"Heyya kayakers," came a man's voice, "this is *Wilderness Swift* on sixteen. Wanna go to channel six-eight?"

"Roger that. Channel six-eight," said Bill.

The captain was only twenty miles away and let us know Judith was aboard and skies were sunny over Stephens Passage.

"We're still pretty socked-in down here in Frederick Sound," Bill told him, "but the fog's looking a little bright."

They agreed to meet in an hour, four miles north of us and sixteen miles south of the *Wilderness Swift*. Soon, patches of light blue sky appeared through the brightening fog, then we reached its edge, with blue sky overhead and cotton candy clouds stuck to the water in all directions. The snowy tops of Admiralty's mountains, over 3,500 feet tall, poked above lower clouds that concealed the island's shores. The mainland mountains were blue and white, almost twenty miles away. Behind us, only the tops of a dozen trees on the islands where we had camped stuck above the fog, which formed a white wall across Frederick Sound. The cruise ship, five miles ahead, was like a twenty-story hotel moving northward in Stephens Passage.

The *Wilderness Swift* was a thirty-foot boat with an aluminum hull and a cabin for up to twelve passengers. Its captain, Lynn Schooler, slid open a window and waved as he slowed to a stop fifty feet from us. Judith's yellow kayak, rented in Juneau, was atop the cabin. A moment later she walked onto the back deck and waved excitedly. As we paddled closer, a German couple in their thirties joined her. They were whale-watching with Lynn for the day.

We had barely greeted each other when two humpbacks sounded half a mile to our east. They exhaled plumes of gray mist ten feet high as their arched backs and low dorsal fins rose slowly from the water. Typical of humpbacks, they surfaced five times in about two minutes, each time letting out a breath and inhaling deeply. After the last breath their big tails, fifteen feet across, rose with a curtain of sparkling water dripping from them, then slipped gracefully below the surface. When a humpback shows its tail after several soundings, it often means the whale is diving. Dives average 200 feet but can approach 500 feet

respond to emergencies. Channel twenty-two is reserved for Coast Guard broadcasts.

Dependent upon location, continuous weather broadcasts generally occur on single-digit channels.

In most areas, a channel in the low twenties can be used to make a phone call using the marine operator.

Paddlers also should be aware of the following common terms used on marine radios.

Securitae: a general warning often given by a large ship such as a ferry or cruise ship traveling through fog, entering a narrow passage or approaching a corner. Because large vessels cannot stop or maneuver quickly, smaller vessels must get out of their way. Securitaes are also given to warn boaters about large floating objects, weather events or other potential hazards.

Pan-pan: a more serious call indicating assistance is required but that the situation is not yet life-threatening. It is an urgent call regarding safety of a vessel or person.

May-day: The most serious call, used only in emergencies involving immediate danger to life or property. Vessels issue a may-day to request immediate help from other vessels or the Coast Guard.

The above is only a partial list of important channels and terms, and kayakers should consult both U.S. and Canadian Coast Guard publications to become familiar with marine radio protocol.

and usually last less than ten minutes, although humpbacks can stay under for more than fifteen minutes.

A minute later another humpback surfaced a quarter mile to our west, close to Admiralty's rocky shore. Its breath was startlingly loud, and it inhaled with a deep sucking sound. Then two more surfaced on the other side of Judith's boat.

"It's Whale Central, boys!" exclaimed Lynn.

Lynn cut his engines, and we floated quietly together for close to two hours watching whales surface in every direction. At one point we counted fourteen, with one rising only fifty feet from Bill's kayak. A mile away, another breached repeatedly, projecting its massive body completely out of the water, twisting in the air, then landing on its back with a great splash. Humpbacks can weigh forty tons, and it sounded like a big rifle in the distance each time the whale struck the water. Reasons for breaching include body language, exercise and a way to knock barnacles from their skin.

"This is different," said Judith, her salt and pepper hair moving in a light breeze, "Two days ago I was in Manhattan, riding in a taxi."

Lynn eventually motored back toward Juneau, and Judith, Bill and I paddled two miles to a Forest Service cabin Judith had reserved for five days. The cabin was next to a shallow lagoon in a big bay that reached ten miles into Admiralty's interior. In warm sunshine, we hauled our kayaks onto grass and carried our gear into the cabin. Smiling broadly, Judith unpacked fresh vegetables, meat, sodas and a bottle of wine. That night we cooked a delicious pasta meal. Later, when I brushed my teeth outside the cabin, I could hear whales breathing in the nearby bay.

The next day we spent three hours watching whales in Frederick Sound. We counted ten individuals, some a few feet from our boats and others three miles away, with one swimming just below the surface only ten feet from Bill. At lunch we went ashore in a small cove, then walked quietly for a mile inside the forest edge, hoping to see a bear. We never saw any, but found massive heaps of their grassy scat in the woods and big holes where they had recently dug for clams and grubs.

Rain began falling that evening as we read our books in the warm cabin. By morning it drummed loudly on the roof and poured past the window in thick streams. While eating breakfast I found a broad, low valley on our map about five miles from the cabin. It had a big stream and stretched inland four miles before reaching 500 feet elevation, a rarity in a region where the land usually rises thousands of feet close to the sea. Alluvial soils in such low valleys create ideal forest habitat, and since most of Admiralty has never been logged I thought the valley might contain enormous trees.

■ ■ ■

Almost all of Admiralty Island is included in the 955,000-acre Kootznoowoo Wilderness, third-largest wilderness area in southeast Alaska after Glacier Bay National Park and Misty Fiords National Monument. Because Glacier Bay and Misty Fiords are mostly on the mainland, Kootznoowoo is the largest example of protected island habitat in southeast Alaska. Although present-day Forest Service managers are committed to protecting Admiralty's wilderness character, it was originally scheduled to be logged.

As early as 1932, the Sierra Club petitioned the National Park Service to preserve Admiralty Island, both as an example of the temperate rain forest ecosystem and in recognition of its dense brown bear population. However, the Forest Service was already the managing agency and was committed to selling the island's timber. For years, against the wishes of vocal sportsmen and conservationists, the Forest Service tried to find a buyer for Admiralty timber who would build a pulp mill in nearby Juneau in exchange for a long-term timber contract. In 1955, with several small timber sales already active on Admiralty, the agency came close to brokering such a contract with Georgia Pacific, but the deal collapsed several years later.

Controversy surrounding Forest Service plans for Admiralty intensified in the late 1960s, when the agency signed a long-term contract with U.S. Plywood Champion. The contract awarded 8.75 billion board feet of Tongass timber over fifty years, much of it from Admiralty Island. However, in 1971 the Sierra Club sued the Forest Service, claiming the agency had ignored its multiple use mandate and offered unsustainable timber rotations on Admiralty. After several years of court battles U.S. Plywood Champion abandoned the project, but Admiralty's forests faced new threats.

By the mid-1970s the Native corporations established by the Alaska Native Claims Settlement Act (ANCSA) were organized and began selecting their lands. Three corporations made selections on Admiralty with the intention of clearcutting its forests for maximum profit. With national attention already on Admiralty following the Sierra Club lawsuit, conservationists from inside and outside Alaska as well as Native activists from the Admiralty village of Angoon pressured Congress to protect the island. Angoon strongly favored making Admiralty a national monument, which would protect it from logging yet preserve native subsistence rights on the island.

The battle for Admiralty became wrapped in the debate over an Alaska Lands Act, which remained contentious throughout 1978. With time running out for Admiralty and other unique places, Jimmy Carter used the Antiquities Act of 1906 to create seventeen national monuments in Alaska, including Admiralty, in December, 1978. Two years later, with the island already protected from logging, ANILCA created the Kootznoowoo Wilderness.

Today's visitors to Admiralty can enjoy almost a million acres of protected rain forest, with healthy populations of deer and bear and streams teeming with salmon. The Forest Service maintains roughly twenty-eight miles of trail on the island and more than twenty public recreation cabins, many built by the CCC in the 1930s. In addition, the Forest Service manages the Pack Creek Bear Viewing Area on the island's east side, where visitors can view brown bears at close range in a natural setting. A limited number of Pack Creek permits are granted each day, which reduces stress on the bears, and Forest Service rangers accompany all visitors to the area, which reduces stress on humans. Visitors spend their time watching as many as twenty bears in a single day feeding and playing around a rich salmon stream. The bears are habituated to human presence, and through years of dedication from Forest Service rangers no human-bear conflicts have occurred in twenty years of management.

■ ■ ■

In continued rain the air was misty and dim at midmorning. Bill and Judith declined my invitation for a hike, and I packed a lunch, then dragged my boat into the water. I paddled ninety minutes through steady rain, pausing for ten minutes at the mouth of a small cove to watch a humpback swim back and forth along a rocky bluff. It came within twenty feet of my kayak and twice rolled onto its side, gently slapping the water with a pectoral fin ten feet long. Its knobby skin was black with small clusters of barnacles.

I reached the mouth of a big stream rolling quietly into the sea. In pouring rain I hurriedly dragged my boat from the water, tied it to a young tree, then ducked through wet alders and spruce into the forest. Inside was a dim collage of greens, with bright skunk cabbage, pale blueberry leaves, dark spruce needles, along with moss, lichen, fern and hemlock. Overhead, patches of gray sky showed between the crowns of giant trees; the rain hissed on the canopy and fell sporadically in big drops that smacked the mossy floor. The stream, twenty feet across and two feet deep, ran in riffles over a cobble bed.

I followed a well-worn bear trail for two miles along the stream, breaking from it occasionally to investigate giant trees. Big spruces and hemlocks leaned against each other or swayed slowly in the breeze, as though drunk on the rain. Many lacked branches below seventy feet, while some had dead branches covered in thick, dark moss, like ghoulish fingers reaching outward. Bits of lichen and scores of hemlock needles drifted downward in occasional gusts of wind. One gust took down a dead branch on the other side of the stream, which hit the forest floor with a thud. Overhead, ravens sounded like monkeys in the trees, and stellar jays screeched like red-tailed hawks.

The forest floor was a messy combination of branches, logs, root wads and understory. A closer inspection revealed cones, needles, rotting feathers and porcupine quills among the moss, lichen and low herbs. Beside a rotting log I found a deer pelvis stained green with moss, almost perfectly camouflaged against the floor. Bear, deer and mink scat littered intersecting game trails. And salmon bones from the previous summer, mostly skulls, lay beside the stream, sinking slowly into the duff. Pink and chum salmon likely filled the stream beginning in July and ending in September, and perhaps an autumn coho run lasted into December.

■ ■ ■

Most salmon spend part or most of their first year in the stream where they were born, nourished by dead salmon and litter from the forest, then follow spring floods into salt water. Depending upon species, they spend one to five years at sea, traveling hundreds and sometimes thousands of miles into the open Pacific before returning to water close to shore. Likely guided by smell, they return to the mouth of their native stream, where in a combination of salt and fresh water they lose their scales, stop eating and even changed shape and color. They eventually enter the stream and, swimming against its current, the males compete for females and the females practice digging redds, or nests, where they will lay their eggs. Then, with the flicker of her tail, the female deposits hundreds of eggs into a shallow depression in the stream's rocky bottom, which the male then sprays with milky sperm. With their one opportunity to reproduce concluded, the salmon spend the next week or more decaying slowly in the stream, their flesh rotting away and their energy decreasing until they lie lifeless in the water.

Salmon are perhaps the best example of interconnectedness in the rain forest. These fish, whose greatest defense mechanism is the enormous number of eggs fertilized each year, feed ducks, heron, trout and mink as juveniles and seals, otters, sea lions, bears and eagles as adults. After spawning, their rotting flesh nourishes eggs and juveniles and feeds scavengers including gulls, crows, ravens, eagles and bears, which crowd salmon streams each summer. Hunters and scavengers, especially bears and birds, bring salmon into the woods. With thousands of fish to choose from, bears often strip their fatty skin or take a single bite from their bellies, leaving the rest to rot on the forest floor. Nitrogen absorbed into salmon flesh in the ocean passes from rotting fish through detritus and tree roots and contributes significantly to the giant trees surrounding salmon streams. Underground capillaries of the streams have the same effect, delivering nutrition from salmon into the forest from below. The trees in turn control erosion, preventing siltification of spawning habitat. Through defecation, birds and bears distribute salmon's nitrogen outside the immediate stream corridor, enriching soils throughout the forest. With more than 2,500 salmon streams in southeast Alaska alone, salmon are an ecological staple in the Inside Passage, cycling nutrition between the ocean, streams and forests and feeding dozens of species, including humans.

■ ■ ■

Showers continued for the rest of our stay on Admiralty, but each day we kayaked or hiked, and each night we ate big meals in our dry cabin. We climbed small mountains and hiked through rolling muskegs, with grouse drumming constantly and low clouds changing the light on the surrounding carpet of forest. We watched many whales from our kayaks but never saw any bears. However, their big prints and diggings in the intertidal areas were palpable reminders of their presence in the woods that surrounded us.

CHAPTER THIRTEEN

Back to the Future—A Visit to Sumdum

Lynn brought our final food supply, mailed to him by Patti, when he returned to Frederick Sound. Under thick clouds threatening imminent rain, we met him near a rocky point and helped him load Judith's kayak aboard the *Wilderness Swift*. Then he and Judith waved goodbye from the wheelhouse and motored north into Frederick Sound as Bill and I paddled ashore to organize our food. Afterward, we paddled northward along Admiralty Island in frequent showers and the following day made a ten-mile crossing of Stephens Passage to the mainland in soggy but calm weather. We camped in a shallow bay that night, and the next afternoon reached Holkham Bay during a cold shower. We were only forty-five miles from Juneau, a distance we could easily cover in two days, but planned to paddle for another nine days.

Holkham Bay is one of six large openings on the east side of Stephens Passage, each with inlets reaching deep into the glaciers and high peaks of the Coast Mountains. It is roughly five miles across at its mouth and opens four miles to the east. Along most of its border, mature forest blankets the lower two-thirds of steep mountains between 2,000 and 3,000 feet, but near its eastern point a series of higher peaks culminates with Mount Sumdum, which rises almost 7,000 feet less than five miles from shore. Glacial ice caps Sumdum and spills from its peak like a bluish teardrop two miles long that terminates in forest only 1,000 feet above the bay. From the bay's northern and southeastern shores two narrow arms, more like broad rivers than seaways, extend close to thirty miles inland and end at the faces of tidewater glaciers.

We paddled to the center of the bay and reached four small islands covered in dark forest, the smallest less than an eighth of a mile across and the largest a mile long and half a mile wide. Tall trees grew to the edge of each rocky bluff and bouldery shore, but we found a narrow beach on one of the smaller islands and set our camp on sand and crushed shells above the high tide line. We spent the rest of the afternoon exploring the islands, finding eagle nests high in trees at the forest edge, fish bones and urchin shells below the trees, and narrow mink and otter trails winding along the mossy forest floor. On the largest island we found remnants of a fox farm, with a wooden rowboat and the foundation of a log cabin covered in moss and fallen branches. On a forested bench above the cabin, wooden cages with chicken wire lay half-sunk in the soft floor.

Limited fox farming probably started in Alaska with the first Russians but did not boom until the early 1900s. Farmers turned red foxes free on hundreds of small islands, often less than one square mile, then trapped them each December when their pelts were thickest. The farmers either homesteaded on the islands or managed them from towns such as Wrangell and Juneau.

Foxes are opportunistic feeders and survived by eating shorebirds, eggs, mussels and clams, but farmers supplemented their diets with tons of meat and grain. Although it was illegal to kill wildlife solely to feed their animals, the farmers escaped scrutiny on their remote islands. In addition, they took advantage of bounties on eagles, seals and sea lions that lasted through the 1950s, a policy game biologists thought would protect salmon stocks. They killed thousands of these and other animals, piling them in the woods to feed their foxes. One farmer reported killing 1,100 porcupines in one year.

By 1930, the year the market peaked, southeast Alaska led the state's industry, and Juneau's newspaper reported that every island suitable for fox farming was occupied. That year the pelts sold for $100 each in Europe, but only two years later the Depression reduced prices to about $10, quickly bankrupting most farmers. Few remained by the 1940s, and today their old homesteads are ruined and covered in moss, sinking into the forest floor surrounded by chicken wire, wooden cages and metal traps.

Like many parts of the Inside Passage now covered in forest, Holkham Bay has a long history of human activity. It probably began with the Sumdum kwan of Tlingits, who had a permanent village and fort there. Sumdum is the English corruption of a Tlingit word that may have referred to the green color of sea water near tidewater glaciers, a result of suspended glacial silt. At some point during the past few thousand years, the tidewater glaciers now thirty miles from Holkham Bay bordered its edge. Harbor seals used their abundant bergs as protected haul-outs, and the village was likely a staging area for seal hunters. Seals provided valuable meat and waterproof clothing; their dried bladders were used as floats at the end of harpoons.

Joseph Whidbey visited Holkham Bay in 1794, four days before meeting James Johnstone on Kupreanof Island at the conclusion of Vancouver's surveys. He reported many icebergs in the vicinity of the islands where Bill and I camped, but poor weather apparently concealed the two arms extending from the bay, which did not appear on Vancouver's charts. Eighty-six years later, John Muir made more extensive explorations, traveling to the end of each arm and detailing the locations of their glaciers. Muir called the area Sumdum Bay and reported a Tlingit fort on one of the small islands where we camped. We looked for signs of it but found only tangled forest over lumpy ground.

Around the time of Muir's visit, the bay became one of many active mining areas in southeast Alaska. Whites established two mining camps that eventually became small towns on the south shore, five miles across from the Tlingit village. By the turn of the century many Sumdum Tlingits had moved to the new towns. The miners built a road eight miles south over rugged mountains to Windham Bay, the location in the 1860s of southeast Alaska's first workable gold discoveries. And the towns' population approached 150 in the early twentieth century, with dozens of other claims and camps in the area. Several successful mines operated in the mountains above the bay, earning tens of thousands of dollars per year, and at least two dozen structures stood on the south shore by the turn of the century, including a saloon, post office and store. While many residents worked the mines, others pursued fox farming, trapping and handlogging; a sawmill eventually opened a few miles to the north, leading to nearby clearcuts.

The most successful mines played out in the early twentieth century. The sawmill closed in the early twenties. The post office closed in the early forties, and although the town's last residents left soon after, sporadic mining continued into the 1970s. Photographs from the forties show many structures still standing on the south shore, but today their remnants are hard to find.

I returned to the area several times in the late 1990s and 2001 and repeatedly looked for ruins, but found only scattered pilings, a few moss-covered foundations and metal scraps lying half-sunk in the intertidal. In the woods, sixty years of rain and forest succession had concealed all but small sections of an old puncheon road and some collapsed cabins, and in the mountains, trees and moss grew over rusted mining equipment and abandoned shafts. Across the bay, the only signs I found of the Tlingit village were faint rectangular depressions that may represent old pit-houses or plankhouses. Any other evidence had sunk into the duff and fed the trees overhead. However, during one of my visits an archeologist used a probe to sample soil beneath the beach of a nearby island. Eighteen inches under ground she found a layer of charcoal and crushed shells that indicated early people regularly used the area. Similar evidence can be found below countless beaches throughout the Inside Passage.

In the early twentieth century, Holkham Bay and nearby Windham Bay were poised to become large modern settlements, just like Juneau, less than fifty miles away. The fact that development stopped there is a testament to the ruggedness of the Inside Passage. And the fact that so little evidence of human activity remains there today reveals the power of the temperate rain forest, which quickly devours everything with moss and rain. Visiting the area, I reflected on mining history in the arid west, where roads, cabins, equipment and bare soil remain clearly visible a century after miners abandoned them. But in the Inside Passage, many places once busily inhabited, like Holkham Bay, are now protected as wilderness and show few signs of past activities.

■ ■ ■

We ate dinner on our beach with maps spread between us as the clouds overhead opened to big patches of blue sky. The maps showed high mountains and glaciers around the arms extending from our bay and shores that rose thousands of feet from the water, leaving few places to camp. We hoped to get closer to the glaciers than we had in LeConte, but knew thick ice could block our progress. Already, big bergs dotted the bay, with one seventy feet long and twenty feet high parked against the back of our island.

After dinner we lay in sleeping bags near sedges at the head of the beach and watched a humpback breaching a mile away. It smacked the sea with its powerful tail and launched from the water repeatedly, landing with huge splashes that sounded like distant rifle fire. We watched it with binoculars for almost an hour, then heard a sudden series of breaths close to the island. Standing quickly, we saw a pod of six orcas swim within 100 yards, with a big male in front. They surfaced in staggered succession while swimming toward the humpback, their sharp dorsal fins cutting the water. A moment later, the humpback breached for the last time and disappeared.

Orcas in the Inside Passage typically travel in two types of pods, residents and transients, which show evidence of being genetically distinct. Residents have comparatively small ranges, which in the Inside Passage include about 500 miles of coastline, and feed primarily on fish, especially salmon. They travel in larger pods than transients, sometimes forming superpods, and use more vocalizations. Transients, on the other hand, are more like the Hells Angels of orcas. They travel in small groups, have larger and less predictable ranges and typically hunt marine mammals such as porpoises, seals and even whales. Holkham Bay, with its relatively small number of salmon, due to steep shores and recent deglaciation, is not a likely spot for residents, but transients visit it for the thousands of seals using its abundant ice bergs. A third type of orca pod spends its time primarily offshore, and while not much is understood about them, they appear more closely related to residents.

We awoke early the next morning to a raucous band of crows and sunny skies. Only a narrow strip of white mist clung to the base of a forested mountain to the north; a thick cloud concealed the top 1,000 feet of Mount Sumdum. With temperatures in the high forties at sea level, snow flurries were possible within the cloud atop Sumdum, where the big ice cap created its own weather. The summit remained hidden as we ate breakfast, packed and shoved our boats into a fast-moving current.

We paddled across the bay and reached the mouth of one of the arms after two miles, then fought a strong ebb over a submerged moraine like the one in LeConte. It formed two-foot standing waves, big whirlpools and spooky boils. Crossing it took half an hour, with the ebb sweeping us far to the north as we tried to maintain an eastward heading. Ahead, the arm averaged between one and two miles wide for thirty miles, which funneled the tide against us. We paddled close to shore all morning, hoping to avoid the strongest current in the middle of the arm, but found only limited eddies. When the tide changed in the afternoon we paddled to the center of the arm, but quickly returned to its edge when a persistent headwind hindered our speed. Although the wind was weaker near shore, we encountered big eddies where the flooding tide spun against us, and we averaged less than three knots. By early afternoon we knew we wouldn't reach the glacier until the following day.

Near four, as we reached the beginning of a twelve-mile stretch of shore too steep for camping, we turned north into a narrow inlet where granite walls rose almost vertically to 2,000 feet. Filthy snow from avalanches filled thin notches down to the sea, bright snow covered mountaintops and sparse vegetation dotted the dark walls. After paddling two miles between towering walls we landed on a tiny beach beside a crook in the inlet only 100 yards wide and a quarter mile long. Beyond our view, the inlet continued five miles and widened to almost a mile.

John Muir visited the same beach in 1880, during what he called "two of the brightest and best of all my Alaska days," and found the fiord almost as impressive as Glacier Bay. Continuing to its end he found a small tidewater glacier that today has receded nearly three miles from the water. A muddy river explodes from below its moraine-covered snout, surrounded by high cliffs, broken rock and a young alder forest. Reaching it requires hours of bushwhacking through dense alders and crossing several strong creeks, but goat, wolf and bear tracks are plentiful on sandbars beside the river.

Behind our camp, polished granite benches rolled upward, covered in a young forest of spruce and mountain hemlock, which clung to mossy soil only four inches deep. Muir's tidewater glacier had covered the area 300 years earlier. During a short walk behind camp I found small ponds filling perfectly circular holes in the granite, evidence of powerful waterfalls that disappeared when the glacier receded. Above, goats ate grass on ledges 1,500 feet above the sea, and later, as we cooked dinner, a river otter glided in and out of the water near the intertidal, and a black bear fed in sedges half a mile away.

13.1: WHITEWATER IN A SEA KAYAK— TIPS ON EDDIES AND RAPIDS

From Puget Sound to northern southeast Alaska, many channels have strong tidal currents that pose serious threats to kayakers. The best defense against these hazards is knowledge of tidal activity in general and local tidal anomalies. However, sometimes kayakers cannot avoid swift water and even whitewater in the Inside Passage and must be prepared to deal with surprises.

Eddy lines, seemingly harmless wrinkles on the water that can easily flip an unsuspecting paddler, are one of the trickiest swift-water obstacles for kayakers. They form where eddies border the main current, often creating distinct lines a few inches tall where opposing currents rub against each other. The currents are often strongest at the eddy line, and when a kayak crosses it the power of the new current can grab the boat's upstream chine and quickly flip it. Safely crossing the line requires paddling aggressively

With big bodies of water on either side, the narrow crook in front of camp was a bottleneck a quarter mile long that turned to raging whitewater between peak tides. We had arrived near high tide, with almost no current moving past our beach, but as we set camp the ebb grew swift, eventually sliding past at eight knots. As its level dropped, standing waves developed that quickly grew to four feet during the second hour of the tide cycle. During the third hour, as we ate dinner above the intertidal, the waves reached twelve feet, with their tops rolling over in gushing whitewater, and deep holes formed near the opposite shore. The rapid roared loudly as occasional icebergs zoomed through it like small boats, bobbing over the waves. It looked more like parts of the Colorado River than an arm of the Pacific Ocean. However, the rapid gradually diminished after the third hour; during the fifth hour the whitewater disappeared.

Shortly after eleven, when the light finally grew too dim for reading, I climbed into the tent and fell asleep, but I awoke three hours later when a rockslide or avalanche released somewhere near camp. I bolted upright, unzipped the door and for a couple minutes peered helplessly into a twilit night as big rocks knocked against mountains. I wasn't afraid the debris would hit us, but with our tent only twenty feet above the high tide, I wondered if it would strike the water and create a big wave.

Signs of massive rockslides commonly scar mountainsides in recently deglaciated fiords, where land takes centuries to recover from the ice. Earthquake-triggered slides are also common, and sometimes scars on nearby walls show where slide-triggered waves destroyed vegetation or created other slides. The best-documented example in southeast Alaska is in Lituya Bay, a recently deglaciated inlet roughly 100 miles south of Yakutat. At ten at night on August 9, 1958, an 8.3-magnitude earthquake centered in the nearby St Elias Mountains triggered a huge landslide in Lituya's northwest arm, and in seconds half a mountainside slipped into the bay and sent water and debris 1,720 feet up the opposite wall, a little more than a mile away. The splash stripped the wall bare, then created a wave 100 feet high that ripped through the inlet at more than 100 miles per hour, removing thousands of trees from its walls before emptying into the Gulf of Alaska.

Lituya Bay is one of few safe anchorages along that portion of the Gulf of Alaska, and that night three fishing vessels were anchored there. Two sank, killing two people, but miraculously one stayed afloat through the turmoil. Its captain later described rising and falling on muddy waves, surrounded by thousands of floating trees. Today, the scars from

and leaning downstream in the new current, which raises the hull to the current's force and prevents it from flipping the boat.

Another common and potentially dangerous phenomenon in the Inside Passage is unexpected swift currents. In a panic, surprised kayakers sometimes attempt to escape the current, bringing their boats sideways to it and risking capsize or collision with downstream obstacles. Although escaping the current is the natural reflex, often it is better to steer for its center, where the water is usually the deepest. Many currents in the Inside Passage fill short constrictions between islands or shoals and are escaped quickest by following their flow to wider water. Of course this can lead to trouble in some currents, which is why paddlers need to study maps carefully before traveling.

Sea kayakers in the Inside Passage should also be prepared for whitewater. Because sea kayaks are long and often heavy with gear, they lack the quick maneuverability of smaller whitewater boats, which makes negotiating a rapid much trickier. Steering across the current is not as easy, and sea kayakers must allow more time to get around rocks, holes and other obstacles to reach the wave trains that usually represent the deepest water.

1958 remain obvious, with mature forest high on the mountains, but bare rock and young forest close to the water. I have thought of Lituya Bay many times when camped along the intertidal in the Inside Passage.

■ ■ ■

When we awoke near seven the next morning a flooding tide was in its last hour, sliding quickly past camp. As we ate breakfast and broke camp the water slowed and eventually became slack for about fifteen minutes, but it quickly began moving in the opposite direction as we packed our boats. By the time we entered the water the waves were three feet tall and breaking. We entered them by forcing through the upstream edge of an eddy near camp, paddling against the main current at a forty-five-degree angle until it swept our bows downstream. Once in the swift current, we struggled to maneuver our heavy boats across the channel to avoid a rock covered in shallow whitewater. Then, sliding past it, we slipped into a V-shaped tongue of smooth water that delivered us into a steady wave train of three-foot waves. Cold water splashed over our bows and smacked our faces as we bobbed through the waves, but a minute later we were in flat water, gliding toward the base of a dark cliff.

We paddled two miles and turned east into the main arm, with the glacier roughly seventeen miles away. Dozens of blue and white bergs dotted the green channel, and hundreds of murrelets, gulls, scoters and guillemots fed where the two fiords met. The skies were clear with temperatures near sixty as we made steady progress through wide paths between the ice. As in LeConte, we paddled deep into the Coast Mountains, with walls rising 4,000 feet within two miles and our maps showing peaks near 7,000 feet only five miles away. Steep waterfalls were abundant; hanging valleys, small glaciers and sharp peaks tugged our attention from one side of the fiord to the other.

We covered nine miles in less than three hours. Whereas the previous morning our island camp was surrounded by mature rain forest, which had not been glaciated in more than 1,000 years, now the forest consisted of much shorter trees and big patches of bare rock, land covered in ice only two centuries earlier. Eventually, the forest became sparse, and we arrived at a point of bare rock angling upward hundreds of feet at a thirty-degree angle. Around the point the arm split, with a small inlet reaching two miles north and the main channel continuing east for eight miles to the glacier.

"I think John Muir camped near this point," I told Bill. "I was looking at the map while reading *Travels in Alaska* last night, and I'm pretty sure he was describing this point." Muir's book did not include detailed maps of his travels.

"He must've had suction cups on his tent. I don't see anything below thirty degrees here."

"Well, he described hauling his tent up about 200 feet while his Tlingit guides slept in their canoe. He found a level bench up there, and I think that could be it." I pointed upward, where a short plateau 200 feet above the water briefly interrupted the steepness. "What's interesting is that he reported seeing two tidewater glaciers from camp, and I bet today you can't see any."

Bill looked at the wall for a moment, then said, "Let's go see."

Polished granite without handholds rose sharply from the water, but after paddling for a few minutes we found a slim notch filled with wiry alders beginning ten feet above the water and leading toward the bench. I paddled to a small wart of rock protruding three inches from the wall, swung my foot onto it, and stood slowly, one foot on the wall and the other in my cockpit. I unhooked my bowline and wadded it into my pocket, then used inch-deep cracks to climb toward the alders, eventually grabbing their thin trunks and pulling myself into the notch. Sitting in damp soil in a nest of alders, I held my bowline taut as Bill tied his boat to mine, then used the rope to scale the wall.

We scrambled upward through an alder-choked notch two feet wide, which narrowed to less than a foot and ended in a sheer cliff 100 feet above the water. On all fours, we grasped tiny handholds to cross a forty-degree slope of polished bedrock, our rubber boots slipping frequently. After fifty feet we reached a crevice three feet wide that wound upward between sheer cliffs and ended in a steep crack filled with loose rocks, which we carefully climbed twenty feet to the level bench.

The bench was thirty feet long and ten feet wide and littered with stones and boulders left by the glacier, avalanches and maybe John Muir. Parallel grooves two inches deep lined the bench, carved by rocks trapped in the glacier. Except for dwarf fireweed and small clumps of grass growing beside a few boulders, it was devoid of vegetation, like most of the surrounding mountainside. Below, white bergs dotted the green fiord, which split to our east, and only patchy forest clung to the bottoms of mountains rising steeply from the water and reaching 5,000 feet two miles from shore.

With a sleeping pad it would have been a great place to camp, and 120 years earlier it afforded views of two tidewater glaciers less than a mile apart. But since Muir's time, the glacier filling the short inlet to the north had receded three miles from the water, leaving a U-shaped valley filled with a light green jungle of alders winding between steep mountains. The glacier filling the main channel, while still tidewater, was now eight miles away and around a corner.

We enjoyed the views for twenty minutes, then carefully returned to our boats. The ebbing tide had left our tiny step two feet above water, revealing sheer bedrock angling into the sea at sixty degrees. While Bill held my bowline taut, I rappelled to my boat and fell clumsily into its cockpit. Once seated, he threw the bowline to me, and I towed his boat fifty feet to the east, where another small step was a few inches above the water. Meanwhile, Bill slowly followed a narrow fissure eastward with his fingers, then lowered himself diagonally through another fissure and plopped into his cockpit.

After paddling for twenty minutes we reached a line of densely packed bergs spanning the one-mile width of the fiord. Most were smaller than our kayaks, but scattered larger ones angled upward above the pack. Forcing our boats into the ice, we paddled diagonally away from the largest bergs, with ice scraping against our beams and crackling around us. Soon we encountered scores of harbor seals lying on flat bergs, some in pairs and others in groups of up to fifteen. We gave them wide berth, trying not to disturb them, but even from 100 yards away a few raised their heads alertly, then hurried across their bergs and slid clumsily into the water.

Mid-May through early July each year is pupping season, when thousands of harbor seals congregate near southeast Alaska's tidewater glaciers to give birth to their young. Birth typically occurs on icebergs, and nursing takes roughly three to six weeks, with mothers lying on their sides on the ice and their small pups at right angles to their bellies, always ready to nurse. The mothers feed on shrimp and small fish near the glaciers, and the thick ice provides protection from orcas, their main predator. After the nursing period mothers and pups separate for life, and mothers are ready to mate again by mid-July. Like bears, they reproduce by delayed implantation, meaning the embryo's development pauses for between six and twelve weeks following fertilization; gestation lasts almost eleven months. After reaching sexual maturity at five years, females potentially spend all but a few weeks each year either pregnant or nursing.

While forcing our way through ice we passed two blood-stained bergs. The first was ten feet across with a big splotch of bright blood on its frosted surface, likely the result of a recent birth. Pups can swim within an hour of birth, and when their mothers lead them into the water, eagles, ravens and gulls quickly descend on bloody bergs to consume their afterbirth. The second berg was smaller and had big clumps of fur mixed with blood stains, likely the result of predation or scavenging. Although orcas occasionally enter the ice to feed on seals, it is more common that eagles, ravens and gulls scavenge abandoned or still-born pups. The birds visit the glaciers more during pupping season than any other time of year, flying low over dense ice teeming with seals and quickly surrounding abandoned or dead pups.

A few years later, in another southeast Alaskan fiord, I watched three eagles surround an abandoned pup, which screamed desperately for its mother and occasionally scurried to the side of its berg, looking nervously at the water. Each time it moved, the eagles jockeyed around it, but maintained a distance of a few feet. The slow courtship with death ended an hour later when one of the eagles hopped forward and delivered the first of many pecks to the pup's head. Pupping season is the most vulnerable time in a seal's life, and once separated from its mother a pup stands no chance for survival. With this in mind, we mitigated our disturbance by keeping our distance from the seals.

In south-central Alaska harbor seal populations have declined sharply since the 1970s. Possible reasons for the decline include increased commercial fishing, warmer water, disturbance from increased vessel traffic and a decrease in tidewater glaciation. Decreased glacial ice also prevents researchers from seeing as many seals, which makes quantifying the population decline difficult. No doubt harbor seals have also declined in parts of Glacier Bay National Park, but their population in the rest of southeast Alaska appears stable, with estimates from the mid-1990s of almost 40,000 animals.

13.2: KAYAKERS AND WILDLIFE HARASSMENT

With a low profile and lack of engine, paddlers in the Inside Passage can get extremely close to wildlife such as humpbacks, orcas, seals and bears. But the closeness also increases the likelihood of harassment. To protect wildlife, paddlers should become familiar with animal behavior and sensitive life phases and never approach so closely that they change an animal's behavior.

Here are some tips:

Surprisingly, research in the Inside Passage demonstrates that kayakers disturb seals on icebergs from nearly 1,000 feet away, not much less than the distance for large cruise ships. The disturbance is particularly harmful during pupping season (late spring and early summer), when panicked mothers and pups can separate after abandoning their bergs. A pup unable to rejoin its mother stands no chance for survival; even brief separation increases susceptibility to predators. Although it is difficult to avoid some level of disturbance when thick ice chokes a fiord, paddlers can minimize their effect by traveling in early morning, when mother-pup pairs congregate in less density, and by carefully planning routes that avoid the highest seal concentrations.

Sea lions also congregate in large numbers, often on rocky and exposed shores. They are

Under continued clear skies we struggled through thick ice for almost a mile, then made better progress through large openings near the north wall. Ice crackled around us and occasionally rolled or split, and seal pups cried loudly in hoarse voices that sounded eerily human. Their cries mixed with crackling ice and echoed slightly against walls of bare rock rising thousands of feet. Alder and willow grew in narrow fissures and tight valleys, but spruce and hemlock were almost entirely absent, making the place look like a half-drowned Yosemite. Muir referred to nearby areas, including the steep mountains near present-day Juneau, as "Little Yosemites," but he never reached the mountains surrounding our kayaks, which were mostly buried in ice at the time of his visit.

We caught our first view of the glacier, still five miles away, after rounding a bare point angling sixty degrees from the water. It was a bluish river of ice almost a mile wide that formed the end of the fiord and wound upward between high mountains covered in snow. Forty-five minutes later, after covering two miles through moderate ice, we could see deep blue cracks in its face and hear low rumbles each time it calved. At that point, a slight headwind we had felt for a few miles suddenly strengthened and turned cold, pressing icily against our hands and faces and slowing our progress. Such winds, called catabatics, commonly occur near glaciers, especially on sunny days: warm air from valleys and fiords rises, enabling cold air from the glacier to spill downward.

We battled the strong headwind and wound through compacted bergs for another ninety minutes and finally arrived within a half mile of the glacier near five. It was a deeply cracked wall of blue and white ice 200 feet high, with tall pillars, spires and precariously balanced piles of crushed ice. A little right of center was a royal blue ice cave fifty feet high; along the glacier's edges, ice almost black with rocky debris clung to steep mountain walls. These lateral moraines are where debris scoured from the mountains collect, along with debris from avalanches and rockslides. Above them, the mountains rose thousands of feet in hulking masses of bare rock lined with steep streams.

We pressed forward through gaps in the ice and stopped paddling about a third of a mile from the glacier. Sitting quietly, we watching small chunks of ice silently free-fall up to 200 feet from its face, smacking the water with sharp cracks that echoed against the glacier. When they splashed water twenty feet high we realized they were the size of cars. After fifteen minutes, an avalanche of ice boulders slid down the right side and splashed into the water with a long roar that sent big waves against the cliffs. Nearby, we noticed a large

extremely sensitive to disturbance. When a kayak or motor vessel approaches too close they tumble over each other in a panicked race for the water that costs important energy and risks injury. Sea lions are listed as threatened by the Endangered Species Act and are protected from harassment by the Marine Mammal Protection Act of 1972. The latter makes harassment, including disturbance, of humpbacks, orcas and all other marine mammals illegal.

Kayakers can also get close to bears feeding in the intertidal, but scaring a bear into the woods costs important calories, especially in early summer when they are still recovering from hibernation and food resources are scarce and in late summer when they are putting on fat for the winter. Kayakers can avoid disturbance by approaching from downwind and closely monitoring the bear's response.

Eagles, otters and terns are only a few examples of other sensitive species that suffer when humans get too close; strong binoculars and zoom lenses provide kayakers a chance to enjoy wildlife without harassing it. And paddlers should keep in mind that bears, seals and other species are common in the Inside Passage-if avoiding disturbance means missing a close encounter, another opportunity will likely soon occur.

circle of brown water boiling at the face, with a dozen gulls and arctic terns circling above it. Monstrous rivers flow within and beneath glaciers, gushing to the surface of the sea at their faces. The constant upwelling creates rich biological communities of small fish and invertebrates, which attract birds, seals and porpoises.

The cold wind and river's current constantly pushed us backward and shifted the ice around us, so that we had to paddle forward to maintain our position and avoid big bergs. The glacier was mostly quiet, but after thirty minutes a column of ice 200 feet tall and almost as wide collapsed suddenly, splashing water more than 100 feet and creating a loud thunder that echoed between the walls. Big, breaking waves radiated from its impact and within seconds exploded against the steep shore, reminding me of the surf by Pine Island. We watched nervously as the waves approached, bobbing the bergs in front of us, but by the time they reached us they were five-foot rollers without breaking tops. They knocked the surrounding bergs against each other loudly as they raised and lowered our boats, and for the next fifteen minutes ice boulders and small spires fell from the glacier, crashing loudly into the water.

Near six, we grew cold in the icy wind and paddled toward a tumultuous river about a mile from the glacier. It was one of only a few places to land in the last eight miles of the fiord and probably the only one flat enough for camping, but as we soon learned, camping there was not easy. We rode ashore on a two-foot wave created by the last calving, which smacked our plastic hulls hard against big cobbles, then carried the heavy boats a few feet from the water.

The beach was 150 feet long and covered with cobbles and boulders, with a violent stream bordering its west side and steep, polished granite between thirty and fifty feet high bordering its other sides. With no camping possible on the cobbles, we climbed the slick granite on our hands and knees, using small fissures as handholds, and reached a plateau of rolling granite covered with patchy moss and lichen fifty feet above the water. Clusters of short willow and alder covered most flat spots, but after a few minutes we found a sloping slab of granite barely adequate for camping. It was 300 feet from our landing and sixty feet above the water, which would require long trips with our gear, but its views of the glacier and surrounding mountains were spectacular. A polished bench close to the water would make a good kitchen, and we could hang our food from a nearby cliff.

As we discussed camp, I looked at the glacier just in time to see a spire 200 feet tall topple into the water, creating a giant splash. Seconds later, a huge spire that had bordered the first crumbled with another big splash. Its thunder vibrated deep in my chest and felt like it could shake the ground. We watched big waves rush through ice bergs and explode against fiord walls, then suddenly realized our boats were still close to shore.

"The boats!" I yelled, and ran fast toward our beach. I half-fell, half-ran through a narrow crevice filled with alders, their wiry branches tangling around my ankles and slapping my face, then, reaching its end, slid on my butt down a steep slope of polished granite thirty feet long. I tried ineffectually to brake with my rubber boots, but after speeding thirty feet tumbled abruptly onto the cobble beach, bruising my elbows and knees. Bill almost landed on top of me, then we hobbled across the beach and dragged our boats over rocks as the first wave rushed ashore. As it receded, the next wave rose five feet and broke where our boats had been a moment earlier. If we hadn't rushed to the beach, the big waves that followed would have pulled the boats into the icy water, stranding us with no gear, food or radio in a remote fiord.

We found no easy route to the plateau. Carrying limited armloads of gear, we scaled a slick granite wall, then struggled through a thin notch of alders. Setting camp took more than two hours. With no vegetation near the beach to determine the high tide line, and considering the threat of waves from calving, we spend another twenty minutes hauling the empty boats twenty feet up steep granite, where we hung them from skinny alders. Finally, at eight-thirty we cooked a burrito dinner while the glacier calved repeatedly, filling the fiord with ice. At nine-thirty, as we did the dishes and hung the food, the setting sun illuminated a 10,000-foot peak near the Canadian border, which was less than twelve miles away. The night remained light enough for reading until after eleven, and with a few stars shining faintly in the twilit sky, we spread our sleeping bags on granite benches and fell asleep outside. All night, the glacier rumbled, cracked and thundered, periodically waking us. Even at two in the morning its crumbling face was clearly visible.

I awoke at six to the crack and rumble of an avalanche a mile to the west. Sitting up quickly, I watched a veil of snow and ice cascade 200 feet over a cliff near the top of a round dome 4,000 feet high. Huge blocks of ice shattered against a ledge below the cliff and joined a stream of snow flowing into a thin gully. I watched for a minute, then looked east toward the glacier and noticed a mountain goat beside some alders 100 yards away.

The skies were clear, with the sun already well above the horizon, and I propped my head against a dry bag and watched the glacier as warm sunlight spread across my sleeping bag. A mile away, a row of 5,000-foot mountains lined the other side of the channel, most of their peaks rounded domes covered in deep snow. Fractures from recent avalanches dotted the snowfields, and an alpine glacier spilled over a saddle between peaks, feeding white streams that fell precipitously down a bare mountain. Valley walls plunged 2,500 vertical feet between mountains, too steep for snow or vegetation, and countless waterfalls fell from high ridges.

After a long breakfast we spent an hour watching the face of the glacier collapse with thunderous explosions, then packed lunches and hiked inland in a narrow valley close to camp. Our topographical maps were useless, with their latest revisions dated 1963. They showed the main glacier filling the fiord beside camp and a tributary glacier filling the valley and covering camp. However, we knew the big stream nearby would lead us to remnants of the tributary glacier. With the valley too recently deglaciated for accurate maps, we knew we were exploring a place few humans had visited.

After hundreds of years buried in ice, the valley had been free for only a few decades. It was raw, like a part of the earth being born, with sparse vegetation and big piles of rocky debris covering a lumpy floor of polished bedrock. Sand, cobbles and car-sized boulders lay strewn haphazardly across its floor, deposited by landslides, avalanches or the receding glacier. Fireweed and lupine grew in cracks in bare bedrock. And a jungle of young alders and willows covered piles of loose rocks. On either side, barren cliffs rose more than 1,000 feet, with tight valleys filled with debris and low vegetation. A boisterous stream cut the middle of the valley, brown with glacial silt.

First we walked beside the stream, which was fifty feet across and deafeningly loud. Its turbid water exploded from boulders, slid across polished granite and burst over sudden drops. After a quarter mile it cut steep walls through a gravelly moraine fifty feet high, where stones avalanched from under our feet and disappeared into the churning water below. The river would crush us if we fell from the unstable slope, and we climbed away from it, eventually arriving in jumbled boulders and a tangle of head-high alder and willow. For nearly a mile we climbed over rocks and struggled blindly through vegetation, gaining only occasional views of the valley from atop big boulders.

It took more than an hour to cover one mile, but the vegetation diminished as we fought closer to the glacier, eventually becoming sporadic thickets across rocky debris. We made better progress for half a mile, then slowed again as we crossed a huge rockslide that left a scar 750 feet up the valley's east wall. It was recent and had released boulders twenty feet high that left divots and skid marks on the gravel floor. With sunshine filling the valley, we took off our shirts as we climbed over the rocks.

The valley narrowed to a quarter mile between steep walls, their barren cliffs smooth and appearing to overhang us. After another hour the alders and willows disappeared, leaving scattered lupine and fireweed among the rocks. With the glacier's face only half a mile ahead, we side-stepped along a gravel slope below a high cliff fifty yards from the river. Stones slid from under our boots and revealed dark ice twenty feet deep, remnants of the retreating glacier. Glaciers do not recede evenly and commonly leave substantial blocks of ice in their path, often insulated by moraine. The shrinking ice eventually creates a kame, a smooth mound of gravel on the valley floor.

The narrowing walls forced us back to the river, where we hiked on bare bedrock above the rushing current until we reached the glacier's moraine-covered snout. It was an uneven cliff of blue and white ice between fifty and 100 feet high covered in deep debris, which came from landslides and avalanches, but also from the glacier's melting process. As a glacier melts, becoming shallower, the silt and boulders locked inside it collect on top, sometimes burying the glacier completely. Mist from the river and a breeze from the ice were refreshingly cool.

The big stream erupted from below the face as brown water poured from its middle through two big holes that looked like sewer pipes. First we tried to climb atop the glacier where it joined the cliff, but a constant stream of falling rocks stopped us. They ranged from pebbles to boulders and skipped along the cliff from a pile of debris 200 feet overhead. Not more than a few seconds passed between falling rocks, which was not enough time to negotiate the uneven pile where they landed. Instead, we backtracked, then hopped carefully between boulders in the raging river, eventually jumping onto a slab of frosted ice at the base of the glacier. Fifty feet above, a boulder thirty feet wide protruded from the ice by more than three-quarters, with loose gravel sliding from its edges as though it would fall at any moment. We quickly climbed over rock and ice to get away from the boulder, but soon realized that small piles of gravel and rocks were sliding from the glacier's face in each direction.

Nervously we hurried up a steep ramp of rock-covered ice to the top of the glacier, knocking gravel and stones into the river below. When we reached the top we discovered cracks above the face ten and twenty feet deep, like it could soon calve. With piles of gravel sliding from the glacier and rocks knocking along the nearby cliff, we ran over uneven ice and rock toward a plateau at the glacier's middle, safely away from the face. As we ran, I expected to be pummeled by rocks from above or carried into the river by collapsing ice.

We felt safer when we reached level ice and gravel about fifty yards from either cliff, then walked up the glacier for half a mile. The layer of gravel diminished, and soon the surface consisted largely of granular ice that crunched under our rubber boots. Scattered boulders littered its surface, and small streams disappeared into azure holes leading to the glacier's inner plumbing. Steep walls rose on either side, with no vegetation. Small rockslides knocked against the cliffs, but never reached the glacier. Rockslides and avalanches are common on sunny days, when warm temperatures melt snow and ice and loosen rocks.

After forty minutes we reached a flat basin fed by two steep ice falls and surrounded by barren cliffs rising 1,500 vertical feet. The main flow of the glacier formed one ice fall, which lay straight ahead and was a quarter mile wide and 300 feet tall. It originated in a cluster of 7,000-foot peaks in the Stikine Ice Field. The other entered at a right-angle from the east and was only 200 feet wide but

750 feet tall. It spilled over a saddle between sheer cliffs and formed a sexy S-curve before joining the main flow. Deep cracks furrowed both falls, a result of their steepness, and made climbing them impossible without crampons, ropes and helmets.

We sat on boulders in the middle of the basin and ate lunch, the surrounding cliffs like cathedral walls below a narrow ceiling of rich blue sky. The basin was eerily devoid of life, with no vegetation in sight and no signs of wildlife. The only sounds were occasional rocks releasing from cliffs, small streams running along the ice and a light breeze. It was easy to imagine we were having lunch somewhere in the Pleistocene. Ten thousand years earlier, most of the Inside Passage still looked like our icy basin, and it is likely the region will look that away again before too long.

■ ■ ■

The Pleistocene ice ages were once regarded as a unique epoch, but today they are considered only a chapter in the earth's long story of glaciation. Due to cyclical climatic changes during at least the last billion years, many global cooling trends created periods of widespread glaciation. Some lasted tens of millions of years, dwarfing the Pleistocene, which began roughly two million years ago. Between ice ages, warming trends eliminated glaciers and at times enabled tropical conditions in today's temperate latitudes and tree growth at the poles. The climatic fluctuations are likely due to combined factors including atmospheric content, solar output, oscillations in the earth's axis, which affect polar distances from the sun, and plate tectonics, which can change ocean currents and weather patterns.

Evidence from past glaciations also demonstrates that the ice ages of the Pleistocene have not yet ended. It is now known that the Pleistocene consisted of many periods of glacial advance and retreat, with advances that spread continental ice sheets as far south as the Great Lakes and retreats when global glaciation was less than it is today. The retreats, known as interglacials, lasted tens of thousands of years, making today's period of relatively light glaciation appear a brief break within a larger cooling trend. In this context, recently deglaciated valleys like the one we hiked will continue their slow recovery in the short term, with lichen, moss and young forest developing in the next century. If the glaciers remain at bay, lush rain forest and abundant wildlife will eventually fill today's lifeless valleys. But at some point snow will increase in the ice fields, or temperatures will cool at sea level, and the glaciers will advance again, pushing mature rain forest into the sea and continuing the excavation of the Inside Passage.

■ ■ ■

We relaxed for more than an hour, then began our return to camp. We quickly but carefully negotiated the face of the glacier, passed the continuing trickle of rocks falling from the cliff, then hiked along the river and eventually re-entered the jungle of alder and willow. After two hours we arrived on polished granite at our camp and snacked and napped in the sun for the rest of the afternoon. Around eight, as we ate dinner, the sun disappeared behind warped mountains, and for the next two hours alpen glow illuminated progressively higher peaks to the east, culminating with a brilliant pink display on a 10,000-foot peak past the Canadian border. A light breeze chased the sounds of dozens of waterfalls around the fiord.

Harbor porpoises and mother seals with pups swam slowly in the green water, sometimes approaching within twenty feet of our kitchen rock. And gulls, arctic terns and swifts flew erratically around nearby cliffs, feeding on insects. The glacier was quiet for a few hours, but near eleven, as we lay in sleeping bags on bare granite, it began a series of enormous calvings that sent big waves crashing against the cliffs below our camp. We slept outside again, but awoke frequently to thundering ice and crashing surf.

We awoke early the next morning to another sunny day and spectacular calvings from the glacier, some sending water and chunks of ice 150 feet into the air and a quarter mile from its face, like shrapnel. A half mile away, scores of seals lay generally motionless on a dense cluster of ice bergs, with random pups crying loudly and eagles making occasional passes. After a long breakfast we hiked east along the steep wall, winding carefully around barren cliffs until we were more than a mile away and 1,500 feet above the glacier. Mountain goats fed on patches of grass 1,000 feet higher, but the only signs of life near us were small clusters of lupine and fireweed growing from piles of gravel mixed with goat pellets.

Illustration 13.2: This complex of glaciers high in the Stikine Ice Field illustrates the formation of lateral and medial moraines. Lateral moraines form along the sides of glaciers and consist of debris scraped from mountainsides or brought down by rock-slides and avalanches. To the right of the photo's center, two glaciers merge, their lateral moraines combining to form a medial moraine. Moraines can pile 100 or more feet above a glacier's surface and consist of material ranging from dust to enormous boulders.

Our hike ended near a bleached and broken goat skull at the edge of a cliff dropping 1,000 feet into a tight valley. Below, in green sea by the glacier's face, an enormous river welled up in a circle of brown and white water, with gulls and terns circling over it as though suspended from a mobile. The glacier creaked and cracked loudly, and tall pinnacles periodically collapsed against each other. On its surface, six deep black lines, like big tire tracks, paralleled the direction of flow. Two were beside each other below us, one was near the center and three were grouped near the outside. They were medial moraines, thick lines of debris that form when the lateral moraines of joining glaciers combine. Representing six tributaries, they illustrated the complexity of the ice field beyond our view.

We returned to camp early in the afternoon, and I bathed in a clear, frigid stream that slid into perfect granite tubs, then dried myself lying on the smooth rock. Throughout the afternoon the glacier's calvings included two enormous shooters, blocks of electric blue ice that rose slowly from under water and stood more than 100 feet before toppling over with big splashes. The evening remained sunny and warm, so we slept outside the tent for the third night. When we turned our backs on the glacier the bare rock and long shadows surrounding us looked more like the Great Basin than the temperate rain forest.

We broke camp the next morning and enjoyed our last views of the glacier. In only three days, constant calvings had drastically changed its shape, creating new features and removing peninsulas, spires and caves. We launched from our rocky beach and after fighting through two miles of thick ice made swift progress, passing shattered bergs from calvings that woke us in previous nights. Under sunny skies we watched bare walls eventually return to thick rain forest, and by seven that evening we covered thirty miles and set our camp on an island near Stephens Passage. Throughout the afternoon clouds approached from the southeast, and rain began that night. Our surroundings returned to a swirling mixture of clouds, forests and white-topped mountains, and we didn't enjoy another perfectly sunny day until two weeks later in Seattle.

CHAPTER FOURTEEN

Taku—Parting Lessons

We followed two humpbacks across our bay early in the morning, then turned north along steep mountains in Stephens Passage. Frequent showers blew north from Frederick Sound. The ceiling hovered around 2,000 feet, with patchy lower clouds clinging to nearby forest and mixing with alpine snows on Admiralty Island, twelve miles to the west. Our progress was slow, and late in the afternoon, after only fifteen miles, we ducked into Port Snettisham, another bay with long arms reaching eastward into the glaciers and high peaks of the Coast Mountains. Under partially clearing skies we set our camp on grass above the intertidal and our kitchen among boulders beside the water, then cooked dinner.

As we ate we enjoyed clear views up the bay's north arm, where barren walls rose 3,000 feet on either side of a narrow channel that zigzagged between steep points. Above it, heavily glaciated peaks near 5,000 feet formed a jagged horizon of deep snow and bare rock. Like so many places we had passed, the arm held vast wildlands offering weeks of remote exploration—again I lamented our limited itinerary.

After Joseph Whidbey's brief visit to Snettisham in August, 1794, Vancouver named it for a Norfolk town not far from his birthplace of Kings Lynn. Whidbey saw "several smokes" in the bay, indicating groups of Tlingits, but apparently did not explore its narrow arms. Nearly 100 years later Snettisham joined other nearby bays as a busy mining area, with two post offices, the last closing in 1931. In the bay's northern arm Alaska's first pulp mill operated for a few years in the 1920s.

Although we saw no evidence of the old settlements, signs of modern civilization were increasing. The previous evening nine boats passed our island in four hours, traveling in and out of Holkham Bay. That day a few float planes buzzed overhead, and more than a dozen boats motored past in Stephens Passage. They included small charters, midsize tour boats, a barge, private yachts and sailboats and an enormous cruise ship with big, black windows.

From our camp in Snettisham, we also saw the power lines leading to Juneau, which like many southeast Alaskan communities gets its power from hydroelectricity. In the 1970s, engineers drilled tunnels beneath two of the many fiord-shaped lakes in the mountains surrounding Snettisham, creating an artificial spillway to turn large turbines that now produce about 80 percent of Juneau's electricity. The power plant, not in view from our camp, includes a dock, airstrip and residential quarters. Its electricity flows through lines running about thirty miles to Juneau, with metal towers placed in a swath cut through the forest. The light green strip, filled with alder, berries and young trees, parallels Stephens Passage at about 500 feet above the sea, and the wires are subject to high winds, falling trees and avalanches, each periodically interrupting power to Juneau. The city has large diesel generators that provide electricity during the outages, important during inclement winter weather.

Our weather the following morning was cool and cloudy, and we packed quickly to stay warm, then entered the water near eight. We made the four-mile crossing of Snettisham and continued north in Stephens Passage in light rain and a southeasterly breeze. At mid-morning we took a short break along steep and broken shores; near noon, as the sun broke through an opening in the clouds, we turned into a narrow inlet with high walls, looking for a good landing for lunch.

After a quarter mile we rounded a rocky point and spotted a black bear in sedges above a long cobble beach. Staying downwind of it, we paddled quietly toward shore until our bows rubbed against rocks at the edge of the water, just thirty feet from the bear. It moved slowly through shoulder-deep sedges, bright green against its jet black coat, and paused for long minutes to rip mouthfuls of vegetation that it chewed loudly. Several times it looked up and stared at us, with long sedges hanging from either side of its mouth as it waved its nose in the air for our scent. But a bear's nose is its window to the world, and with our scent blowing away, it apparently felt no threat and resumed eating.

"Another," Bill whispered, nodding his head to the east.

Another black bear, this one cinnamon-colored, ambled slowly toward us along cobbles 100 yards away. It paused for ten minutes at the water's edge, and with our binoculars we watched it roll large rocks together with big forepaws, crushing hundreds of barnacles. It rubbed the rocks, then licked barnacle goo from its paw, exhaling a stringy combination of saliva and barnacles that momentarily shone silver in the sun. Especially in spring, before salmon arrive, piles of bear scat loaded with barnacle shells litter the forest near beaches in the Inside Passage. After a year, all that remains are small piles of off-white shells sinking into the moss—another mingling of ocean and forest.

The first bear had his back turned and head down in the sedges as the other continued toward us along the water. When it reached fifty feet away, only a minute from bumping into us, we slowly raised our paddles to back away from shore. But then it knocked cobbles together with its steps, and the first bear lifted its head quickly and stiffened, then bolted through sedges, hopped over a dead tree and crashed into the woods through a curtain of alders. The thrashing vegetation startled the approaching bear, which also ran noisily into the woods. We never saw the first again, but for five minutes we watched the second peer at us from 100 feet up a hillside, obscured by dark branches. As we paddled away, it returned cautiously to the beach, seeping into view through a film of alders.

That night we set our camp above broken boulders along Stephens Passage as the clouds rifted, revealing big patches of blue that turned dark purple around eleven. We lay against drift logs as three whales swam back and forth along a steep bluff only fifty feet away, their loud breaths echoing against the bluff and mixing with the steady calls of a great horned owl in the steep woods behind camp. A light breeze rustled the sedges above the intertidal as Stephens Passage, ten miles across but as still as a lake, lapped gently against broken boulders. The sounds of the coast seemed especially vivid, and I knew in five or six short days the city sounds of Juneau would reduce them to memories.

A little after eleven the enormous white bow of a cruise ship slid silently into view from around the bluff to our south, seeming very close to shore. It quickly moved into full view, twenty stories tall, 700 feet long and covered in bright white and yellow lights. It was like Juneau had suddenly come to us, floating on the inky water of Stephens Passage. Soon, the low rumble of diesel engines and the rush of water along its bow and stern reached our camp, and after a few minutes waves three feet high crashed against the nearby rocks. The ship took ten minutes to pass our beach, disappearing around a bluff to the north, but left a plume of light blue smoke that hovered above the water for an hour.

Cruise ship traffic in the Inside Passage nearly tripled between 1990 and 2002, eventually bringing more than 700,000 annual visitors to the region. At any one time between Memorial Day and Labor Day, 45,000 people may be aboard the ships between Seattle and Skagway. On some days they bring crowds of up to 10,000 to small downtown areas in Ketchikan and Juneau. While the massive industry brings millions of dollars and thousands of seasonal jobs, it also raises controversy about air and water pollution and effects on solitude and community infrastructures.

During a week's voyage, a typical cruise ship generates about 210,000 gallons of raw sewage, 50,000 gallons of oily bilge water and lesser amounts of hazardous waste and heavy metals, the product of photo development shops, dry cleaners and incinerators. Before dumping, sewage is treated at onboard waste treatment plants, called Marine Sanitary Devices (MSDs); bilge water is filtered until only minimal amounts of oil enter the water. Hazardous waste is disposed onshore according to federal and local regulations. However, each cruise ship also generates more than a million gallons of gray water in a week, from dishwashers, showers and cooking and laundry facilities. Gray water was historically dumped without regulation or oversight, but that began changing in 1999, when Royal Caribbean pled guilty to discharging hazardous waste with its gray water over a period of years in Alaskan waters. That same year, Holland America paid $2 million in fines and restitution for illegally polluting Alaskan waters.

Money from both settlements funded a wastewater testing program in southeast Alaska in the summer of 2000, which revealed widespread violations: All thirty-six samples of treated sewage failed to meet federal regulations, and 70 percent of gray water samples revealed unacceptable levels of fecal coliform bacteria, some 100,000 times federal standards. The results created outrage in a state that relies on clean water for its fishing, recreation and tourism industries; its governor and congressmen were quick to act. They supported strong legislation that passed in late 2000, requiring restrictions on wastewater discharges and increased wastewater testing and authorizing the Environmental Protection Agency (EPA) to set the nation's first standards for gray water. In addition, it banned discharging treated sewage and gray water within a mile of shore and releasing untreated sewage anywhere in Alaskan waters. Previously, untreated sewage could be dumped three miles from shore, which in the Inside Passage led to dumping in "doughnut holes," the middle parts of passages wider than six miles, like Stephens Passage. In 2001, the Alaska legislature put additional pressure on the industry by passing the first state bill to address cruise ship pollution. It set wastewater pollution limits, created reporting requirements and wastewater sampling schedules and charged a fee for state oversight.

In addition to water pollution, cruise ships emit large quantities of carbon monoxide, carbon dioxide, nitrogen oxides, particulate matter and ozone, emissions monitored by Alaska's Department of Environmental Conservation (DEC) and the EPA. In response to violations by two companies in 1999 and complaints of smog in Juneau and other cities, DEC used money from the 1999 Royal Caribbean and Holland America settlements to begin an air quality testing program in July, 2000. By the end of September, after eighty-one tests, DEC issued violation notices to Princess, Norwegian, Holland America, Crystal, Celebrity and Carnival cruise lines, alleging eleven of their ships violated air quality fifteen times in Juneau. The next year, Princess began a pilot program that involved shutting off its engines while in Juneau and buying surplus electricity from the city at a cost of thousands of dollars per day to keep the ships functioning.

In response to the myriad concerns, citizens in Juneau voted in 1999 to tax cruise ship companies $5 per visitor, bringing millions of dollars of additional revenue to the city. But in British Columbia, where cruise ships typically only stop in Vancouver and Victoria, controversy is at a much lower level. And so is regulation. While British Columbia recently created raw sewage non-dumping zones along its coast, very few of them are along cruise ship routes. In addition, MSDs are not inspected and wastewater discharges are not monitored. However, after recent findings in southeast Alaska some British Columbia residents are pushing for stronger legislation.

■ ■ ■

The following morning we continued north in cold showers and reached the intersection of Stephens Passage, Gastineau Channel and Taku Inlet. Stephens Passage, after running north-south for fifty miles, turned almost due west between Douglas and Admiralty Islands, forming the elbow that when viewed from the north in July, 1794, led Joseph Whidbey to consider Admiralty part of the mainland. To its east, Gastineau Channel was only a mile wide, running north-northwest between snowy mountains on Douglas Island and the mainland. It was busy with boat traffic, and ten miles ahead we saw the buildings of downtown Juneau, which created mixed emotions. After two wet months, it would have been easy to paddle to town, dry off and congratulate ourselves on completing the trip—it was only a few hours away. But above all, our two months had demonstrated the vastness of the Inside Passage, every day providing countless bays and mountains that invited exploration and promised wilderness. While returning to civilization was tempting, I felt enough energy and curiosity for at least another two months of kayaking.

Taku Inlet ran northeast between steep mountains, and with jagged peaks above it and a fragment of the Taku Glacier in view, it offered a perfect last chance for exploration. Although only a few miles from Alaska's capital, Taku Inlet is surrounded by some of the most forbidding and fascinating land in the Inside Passage. Fifteen miles from its mouth, the Taku Glacier spills thirty miles from the Juneau Ice Field, forming a face five miles wide along the side of the inlet, and past the glacier the inlet tapers to the mouth of the Taku River, a transboundary river that slices through the Coast Mountains from northwestern British Columbia. On either side of the inlet, steep mountains surround fiord-shaped lakes and rise more than 5,000 feet, disappearing into vast seas of ice and snow. Before paddling to Juneau, we planned to spend three days in Taku, exploring its lakes and camping near its glaciers.

The Taku River begins about 105 miles northeast of Juneau and drains 7,000 square miles of British Columbia's northwest corner. Hundreds of creeks and small streams feed its main stem from the mountains of northern British Columbia. The watershed is bordered

310

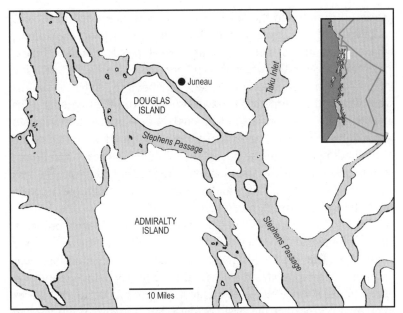

Map 14.1. Stephens Passage, Gastineau Channel, and Taku Inlet.

on its north by the headwaters of the Yukon River and on its south by the headwaters of the Stikine River. Like the Stikine, Nass, Skeena and Fraser, the Taku hosts huge runs of steelhead and all five species of Pacific salmon; its inland corridor provides habitat for moose, wolves and brown and black bears. It has provided ecological exchange between the coast and interior since the end of the last ice age and was an important trade route for the Taku kwan of Tlingits. And like other big rivers in the Inside Passage, it did not appear on Vancouver's charts.

With the *Chatham* and *Discovery* still anchored in Port Conclusion, Whidbey entered Taku Inlet on August 10, 1794. Two days earlier he had fired shots at an unfriendly group of Tlingits near Juneau while completing his circumnavigation of Admiralty Island, and in another six days he would meet James Johnstone on Kupreanof Island, nearly 100 miles to the south, to conclude the surveys. Whidbey spent the 10th and most of the 11th in Taku, which he reported as thirteen miles long and ending in a wide bay near a big glacier. Vancouver later wrote:

"The weather here was severally cold, with frequent showers of sleet and rain.... A compact body of ice extended some distance

311

nearly all round; and the adjacent region was composed of a close connected continuation of the lofty range of frozen mountains, whose sides, almost perpendicular, were formed entirely of rock, excepting close to the water side, where a few scattered dwarf pine trees found sufficient soil to vegetate in; above these the mountains were wrapped in perpetual frost and snow. From the rugged gullies in their sides were projected immense bodies of ice, that reached perpendicularly to the surface of the water...[and] which admitted of no landing place for the boats, but exhibited as dreary and inhospitable an aspect as the imagination can possibly suggest. The rise and fall of the tide in this situation was very considerable, appearing to be upwards of eighteen feet."

Poor weather, shallow mud and the huge Taku Glacier probably all contributed to Whidbey's failure to see the significance of the Taku River. But like the Stikine, Fraser and others, the mudflats near its mouth and rapids upstream would have prevented navigation by ocean-going ships of the late eighteenth century. Although Meares expressed regret over the haste of these late surveys, Whidbey had followed the instruction the British Admiralty gave Vancouver.

Although the Taku appears much the way it did when Whidbey visited, it faces modern threats. For years legislators and developers on both sides of the border have proposed a road to Juneau through the Taku's pristine valley, and currently a Canadian mining company is going through the process of re-opening the Tulsequah Chief Mine, about fifty miles from the Taku's mouth. The threats from the mine, including tailings dumps and a 100-mile road, recently prompted conservation groups to nominate the Taku as one the most endangered rivers in the United States.

■ ■ ■

Juneau's buildings slipped behind a forested point to the north as we paddled into Taku. Cold rain beat against our rain gear and hissed on the water. To the west thick clouds swallowed the snowy mountains and forested shores of Admiralty Island, now only five miles away. To the south dark clouds dragged toward us along the surface of Stephens Passage. But to the northeast the clouds were high above Taku, with occasional breaks that sent bright splashes of sunlight onto snowy peaks and ridges. In the distance, huge mountains tapered around the Taku's narrow valley, which wound toward Canada, and on the border, about forty miles away, Devils Paw stood nearly 9,000 feet high, like a gray fist protruding from ice and snow. Beside it, a barren spire, sheer on all sides, rose like a sword above snowy peaks.

The rain turned to showers as we paddled beside steep forest on the south shore, eventually reaching long sections of bare rock too steep for much vegetation, with one cliff rising 3,000 feet in less than a mile. Our progress was moderate through the morning, but around noon we rounded a rocky headland and met a stiff breeze blowing from the Taku's valley. Winds from the interior are common, and stunted spruce and mountain hemlock stood retreated from the grassy headland, with few branches on their windward sides. Across the fiord, the clouds lowered to touch the tops of mountains between 3,000 and 4,000 feet and covered in deep snow.

We took a brief lunch break, then paddled against increasing wind toward a beach near a lake five miles away. But an ebbing tide gained force, magnified by the Taku River's strong current, and even while hugging the steep shore our progress was torturously slow. We covered less than two miles in an hour, our slowest speed since Prince Rupert, and considered setting camp early. But our maps indicated the edge of some mudflats and marshes in three more miles, which would provide a chance to hike that afternoon and put us in a good position to cross the fiord to the glacier the next day. Already, the glacier was partially in view, a blue and white river of ice filling a wide valley between steep mountains.

Our shoulder and back muscles cramped as we fought forward, taking another hour to cover two miles along steep shores. Although our maps indicated the mudflats were still a mile away, the water suddenly turned caramel colored; we began periodically testing its depth with our paddles. After fifteen minutes Bill turned to me from 100 feet ahead, jabbing his paddle perpendicularly into eighteen inches of water.

"It's too shallow here," he called. "We should turn back for that beach." He pointed at a small patch of grass and cobbles below a steep mountain about a third of mile behind us. As he turned his boat around, I stuck my paddle into the water and realized it was only four feet deep.

Like the vicinity of the glaciers we had recently visited, our topographical maps were obsolete in Taku, this time due to the combined forces of isostatic rebound and the Taku River. Northern southeast Alaska is much more recently deglaciated than the rest of the Inside Passage and continues to rebound significantly from the massive weight of the ice. Near Juneau the land rises about half an inch annually. In parts of Glacier Bay the rate exceeds an inch and a half per year. Over a period of years the rebound turns deep water to mudflats, mudflats to marshes, and marshes to stands of young alder and spruce—significant changes that had occurred in Taku since our maps were last revised several decades earlier. In addition, annual variations in the Taku River's current constantly change the size and shape of the mudflats, and even if the maps were more recent, they might not have shown the exact location of the mud from year to year.

With the Stikine Flats still fresh in our minds we paddled hard for shore, but within a few minutes our bows rubbed against a muddy bar under only six inches of water. Still more than half a mile from land, we poled over the mud with our paddles, then paddled quickly toward shore in murky water three feet deep. The wind urged us forward for ten minutes, but when we reached 200 feet from shore our bows ran aground again. We tried poling forward, but the water quickly disappeared as the mud extended to the beach.

In light rain we towed our boats through greasy mud to a lumpy beach barely suitable for camping. It was a combination of mud, grass and cobbles lined on three sides by bedrock walls between three and five feet high. A thick jungle of alder and spruce overhung the walls. We weren't sure the beach was above the high tide line, but the forest above it looked too thick for camping and the expanding mud made looking for another beach impossible. We set our tent at the extreme head of the beach on the smoothest ground we could find, which had three round boulders protruding a few inches from mud and grass, then set our kitchen in intertidal mud a safe distance away. Our hands, pants and gear quickly grew muddy from setting camp, and we knew hanging the food would be a struggle in the thick woods. It was one of the least comfortable camps of the trip.

After setting camp and snacking, we walked east through marshes and mudflats, with broken clouds strewn throughout Taku, partially blocking our view of the glacier. Saturated ground squished beneath our boots as we followed sporadic bear paths through the marshes. Where the paths faded, we walked through waist-high grass soaked from the recent rain. After an hour we turned inland in a narrow valley between mountains rising quickly to 4,500 feet. We entered dim forest and followed a well-worn bear trail beneath towering spruce trees, and soon arrived at the shores of a narrow lake winding for miles between steep forest and sheer walls. Several peaks reached more than 5,000 feet within a mile of its shores, and our map showed alpine glaciers and small lakes feeding dozens of streams that fell precipitously into the lake. In the distance, avalanched snow filled gullies and formed white cliffs at the water's edge.

We explored the lake for an hour, but returned to camp when low clouds swallowed the surrounding mountains. Back at camp, a thick squall blew toward us from Stephens Passage. Fat raindrops smacked the mud as we set our tarp in the intertidal, erecting it at an angle using our paddles and the bows of our boats. Although the tarp kept us dry, it also provided shelter for hundreds of no see'ums, white socks and mosquitoes, which swarmed our faces as we crouched in mud above the stoves, cutting onions and cheese for quesadillas. They dove into our ears, eyes and food as we ate, pacing in circles and waving our arms. The only relief came when cold breezes blew rain under the tarp. By traveling in early spring we had avoided the height of the bug season, but by early June they are thick throughout the Inside Passage, especially near marshes.

The rain stopped after dinner, which increased the bugs, and we hurried to clean the dishes, secure the boats and hang the food. The only tree high enough for the food was a single spruce surrounded by thick alders, their leaves soaked from the rain. Carrying dry bags of food, we pushed through the wet brush, then Bill climbed the tree and ran our rope over a sturdy limb twenty feet high. Soaked, cold and with bugs assaulting our faces, we pulled the rope to get the food above the ground, then used another rope to pull it away from the trunk of the tree.

Back on the beach, the sun broke through holes in quickly shifting clouds, illuminating pieces of snowy ridges and jagged peaks and forming moving puddles of sunlight on the surface of the Taku Glacier. Although it was spectacular scenery, and some of the last of our trip, the bugs were unbearable and forced us into the tent before eight. Two dozen bugs followed us inside, and we slowly lowered their population with our fingers as we spread maps between us and plotted our route to the glacier. With mudflats on either side of the inlet, it could be a tricky crossing.

I read for a while, then fell asleep before dark, but Bill woke me a few hours later. When I sat up I heard the familiar sound of water lapping near our tent.

"We're going to get wet if we stay here," he told me. "High tide's not for another ninety minutes." Calm water lapped against mud and cobbles only a few feet from our door, and light rain crackled on the tent. It was one-thirty.

We quickly packed our sleeping bags and stuffed our clothes, maps and books into dry bags, then climbed from the tent and piled the gear on a nearby bedrock wall. In dusky light we climbed atop the wall and struggled through wet woods looking for a flat spot for the tent, and after ten minutes we found a lumpy patch of wet earth between alders fifty feet away. Returning to the shrinking beach, we half-collapsed the tent, then carefully squeezed it through the dense woods. Bill reassembled it as I bent branches from the way, and when I released the branches they depressed its walls.

It was 2:30 when we finished. In strengthening daylight the glacier was powder blue and the snowy peaks were soft white. Creamy bands of mist floated above the calm inlet, as gray and white clouds encircled patches of light blue sky. We walked along the remaining sliver of beach to check the boats, which were floating but tied securely to alders, then climbed through woods to the tent. Inside, we struggled to sleep comfortably atop roots and rocks, the tent walls bent close to our faces.

We climbed from the tent at nine the next morning and pried through knotted alders to our beach, where we found partly cloudy skies and temperatures near fifty Fahrenheit. The tide was low, with the mud appearing to reach the marshes and glacier on the other side of the inlet. After wrestling through alders to get our food, we ate bagels and cream cheese in a patch of sun on our beach. Half a mile away, a brown bear moved slowly through the marshes where we hiked the previous day, pausing frequently to eat grass and dig in the mud. With our binoculars we saw the large hump on its back between its front shoulders, a mass of muscle that is one of the identifying characteristics of a brown bear.

Since the tide would not reach our beach for close to five hours, we spent the morning reading and taking separate hikes in the marshes. When the bugs grew too fierce we set up the tent and read and relaxed, still tired from the previous night's disrupted sleep. After lunch, we dragged the empty boats onto the mud, then packed them as the water approached from a quarter mile away. Finally, at one, it was six inches deep fifty feet away, and we dragged the boats through a few inches of water and began paddling.

High tide was only an hour away, which gave us roughly two hours to cross the mud on our side of the inlet, paddle across its deeper middle, then cross another big mudflat six miles away at the other shore. If we traveled at anything less than three knots we would get stuck on mud again, but if we made it across we would land on a flat bar covered in grass and forest about a mile and a half from the Taku Glacier. We probably would not have time to paddle along the bar to set our camp close to the glacier, but the next day we could hike across it to the glacier's face.

We made swift progress into the inlet, with the incoming tide blocking the current from the Taku River and only slight breezes blowing from its valley. Devils Paw and the snowy peaks of the Juneau Ice Field came into view above the Taku's narrow valley, and soon we counted four large glaciers flowing to sea level on the west side of the valley. The Taku was by far the largest, spilling into the valley in a bulbous snout almost five miles across, with dark moraine and young trees growing along its face. Immediately to its west, the Norris Glacier was about a mile wide and steeper, with more crevasses revealing dark blue ice. As we crossed the middle of the inlet, dozens of harbor seals surfaced around us, some peeking above the water only a few feet behind our boats.

In a little less than two hours we reached a grassy meadow on the other side of the inlet. It stretched half a mile ahead to an abrupt spruce forest, which covered flat ground for another mile before reaching steep mountains and the pale blue Norris and Taku Glaciers. Gray mud already surrounded parts of the shore, but we followed a narrow slough running through the grass toward the forest. It was only two feet wide in places, but by poling forward with our paddles we traveled a quarter mile before reaching mud, then climbed from our boats and emptied our gear onto the grass.

Lupine, paint brush, shooting stars and chocolate lilies colored large parts of the green meadow purple, white, red and pink, separated by broad swaths of flattened grass from the recent high tide. With our tide books indicating the next high tide would flood even further, and fearing a repeat of the previous night's interrupted sleep, we hauled our gear 100 yards to the closest clump of spruce trees. After clawing through a thicket of young spruce at its border we set our tent on flat ground shaded by the sprawling branches of a fat spruce and hung our food from another spruce 150 feet away. As we worked, thick clouds lowered over the mountains across the inlet.

It was late afternoon when we finished setting camp. After snacking at the edge of the meadow, we hiked north through spruce forest, hoping to find an easy route to the Taku Glacier. The forest was around a century old, with a dense canopy that prevented thick understory. For half a mile we followed game paths that wound between trees and cut through a low carpet of moss and herbs. In addition to the usual deer and bears tracks, big moose tracks were common, a result of the Taku River's nearby corridor to interior British Columbia. We also found patches of granular snow under an opening in the canopy, vestiges of deep winter snow the Taku's cool temperatures bring to the coast.

After fifteen minutes of relatively quick progress we reached a boundary where the forest opened to scattered patches of young spruce and cottonwoods growing from sandy soil. A thin layer of moss and lichen covered the soil, turning the ground to a mosaic of yellow, orange, red, green and black. Clumps of knee-high alder and willow sprouted from the soil between clusters of larger trees, and half a mile ahead the glacier loomed pale blue above young forest. Overhead, the sky was dishwater gray.

For a short distance we strolled easily through wide openings, then hit a wall of knotted willow and alder ten feet high, with scattered cottonwoods reaching twenty-five feet. We picked along its edge for a few minutes, looking for openings, then took deep breaths and dove into the thick brush, hoping to emerge close to the glacier after a short fight. Wiry branches slapped our faces and wrapped around our arms and legs as we pried willow and alder apart with every step, often crawling long distances across trunks and branches without touching the ground. The dense brush blocked our views, so occasionally we climbed thin cottonwoods to orient our direction toward the glacier. But after thirty minutes of constant

318

wrestling we were still tangled in brush. Hungry, tired and beat-up, and with raindrops tapping the leaves, we turned back for camp, agreeing to hike along the forest's perimeter the next day.

After struggling out of the jungle we chose a poor route through the spruce forest, which required clambering through thick blow-down and young trees with sharp needles and stiff branches. An hour later, when we finally reached camp, our arms and faces were scratched from the brush, and needles, leaves and twigs stuck to our clothes and hair. With Taku Inlet concealed in a gray cloud and hard rain hissing on the canopy, we let our food down from its tree and cooked dinner near the base of a fat spruce. Although it protected us from the rain, we constantly swatted at hundreds of bugs as we ate. Afterward, we retired to the tent as an early dusk swallowed the meadow and driving rain assaulted the canopy, with big drops smacking the forest floor. It was dreary weather for the beginning of June.

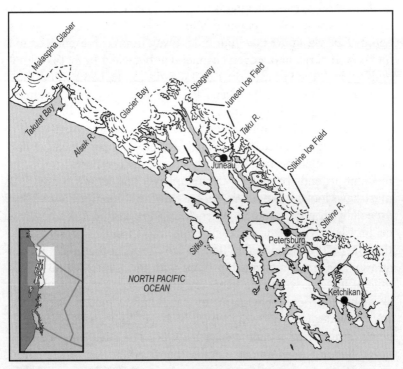

Map 14.2: Coast Mountains of southeast Alaska showing three major ice fields.

■ ■ ■

Taku Inlet and the Taku River cleave the Coast Mountains and mark the southern boundary of the 1,500-square-mile Juneau Ice Field, one of southeast Alaska's three major ice fields. The largest ice field is the Brady, which feeds the glaciers of Glacier Bay, while the Stikine ice field feeds the ice in Holkham, Thomas and LeConte Bays. The ice fields are lifeless seas of ice and snow that straddle the Coast Mountains at around 5,000 feet, with jagged and barren peaks rising 1,000 to 5,000 feet above them. They have depths of more than 4,000 feet and glaciers pouring for miles from all sides. Between them, and along the Coast Mountains of British Columbia, alpine glaciers and smaller ice fields cover high peaks and feed big valley glaciers.

The Taku Glacier flows from the southern edge of the Juneau Ice Field and is the only one of its glaciers that advanced for much of the last 200 years, making it the only glacier that is longer today than it was when Whidbey and Muir visited it. Two hundred years ago its face was more than four miles away from its present location and calved bergs into a deep channel that branched from Taku Inlet and is now buried in ice over 1,000 feet deep. The bergs filled Taku Inlet and floated into Stephens Passage and Gastineau Channel, which could never happen today.

In August, 1794, Whidbey encountered icebergs from the Taku Glacier clogging Gastineau Channel near present-day Juneau. A day later he traveled up the Taku's old channel and reported a glacier blocking its end. To its east, the Taku River and its broad mudflats must have looked like a small river flowing through a low valley, especially in poor weather. When John Muir visited Taku nearly a century later, the glacier was still four miles from its present location. In 1879 he reported a "fleet of ice bergs" at the inlet's mouth and in 1890 rode a steamship filled with tourists to within a half mile of its face, where big bergs fell into the sea. Today, even small skiffs have difficulty navigating over the shallow mud in Taku Inlet.

In the decades following Muir's visit the Taku advanced rapidly, nearly swallowing its entire inlet by 1950. The advancing ice bulldozed forward an enormous moraine that filled the deep water ahead and partially buried its snout, preventing further tidewater calving.

Since that time, no bergs have floated in Taku Inlet or Gastineau Channel. However, the glacier continued advancing and as recently as the late 1980s was reported to move forward several hundred feet per year, a rate that would block the Taku River in forty years.

Although the glacier is presently stalled alongside the Taku River, about a mile from blocking it, old lake shores on nearby mountains show that it dammed the river not long before Whidbey's visit, creating a lake that extended miles up the Taku Valley. The lake drained through the glacier in big channels, much like the Stikine did when the Great Glacier dammed it. Such glacial dams are not uncommon; several still form each year in British Columbia and southeast Alaska, sometimes leading to dramatic outburst floods. One of the most well-known is a branch of the Tulsequah Glacier in British Columbia, about fifty miles from the mouth of the Taku River. Rain and meltwater fill a lake behind the glacier each year, eventually draining in midsummer by floating the dam. Water flowing under the dam quickly erodes the ice and leads to several days of flooding that doubles and even triples the Taku River's mid-summer average of about 30,000 cubic feet per second. Similar floods occur regularly near the Patterson and Baird Glaciers near Petersburg and on the Salmon Glacier near Hyder.

Glacial dams were common during the Pleistocene, too, some creating cataclysmic floods called Jokulhlaups that altered the land-scape. One of the most well-known examples was the Missoula Flood, which occurred 15,000 years ago when a glacial dam 2,500 feet high released a lake stretching more than 100 miles from Lake Pend Orielle, Idaho, to Missoula, Montana. The flood carved the Grand Coulee and other dry valleys in eastern Washington, scoured the Columbia River Gorge and covered the area near Portland in 400 feet of water, depositing rocks there from far to the east. It probably occurred dozens of times, much like the smaller outbursts that occur today in southeast Alaska.

■ ■ ■

We awoke the next morning to damp air and low clouds hovering above Taku Inlet, and after breakfast we packed lunch and rain gear and walked north through lumpy meadow along the edge of the for-est. By hiking north for a mile, then west for another mile or two, we thought we could reach the face of the glacier without bushwhacking. But the new route had challenges of its own: puddles, slippery mud and grassy mounds slowed our progress across the meadow, and deep sloughs forced us into the woods, where we moved slowly through moderate brush. When we finally reached the north end of the meadow we turned west, hiking clumsily along uneven cobbles and boulders beside a wide estuary where salt water from the inlet met fresh water from the glaciers. Part of the Taku's broad face was visible a mile to the north, sloping steeply into water and mud and covered with debris, but we knew we could get closer by continuing west.

We followed the narrowing estuary, finding frequent wolf, moose, deer and bear tracks in sandy patches and near small clusters of willows. Tiny cub prints followed alongside some of the bigger bear tracks, and several paths disappeared into thickening brush bordering the rocks. After twenty minutes we reached an embankment six feet above the estuary, covered in stiff willows mowed thigh-high by moose. As we pushed forward the woody growth grabbed our bibs and coats, and we stumbled frequently on cobbles concealed below their branches. Soon the glacier was only 200 yards across the estuary, its blue and white snout filthy with moraine and sloping sharply into gravel bars and murky water, but thickening brush obscured our view, with tangled alder and willow growing ten feet high to the edge of the embankment. Leaning over the water, we saw a rocky bar another half mile to the west that provided a closer and clearer view of the glacier, but required entering thick jungle.

We entered the brush on a well-worn moose trail, hoping it would provide clear passage, but it soon branched into three trails that disappeared quickly into knotted brush. We dove forward, crashing through the trees with our chests, arms, legs and faces, prying them apart with each step and tripping frequently over their tangled branches and trunks. Between grunts and breaking branches we heard loud pops and cracks from the glacier, like gunshots and car wrecks, but hundreds of brown branches and green leaves were always inches from our faces, blocking our views and poking our eyes and mouths.

Every ten minutes we struggled up thin cottonwoods to mark our progress toward the glacier. It was the kind of travel Muir called a "wet, weary battle" while near the Stikine in 1879. "For over an

322

hour I had to creep and struggle close to the rocky ground like a fly in a spider web without being able to obtain a single glimpse of any guiding feature of the landscape."

Finally, after forty-five minutes, we spilled from the jungle onto a cobble and boulder outwash only 150 feet from the Taku's face. It formed a giant wall of blue and white ice varying between seventy and 100 feet tall, with deep fractures and crisscrossing veins of brown moraine. Big piles of moraine covered parts of its top, with alders and willows growing from their cold mud. A milky river seventy-five feet across ran swiftly past and undercut the glacier below dark blue ice that had recently calved. Several icebergs three feet tall and five feet long lay on the outwash thirty feet from the river, thrown there by big calvings. A mile away, the Norris Glacier had a taller face that fed the river flowing past us, which ran from the ice in white and brown rapids. Beyond, cobweb clouds framed snowy mountains, patches of forest and jagged peaks.

Only moments after leaving the alders, a section of ice forty feet tall and sixty feet across collapsed into the water with a loud crash, sending big bergs flying to the middle of the river. The largest bergs remained anchored in the swift current, but smaller ones drifted quickly downstream, colliding with boulders and other icebergs. On the glacier's face the calving revealed a triangle of dark blue ice, the compacted snowflakes from eighty or more winters earlier.

We sat on boulders forty feet from the river and ate lunch with clear views of the glaciers. The Norris, which had receded for 200 years, had bare rock and scant vegetation along its mountainous sides, the same recently deglaciated landscape we saw near other glaciers. But the Taku, with its recent advances, had mature forest growing to its edges. If the glacier moved forward again, it would break the big trees like twigs and dump them into the river. Big mountains surrounded the glaciers and rose over the jungle behind us, with tattered low clouds shifting constantly and clinging to their forests.

Resting at the face of the Taku represented the conclusion of our last excursion. All that remained was the hike back to camp, one more night in the tent, then a day of paddling to Juneau. It was possible that in twenty-four short hours we would be out of our boats and hanging around Alaska's capital city, making plans to fly to Seattle. After more than eight weeks it was time to begin thinking seriously about our normal lives.

14.1: LOW IMPACT CAMPING

The Inside Passage is vast and largely unspoiled by development and overuse, offering a rare chance to see the earth as it was thousands of years ago. However, each year more people visit by kayak, pleasure boat and commercial tour, and impacts are increasing throughout the region. Visitors can help protect the area and ensure future visitors enjoy the same unspoiled coast by becoming familiar with leave-no-trace camping and travel techniques. The National Outdoor Leadership School (NOLS (307) 335-2213) offers leave-no-trace literature for all North American ecosystems. Here are a few common rules:

Campers can protect wildlife by following the food-related precautions outlined in Sidebar 9.2.

Campers can protect fragile vegetation by camping close to the intertidal on gravel, sand and bedrock rather than further inland on meadows and beach grass. Impacts to vegetation are invitations to the next visitors, and soon a permanent tent site replaces wilderness character.

Campers can further minimize their impact to vegetation by establishing camp so that repeated travel between the kitchen, latrine, food-hang and tent occurs on hard surfaces like beaches and bedrock rather than sensitive vegetation. Storing kayaks on hard surfaces also protects vegeta-

Confirming our closeness to civilization, a helicopter suddenly sped over the glacier's horizon and passed only a few hundred feet above us with a deafening engine. Seconds later, before its sound faded, another followed the same course low over our outwash, and two more followed in the next minute, like something out of a war movie. But people in sunglasses pointed their cameras through the windows, cruise ship passengers enjoying their flightseeing tour of the ice field. At the end of the first week of June southeast Alaska was near the height of its tourism season; Taku was on the flight path of one of the most popular tours. The helicopters took part of the Taku's wilderness feeling with them and made us suddenly aware of Juneau's close proximity.

We took two hours to get back to camp and cooked dinner at the edge of the meadow, our arms and faces scratched and bruised from bushwhacking. Although low clouds clung to the steep mountains across the inlet, holes opened overhead and sent evening sunlight over our camp. After cleaning dishes and hanging the food we relaxed at the edge of the meadow, but intense bugs drove us inside the tent before nine. An hour later we heard wolves howling somewhere north of camp.

The next morning was cloudy but dry, and after breakfast we spent two hours hauling our gear across the meadow to a narrow slough. Its muddy bottom snaked through grass and wildflowers for a quarter mile before reaching the mudflats in Taku Inlet. After packing our boats we still had almost four hours before the tide would reach us. Although misty rain clouds veiled the snowy peaks on Admiralty Island, almost twenty miles away, big gaps in high clouds overhead periodically let sunshine onto our meadow. With the boats lying in grass far from the water, we took walks, read and watched the light change on the steep mountains that surrounded us.

Near noon a small tongue of water a quarter inch deep crept into our slough. During the next ninety minutes it grew to two feet of murky water. We slid our boats across grass and into the slough, then used our paddles to pole through the narrow passage. After fifteen minutes we entered the inlet, with Juneau about twenty miles away. We paddled across the shallow mudflat as the tide turned, then enjoyed a strong boost toward Stephens Passage provided by the ebbing tide and the Taku River. Dozens of seals surfaced around us, and while barely paddling the snowy mountains on either side swept past quickly. In a little more than two hours we traveled twelve miles to the mouth of Taku, with Juneau only eight miles to the north. It was only four in the afternoon, and we could have easily reached the city by dinner.

"I'm not ready for Juneau," I told Bill, "It feels like it's coming up too fast."

tion.

To protect pristine fresh water, human waste should be deposited below the high tide line, where the deep water and powerful tides of the Inside Passage will quickly flush the area clean. Further inland, human waste should be buried in a cat-hole eight inches deep and 200 feet from fresh water.

If campers prefer a fire, building it on rocks and sand below the high tide line will prevent permanent damage to vegetation. Before leaving, scattering wood, ashes and fire rings leaves a beach pristine for the next visitors. Foil, plastic, glass and tin do not burn well and are often left as litter in fire rings.

Kayakers can minimize their garbage and potential for litter by repackaging food into zip-sealed bags before a trip. Removing twist ties and other small packaging reduces the chance of inadvertent litter.

Packing out food scraps protects wildlife from food conditioning and leaves beaches pristine for the next campers. Tupperware is great for leftovers, and disciplined cooking can minimize food scraps.

Kayakers go ashore often and can keep shores clean by "sweeping" each beach they use, carefully inspecting them for pieces of gear or litter that are easy to leave behind.

Leaving beaches in pristine condition, with no fire rings, trash or damaged vegetation, can be a great source of pride for any visitors to the Inside Passage.

"Yeah, me neither. It's too abrupt. Let's camp another night, then do it tomorrow."

We paddled to a point near the convergence of Taku, Stephens Passage and Gastineau Channel and set camp on a sandy beach facing south. A nearby point marked the end of a popular hiking trail that ran eight miles from Juneau and showed signs of use, including fire rings, trails and a little litter. We set our tent on gravelly sand at the head of the beach, put our kitchen in the intertidal and hung the food rope from a nearby hemlock. With our chores completed and a cool breeze keeping the insects to a minimum, we lay against big drift logs and enjoyed our last hours along the Inside Passage.

The clouds remained high and broken. The ebbing tide lapped gently at dark rocks in the intertidal as we lay against our logs. Like scores of other landings, our beach was rich with Tlingit history and was near points named by George Vancouver and visited by members of his crew. John Muir had passed it several times, and during the late nineteenth century miners camped and prospected nearby. Early twentieth century handloggers had removed its biggest trees.

To the east big mountains covered in snow towered over Taku Inlet, while to the west Admiralty's mountains rose directly from the sea, with snow covering everything above a low tree line. And to the south lay the Inside Passage and two months of adventure. Although Stephens Passage disappeared in less than twenty miles, I could see it meeting Frederick Sound, where whales breached between the mainland and Admiralty. I let my mind travel over the sound and south to the Stikine Flats, Wrangell Island, Behm Canal, Dixon Entrance. I recalled the narrowness of Grenville Channel, the driving rain in Princess Royal and bursting surf near Cape Caution. I remembered specific beaches, points and mountains across close to 1,000 miles of shattered coast—detailed images of streams where we filled our water bottles, slabs of rock where we cooked dinner and branches we used to hang our food. I knew the mellow passages, steep coast and dark forests were similar for hundreds of miles to the south, past Vancouver Island and even Seattle, where somewhere in Capitol Hill my battered truck awaited the long drive back to Colorado.

CHAPTER FIFTEEN

Culture Shock—Learning to Walk Again

After a relaxing morning and a short hike, we left our last camp early in the afternoon and paddled north in Gastineau Channel under cloudy skies. Steep mountains with their tops covered in snow lined both sides of the water as Juneau's buildings slowly gained detail, clumped together at the base of steep mountains. Skiffs and pleasure boats passed frequently on their way in and out of town. After almost three hours of leisurely paddling, we arrived close to downtown and veered west toward a sandy beach on Douglas Island, where we had arranged via marine radio to meet some friends.

After blasting its horn twice a giant cruise ship motored slowly out of Juneau and passed within a quarter mile as we paddled toward the beach. Moments later its big wake stood four feet over a shallow bar, lifting our boats quickly from behind, and we responded with panicked braces as our friends watched from shore. Regaining our composure, we paddled the remaining quarter mile and drove our bows into wet sand, stepping ashore for the last time, after more than eight weeks and 1,000 miles of paddling. For the next couple hours we barbecued salmon, halibut and venison on the beach, then drove to a friend's apartment when a cold shower blew north from Stephens Passage, swallowing the mountains around Juneau.

Mark Johnson, a longtime resident of Juneau and friend from my days with the Forest Service, generously offered us room at his apartment and use of his car for the next week. He went to work most days, providing Bill and I space as we reacquainted ourselves with civilized life. We took frequent showers, watched television and made phone calls; frozen pizzas, ice cream and fried food seemed like delicious delicacies. Mark's hospitality was a perfect complement to our experiences at lighthouses, Hartley Bay and even Prince Rupert, and each night we cooked big meals with friends and talked about the Pacific coast.

Juneau is the largest coastal settlement north of Vancouver Island, with malls, movie theaters, supermarkets and nearly 30,000 residents. After thousands of years of use by Auk Tlingits, prospectors discovered gold near what is now downtown in 1880—a bustling mining town soon developed. In 1900 Alaska's capital moved from Sitka to Juneau, and although periodic motions arise to move the capital to Anchorage, Alaska's largest city, Juneau remains the only mainland American capital that cannot be reached by automobile.

Juneau occupies a thin strip of flat land about forty miles long between the narrow channels of the Inside Passage and the ice and steep flanks of the Coast Mountains. Thick rain forest with healthy populations of deer and brown and black bear surrounds the city, and opportunities for real wilderness adventure lie within only a mile of its road. Bears commonly walk into town, occasionally raising a stir near schools or supermarkets. Bald eagles are everywhere, perched atop streetlights and rooftops and filling neighborhoods with their calls. Each August salmon choke streams running through downtown and residential neighborhoods, filling parts of town with the stink of rotting fish. Winters are a cold and damp combination of snow, wind and rain, but at 1,400 feet, the base of the local ski area usually has enough snow by mid-December for a ski season that lasts into April. Deep snow remains on nearby mountains throughout the summer, providing spectacular scenery and abundant backcountry skiing within a short distance of town. In addition, more than fifty miles of well-maintained trails lead to glaciers, pristine lakes and spectacular mountain vistas. The surrounding waters provide limitless opportunities for fishing.

■ ■ ■

In showery weather we hiked Juneau's trails, visited the twelve-mile glacier that flows into town and enjoyed the amenities of civilization. But we shared an awkwardness near people that we had not expected. Since shortly after leaving Port Hardy, we grew accustomed to long hours of comfortable silence, broken only by the water, wildlife and occasional boats of the coast. Of course, we joked and talked about the chores, rain and scenery, but it was nothing compared to the level of conversation required in Juneau—phone calls to friends, family, our banks; dinners with friends in Juneau; mornings and evenings with Mark and his girlfriend. Conversation seemed constant and didn't always come easy for us.

The lack of work was also disconcerting. For more than eight weeks, breaking camp, setting camp, hanging food, cooking, cleaning dishes, tying boats and paddling occupied most of our waking hours. The energy required to keep warm and dry in frequently poor weather compounded the work load, and even during days of supposed relaxation we often undertook arduous hikes or explored rocky shores. Each day, paddling and keeping warm provided clear purpose, but that sense of purpose disappeared when we arrived in Juneau and the busy activity abruptly ended. In the following days, we tried to fill our abundant free time with hikes, walks into town and car rides, but their comparative lack of purpose contributed to an uneasy limbo between the trip and our real lives. We thought increasingly of leaving Alaska.

Even exploring the forest and mountains was anticlimactic, with constant signs of human use and a lack of challenge that paled in comparison to bushwhacking in Taku or climbing cliffs looking for John Muir's old campsites. In addition, the cool, showery weather kept us increasingly indoors; from the windows of Mark's apartment the Inside Passage grew bleak and distant. In later years I would return to Juneau many times and look with amazement at its surrounding wilderness and the views from downtown, but that week, after many days living intimately along its shores, I felt oddly removed from the Inside Passage.

Our original plan involved taking the ferry from Juneau to Bellingham, Washington, covering in three days what had taken two months to paddle, but nearly a week after arriving in Juneau we changed plans and bought plane tickets to Seattle. Two days later we put our kayaks on a barge to Washington. Mark dropped us at the Juneau International Airport in pouring rain, and we climbed aboard a 737. As the plane lifted we peered through the window at steep mountains, dark forest and the Mendenhall Glacier winding away from town, but less than 1,000 feet above the ground we entered a thick layer of cloud and southeast Alaska disappeared. A few minutes later the plane rose above the clouds, and as bright sunshine warmed our faces I began looking forward to summer weather. For the next thirty minutes an unbroken sea of thick clouds concealed the Inside Passage, but somewhere near Petersburg it dissolved, revealing narrow fingers of ocean running between dark islands, bordered on their east by an immense jumble of snowy mountains and flowing glaciers.

We arrived in Seattle at eleven that night and took a taxi to Capitol Hill, where we found my truck parked on a side street and covered in leaves and dust. We had been unable to reach Stephanie and Brian from Juneau, but under the windshield wiper we found a note from them telling us they'd moved and providing directions to their new home about a mile away. Since it was late, we broke into the truck and spread our sleeping bags under the camper shell for a final night sleeping in tight quarters. Then we lay awake for hours reminiscing about the trip.

"Were they really twelve-foot waves," asked Bill, doubting his memory.

"I think they were. And I can't believe we paddled through them."

"Remember that bear near Snettisham? It was thirty feet away!"

"Remember the Stikine Flats?"

"We'll have to send gifts to Belle, the lightkeepers, Mark. And we have to do something big for Patti."

The next night we had dinner with Stephanie and Brian. As we paced around their apartment Brian asked if we felt restless indoors, a question Mark had asked in Juneau. Only a week after ending the trip, apartments still seemed small, with low ceilings, close walls and particularly tiny kitchens. For two months our kitchens had been enormous, and we often ate pacing in order to keep warm or escape bugs. The change to eating indoors was disconcerting. And everything seemed too easy. We didn't have to climb trees after dinner, wash dishes with cold sea water, or wake up in the middle of the night worrying about rock slides, bears or flooding tides.

After two days in Seattle we picked up our kayaks from the barge, divvied our camping gear and drove to SeaTac, where Bill caught a nonstop flight to New York. After saying goodbye at the gate, I drove south on I-5, then east through the Columbia River Gorge, leaving the northwest coast the same way we had entered it almost three months earlier. In eastern Oregon I changed into shorts, revealing frighteningly white legs, and for the next two days I drove long hours across increasingly arid land, surrounded by lodgepoles, pinions and sagebrush. Hot sunlight filled the truck's cab, and I hung my bare arm out the window, where it quickly burned in the sun.

All across the desert I relived moments from the Inside Passage, with images of Douglas firs, red cedars and straight Sitka spruces contrasting the sunburned land surrounding me. In Nevada I picked the last devil's club pricker from my thumb, a remnant of Taku, and at a truck stop in Utah I threw out my gumboots, which were stinking up the back of the truck.

In the following months the memories only sweetened, and I enjoyed an intimacy with the Inside Passage that I knew would never fade. No matter how far from it, I knew I would always hear the canopy release fat rain drops onto the forest floor, see mink busy in the intertidal and feel the rumble of glacial ice falling into the cold sea. And in the following years, while looking at photos or riding the ferry between Washington and Skagway, I looked at the rocky shores and recalled vivid images from our trip, with breezes rustling sedges along small beaches, tiny waves lapping against intertidal rocks and big eagle wings beating the air. Loyal rain wrapped each image in an intimate blending of land and sea.

Bibliography

Adney, Edwin Tappan and Howard I. Chapelle. *The Bark Canoes and Skin Boats of North America*. Washington, D.C.: Smithsonian Institution Press, 1983.

Broze, Matt and George Gronseth. *Sea Kayaker: Deep Trouble*. Camden, ME: Ragged Mountain Press, 1997.

Burch, David. *Fundamentals of Kayak Navigation*. Chester, CT: Globe Pequot, 1987.

Durbin, Kathie. *Tongass: Pulp Politics and the Fight for the Alaska Rain Forest*. Corvallis: Oregon State University Press, 1999.

Ferguson, Sue A. *Glaciers of North America: A Field Guide*. Golden, CO: Fulcrum Publishing, 1992.

From Maps to Metaphors: The Pacific World of George Vancouver. Edited by Robin Fisher and Hugh Johnson. Vancouver: University of British Columbia Press, 1993.

Graham, Donald. *Lights of the Inside Passage: A History of British Columbia's Lighthouses and Their Keepers*. Madeira Park, BC: Harbour Publishing Company, 1986.

Harris, E. A. *Spokeshute: Skeena River Memory*. Victoria, BC: Orca Book Publishers, 1990.

Kenneth M. Ames and Herbert D.G. Maschner. *Peoples of the Northwest Coast: Their Archaeology and Prehistory*. London: Thames Hudson, 1999.

Mackenzie, Alexander. *Journal of the Voyage to the Pacific*. New York Dover Publications, 1995.

Muckle, Robert J. *The First Nations of British Columbia*. Vancouver: University of British Columbia Press, 1998.

Muir, John. *Travels in Alaska*. New York: Houghton Mifflin Company, 1915.

O'Clair, Rita M., Robert H. Armstrong, and Richard Carstensen. *The Nature of Southeast Alaska: A Guide to Plants, Animals and Habitats*. Seattle: Alaska Northwest Books, 1992.

Raban, Jonathan. *Passage to Juneau: A Sea and Its Meanings*. New York: Pantheon Books, 1999.

Schooler, Lyn. *The Blue Bear: A True Story of Friendship, Tragedy and Survival in the Alaskan Wilderness*. New York: Harper Collins, 2002.

Sharp, Robert. *Living Ice: Understanding Glaciers and Glaciation*. Cambridge: Cambridge University Press, 1988.

Stanley Sr., Robert E.. *Northwest Native Arts: Basic Forms*. Blaine, WA: Hancock House, 2002.

The Book of Tongass. Edited by Carolyn Servid and Donald Snow. Minneapolis: Milkweed Editions, 1999.

The Rain Forests of Home: Profile of a North American Bioregion. Edited by Peter K. Schoonmaker, Bettina con Hagen, Edward C. Wolf. Washington, D.C.: Island Press, 1997.

The Voyage of George Vancouver 1791-1795. Edited by W. Kaye Lamb. London: The Hakluyt Society, 1984.

Index

A

Admiralty Island 201, 226, 258, 259, 260, 261, 262, 263, 268, 271, 273, 277, 282, 305, 311, 312, 325
Alaska National Interest Lands Conservation Act 201, 202, 203, 278
Alaska Native Claims Settlement Act 201, 277
Alaska Pulp Company 200, 202, 205, 226
alpine glaciers 249, 315, 320
ANCSA. *See* Alaska Native Claims Settlement Act
ANILCA. *See* Alaska National Interest Lands Conservation Act
APC. *See* Alaska Pulp Company
avalanche 137, 142, 169, 217, 245, 288, 295, 298

B

Babine River 178
bald eagle 22, 32, 63, 64, 116, 153, 176, 228, 328
bear 7, 20, 22, 32, 41, 80, 87, 89, 91, 120, 144, 146, 147, 153, 154, 155, 157, 159, 163, 164, 166, 169, 170, 176, 204, 213, 218, 220, 223, 229, 234, 271, 272, 276, 278, 279, 280, 281, 287, 293, 307, 315
  black bear 22, 154, 159, 216, 217, 230, 272, 287, 306, 311, 328
  brown bear 22, 153, 154, 201, 224, 229, 234, 271, 272, 277, 278, 316
  grizzly bear 271
  Kermode bear 154
  mother bear 164
  spirit bear 8, 154
Behm Canal 207, 208, 210, 211, 217, 234, 235, 258, 326
Bering Land Bridge 79, 80
Bering, Vitus 54
Beringia. *See* Bering Land Bridge
British Columbia 9, 19, 24, 38, 39, 54, 55, 65, 72, 73, 74, 83, 84, 118, 119, 146, 154, 160, 162, 163, 178, 186, 187, 207, 217, 219, 225, 229, 246, 309, 310, 318, 320, 321

Bulkley River 178

C

California 22, 54, 71, 80, 82, 118, 131, 133, 160, 166, 179, 221, 237
Calvert Island 29, 30, 31, 56, 58, 60, 62, 63, 64, 65, 66, 71
canoes 16, 18, 43, 134, 135, 138, 139, 140, 146, 148, 179, 209, 210, 264
Cape Caution 29, 30, 33, 42, 44, 45, 48, 56, 58, 59, 326
Cape Decision 237, 259, 260, 261
carving 139, 220
Cascade Mountains 13
Chatham 55, 56, 67, 132, 133, 135, 175, 208, 234, 236, 237, 260, 311
Chatham Sound 176, 177, 180, 182, 183, 184, 186, 191
Chatham Strait 215, 262
Chirikov, Aleksei 54
clearcuts 169, 172, 202, 206, 218, 263, 284
Coast Mountains 72, 73, 74, 79, 80, 82, 118, 119, 156, 176, 178, 229, 242, 246, 249, 263, 282, 290, 305, 310, 319, 320, 328
Columbia River 13, 67, 78, 131, 144, 160, 321, 330
compass 211, 212, 213, 214, 269, 273
Cook Inlet 22, 55, 132, 237, 259
Cook, James 37, 55, 56, 138, 259
Cross Sound 260, 261
cruise ships 16, 83, 84, 294, 309

D

Department of Environmental Conservation (DEC) 204, 309
Discovery 55, 56, 58, 59, 67, 132, 133, 135, 208, 234, 236, 237, 259, 260, 311
Dixon Entrance 29, 154, 176, 183, 191, 197, 207, 208, 209, 210, 225, 234, 262, 326
Douglas fir 13, 71, 162, 166, 331
Dry Strait 226, 234, 235, 236, 237, 262, 264, 268

E

Environmental Protection Agency
(EPA) 204, 309
Eskimo 31, 44, 60

F

fireweed 254, 291, 298, 299, 302
Fitz Hugh Sound 62, 63, 64, 66, 70,
71, 86
forest succession 255, 256, 285
fox farming 283, 284
Fraser River 72, 73, 80, 131, 139, 178,
179, 237, 311, 312
Frederick Sound 226, 227, 234, 236,
240, 241, 243, 253, 258, 261, 262,
263, 264, 266, 267, 268, 269, 272,
274, 275, 276, 282, 305, 326
fur trade 19, 54, 264
fur traders 16, 19, 37, 54, 225

G

Gastineau Channel 310, 311, 320, 321,
326, 327
glacial dams 321
glacier 8, 21, 72, 84, 156, 174, 176,
191, 202, 219, 222, 226, 227, 229,
240, 241, 243, 245, 246, 247, 249,
250, 251, 252, 253, 254, 255, 256,
257, 258, 260, 263, 277, 287, 290,
291, 292, 293, 294, 295, 296, 297,
298, 299, 300, 302, 303, 304, 310,
311, 312, 313, 314, 315, 316, 317,
318, 319, 320, 321, 322, 323, 324,
328, 329
Glacier Bay 8, 84, 174, 202, 222, 250,
260, 277, 287, 293, 314, 320
Grenville Channel 154, 155, 156, 157,
167, 173, 174, 175, 176, 177, 179,
211, 326

H

Haida 131, 139, 150, 187
Haida Gwaii 16, 74, 83
Haines 17, 24, 260
handloggers 160, 163, 180, 199, 206,
218, 225, 326
harbor seals 284, 292, 293, 317
Hartley Bay 6, 23, 43, 62, 123, 136,
137, 138, 140, 141, 142, 148, 149,
150, 151, 152, 154, 158, 328
Holkham Bay 282, 283, 284, 285, 286,

305
Hudson's Bay Company 19, 55, 57,
179, 186, 225
humpback whales 22, 32, 64, 85, 263,
265, 275, 276, 305
Huroshio Current 117, 118
hypothermia 7, 12, 17, 18, 30, 31, 32,
36, 38, 96, 114, 128, 129, 134, 232,
248

I

ice fields 156, 242, 249, 302, 319, 320
interglacials 301
isostatic rebound 131, 314

J

Johnstone, James 234, 235, 236, 237,
261, 264, 267, 268, 284, 311
Jokulhlaups 321
Juneau 6, 7, 24, 36, 83, 84, 118, 124,
146, 149, 181, 190, 200, 201, 207,
226, 250, 258, 261, 263, 264, 267,
272, 275, 276, 277, 282, 283, 285,
294, 306, 307, 308, 309, 310, 311,
312, 314, 317, 320, 323, 324, 325,
326, 327, 328, 329, 330
Juneau Ice Field 310, 317, 320

K

kame 299
Ketchikan 6, 83, 84, 197, 200, 201,
203, 204, 205, 206, 207, 308
Ketchikan Pulp Company 218
Kitimat 24, 135, 154
Klemtu 6, 120, 121, 122, 123, 138,
140, 150, 180, 194
Kootznoowoo 271, 277, 278
Kuiu Island 236, 261, 267
Kupreanof Island 236, 267, 284, 311

L

LeConte Bay 227, 228, 230, 240, 242,
243, 245, 250, 253, 263, 264, 265
LeConte Glacier 191, 219, 226, 243,
253, 257, 263
Little Ice Age 242, 246
Lituya Bay 289, 290
lupine 254, 268, 298, 299, 302, 317
Lynn Canal 260

M

Mackenzie, Alexander 55, 133
marine radio 14, 18, 37, 40, 49, 89, 94, 114, 124, 190, 272, 273, 274, 275, 327
Mendenhall Glacier 250, 329
Archibald Menzies 264
miners 8, 19, 225, 284, 285, 326
mines 206, 284
mining 19, 20, 187, 199, 284, 285, 305, 312, 328
mink 7, 22, 32, 117, 152, 166, 279, 280, 283, 331
Missoula Flood 321
Misty Fiords 191, 197, 208, 277
Mitkof Island 226, 234, 236, 263, 264, 265
moraine 176, 242, 243, 246, 252, 253, 264, 286, 287, 299, 303, 317, 321, 322, 323
mountain goat 298
mudflats 181, 182, 183, 226, 227, 228, 230, 234, 237, 312, 313, 314, 316, 320, 325
Muir, John 81, 82, 172, 195, 220, 221, 222, 225, 258, 284, 287, 291, 294, 320, 323, 326, 329

N

Namu 76, 77, 78, 82, 86, 120
Nass River 150
Native corporations 201, 202, 204, 218, 277
nautical charts 14, 15, 24, 158, 183, 256, 257
New Hazelton 179
Nootka Sound 55, 67
Norris Glacier 317, 323
northwest coast culture 78, 131, 132
northwest coast Native art 131, 135, 144, 146, 220
Northwest Passage 19, 54, 55, 56, 134, 259, 264

O

Olympic Peninsula 160
orca 32, 81, 173, 174, 175, 286, 292, 293, 294, 295, 332
Oregon 13, 55, 66, 71, 78, 82, 118, 160, 161, 162, 163, 179, 199, 202, 203, 331, 332

P

Petersburg 6, 84, 258, 265, 266, 267, 321, 330
Pine Island 30, 33, 34, 35, 36, 38, 39, 40, 41, 43, 48, 49, 50, 59, 60, 61, 66, 72, 92, 113, 122, 296
Pleistocene 74, 80, 156, 157, 176, 178, 242, 246, 255, 301, 321
Point Retreat 261, 263
Port Conclusion 268, 311
Port Essington 179, 180, 186
Port Hardy 6, 12, 17, 19, 20, 21, 23, 24, 27, 28, 36, 40, 62, 64, 66, 83, 118, 120, 136, 158, 187, 188, 328
Prince of Wales Island 201, 206, 210, 217
Prince Rupert 6, 24, 36, 38, 39, 78, 83, 84, 118, 127, 130, 137, 147, 148, 154, 163, 168, 175, 177, 178, 180, 182, 183, 184, 185, 186, 187, 189, 191, 193, 197, 313, 328
Prince William Sound 44, 259
Promyshlenniks 54
Puget, Peter 179, 209, 210
Puget Sound 17, 20, 21, 24, 55, 56, 58, 81, 132, 156, 160, 173, 174, 179, 288

Q

Queen Charlotte Islands 16, 237
Queen Charlotte Sound 16, 17, 25, 27, 29, 30, 35, 36, 37, 38, 40, 43, 44, 52, 64, 66, 197
Queen Charlotte Strait 16, 17, 28, 29, 30, 33, 40, 42, 53, 57, 58, 62, 63, 71, 137

R

rain forest 5, 7, 13, 18, 20, 22, 32, 39, 63, 68, 69, 70, 71, 72, 74, 77, 80, 91, 113, 117, 146, 152, 154, 158, 169, 176, 178, 198, 204, 223, 242, 262, 263, 277, 278, 280, 285, 290, 302, 304, 328
Revillagigedo Island 206, 208, 210
Russia 54, 225
Russian 19, 37, 54, 55, 57, 225, 259, 283

S

salmon 18, 22, 32, 77, 78, 84, 85, 87, 91, 131, 132, 134, 139, 144, 146, 148,

150, 153, 154, 156, 158, 159, 163, 166, 169, 174, 178, 179, 187, 204, 205, 208, 210, 218, 221, 222, 224, 234, 265, 266, 271, 278, 279, 280, 283, 286, 307, 311, 321, 327, 328
sea lions 7, 22, 32, 34, 45, 174, 229, 280, 283, 294, 295
Sierra Club 81, 201, 277, 278
Sitka 8, 13, 54, 71, 84, 87, 159, 160, 162, 163, 166, 178, 199, 200, 203, 205, 212, 218, 220, 262, 328, 331
Sitka black-tailed deer 154
Sitka spruce 87, 159, 166, 199, 262
Skagway 16, 17, 21, 24, 83, 84, 85, 173, 225, 308, 331
Skeena River 73, 131, 177, 178, 179, 180, 181, 183, 186, 229, 237, 311
Snettisham 305, 306, 330
Stephens Passage 261, 264, 267, 272, 274, 275, 282, 304, 305, 306, 307, 309, 310, 311, 312, 315, 320, 325, 326, 327
Stikine Flats 226, 227, 232, 234, 235, 243, 249, 263, 264, 314, 326, 330
Stikine Ice Field 219, 224, 263, 300, 303, 320
Stikine River 73, 80, 131, 178, 179, 219, 224, 225, 226, 227, 229, 230, 233, 235, 237, 239, 264, 311, 312, 321, 323
Strait of Juan de Fuca 56, 156, 237
Sumdum 225, 282, 283, 284, 286

T

Taku Glacier 310, 312, 315, 317, 318, 320
Taku Inlet 310, 311, 319, 320, 321, 325, 326
Taku River 310, 312, 313, 314, 317, 318, 320, 321, 325
tidal exchange 32, 232
tidewater glaciers 121, 242, 249, 252, 282, 284, 291, 292
Tlingit 131, 144, 150, 206, 234, 264, 283, 284, 285, 291, 326
Tongass 6, 198, 199, 200, 201, 202, 203, 204, 205, 206, 207, 208, 225, 277
Tongass Timber Act 200
Tongass Timber Reform Act 204
topographical maps 15, 298, 314
tourism 19, 20, 84, 85, 187, 205, 226, 266, 308, 324
Tsimsian 131, 141, 150, 172, 178

U

U.S. Forest Service 7, 21, 162, 197, 199
Ursus arctos. See brown bear

V

valley glaciers 242, 249, 265, 267, 320
Vancouver 38, 39, 84, 160, 161, 163, 186, 187, 194
Vancouver Canucks 142
Vancouver Island 7, 12, 14, 15, 16, 18, 19, 21, 24, 25, 27, 28, 29, 30, 31, 35, 37, 38, 40, 55, 58, 66, 71, 73, 74, 83, 85, 86, 118, 122, 139, 141, 153, 160, 163, 178, 187, 198, 326, 328
Vancouver, George 8, 19, 55, 56, 58, 59, 67, 132, 133, 134, 135, 138, 172, 179, 208, 209, 210, 211, 217, 222, 225, 234, 235, 236, 237, 258, 260, 261, 262, 264, 268, 259, 284, 305, 311, 312, 326

W

Washington 16, 71, 78, 83, 118, 119, 160, 161, 162, 163, 199, 200, 201, 202, 203, 321, 329, 331
western hemlock 166, 223, 262
Whidbey 135, 137, 210, 236, 237, 261, 264, 267, 268, 311, 312, 320, 321
Whidbey, Joseph 134, 135, 179, 209, 234, 260, 261, 263, 284, 305, 310
Windham Bay 284, 285
wolves 7, 22, 32, 87, 144, 150, 154, 155, 166, 170, 204, 224, 229, 287, 311, 322, 324
Wrangell 6, 54, 73, 82, 205, 219, 220, 221, 222, 223, 224, 225, 226, 227, 229, 230, 234, 235, 268, 283, 326
Wrangell Narrows 236, 262, 265, 266, 268

Y

Yakutat 55, 78, 289
Yukon River 73, 311